Nikki Halford

Shrewsbury

General Studies

An A-Level Coursebook

Summer '99

Colin Swatridge

Collins Educational
An Imprint of HarperCollinsPublishers

Published by CollinsEducational
77–85 Fulham Palace Road, London W6 8JB
An imprint of HarperCollins*Publishers*

First published 1995
Reprinted 1996 (three times), 1997, 1998

ISBN 0–00–322413–9

British Library Cataloguing-in-publication data
A catalogue record for this book is available from the British Library

Edited by Patricia Briggs
Maths items by Helier Dreux
Design and typesetting by Derek Lee and Patricia Briggs
Based on an original design concept by Colin Swatridge
Illustrations by Julia Osorno, Mark Norcutt and Derek Lee
Cover artwork by Caroline Smith
Cover typography by David Jones
Project management by Patricia Briggs
Production by Jane Bressloff
Printed and bound in Hong Kong

Contents

Unit 13 Painting

Unit 14 Philosophy

Unit 15 Psychology (Cognitive)

Unit 16 Religion

Unit 17 Science

Unit 18 Society

Unit 19 Sport and Leisure

Unit 20 Technology

Unit 21 Universe

Unit 22 World

Acknowledgements

Helier Dreux is due the entire credit for the mathematical sections of the book, and for advice and support diffusely given besides. Monique Pottage lent ready, mother-tongue help in respect of the French items.

My wife, Sue Swatridge, and two students, Emily Shaw and Kate Percival, answered all the questions, and alerted me to those which were obscurely worded, too difficult, or frankly impossible.

I am indebted to Pat McNeill and Emma Dunlop for editorial encouragement, and for the enormous discretion that I enjoyed where the contents of the book are concerned. Finally, I should like to pay homage to the patience with which Melanie Norcutt committed to typescript text that I am backwoodsman enough to have submitted entirely in manuscript.

The author and publishers would like to thank those who granted permission to reproduce the following material:

All-Purpose Essay Plan
Tony Benn, *Arguments for Socialism*, Jonathan Cape Ltd, 1979
William Davis, *It's No Sin to Be Rich*, Osprey, 1976
Susan George, *How the Other Half Dies*, Penguin Books, 1976
F.A. Hayek, *The Road to Serfdom*, Routledge and Kegan Paul, 1976 (1st edn 1944)

Unit 1
P.M. Bardi, *Architecture*, Collins/Watts, 1972
John Burnett, *A Social History of Housing 1815–1970*, Routledge, 1978
Theo Crosby, *How to Play the Environment Game*, Penguin Books, 1973
Reinhard Gieselman, *Contemporary Church Architecture*, Thames and Hudson, 1972
Jonathan Glancey, New British Architecture, Thames and Hudson, 1989
Nikolaus Pevsner, *An Outline of European Architecture*, Penguin Books, 1943
Michael Raeburn (ed.), *Architecture of the Modern World*, Orbis Publishing Ltd, 1980
Richard Rogers, *Architecture: A Modern View*, Thames and Hudson, 1990
Deyan Sudjic, *Norman Foster, Richard Rogers, James Stirling*, Thames and Hudson, 1986

Unit 2
A.D. Edwards, *The Changing Sixth Form in the Twentieth Century*, Routledge and Kegan Page, 1970
T.H. Huxley, 'Science and Culture' in *The Victorian Mind*, Gerald B. Kauvar and Gerald C. Sorensen (eds), Simon and Schuster Inc., 1969
Gordon Higginson, 'On the Wrong Track', in *Times Educational Supplement*, 17 June 1988
Department of Education, *15–18* (The Crowther Report), HMSO, 1959
Department of Education and Science:
  The Dainton Report, HMSO, 1968
  Education for 16–19 year olds (The Macfarlane Report), HMSO, 1981
  Better Schools (Cmnd 9469), HMSO, 1985
Jean McGinty and John Fish, *Further Education in the Market Place*, Routledge, 1993
Alan Smithers and Pamela Robinson, *General Studies: Breadth at A Level?* The Engineering Council, 1993

Unit 3
David Begg *et al.*, *Economics*, McGraw-Hill Book Company Europe, 1984
Peter Donaldson, *A Question of Economics*, Penguin Books/Channel Four, 1985
Milton and Rose Friedman, *Free to Choose*, Secker and Warburg, 1980
David Howell, *Freedom and Capital*, Basil Blackwell, 1981
Richard G. Lipsey, *An Introduction to Positive Economics* (2nd edn), Oxford University Press, 1966
Joan Robinson, *Contributions to Modern Economics*, Basil Blackwell, 1978
Michael Stewart, *Keynes and After* (3rd edn), Penguin Books, 1986
A.J.P. Taylor, *English History 1914–1945*, Oxford University Press, 1965

Unit 4
R.S. Atterbury (ed.), *A Golden Adventure: The First 50 Years of Ultramar*, Hurtwood Press, 1985
Peter Chapman, *Fuel's Paradise: Energy Options for Britain*, Penguin Books, 1979
F.J.P. Clarke, from a speech to the BAAS at Aston, Birmingham, 1977
S.F. Goodman, *The European Community* (2nd edn), Macmillan, 1993
Walter C. Patterson, *Nuclear Power* (2nd edn), Penguin Books, 1983
Mike Wild (ed.), *Energy in the 80s*, Longman Group Ltd, 1980

Unit 5
Tony Aldous, *Battle for the Environment*, Fontana, 1972
Rex Bellamy, *The Peak District Companion*, David and Charles, 1980
Melvyn Bragg, *Land of the Lakes*, Hodder and Stoughton, 1990
J.M. Brereton, *The Brecon Beacons National Park*, David and Charles, 1990
Hunter Davies, *A Walk around the Lakes* (3rd edn), J.M. Dent, 1993
Phil Drabble, *A Voice in the Wilderness*, Pelham Books, 1991
John Hillaby, *John Hillaby's Yorkshire*, Constable Publishers, 1986
Harry Reé and Caroline Forbes, *The Three Peaks of Yorkshire*, Wildwood House, 1983
John Weir (ed.), *Dartmoor National Park, Official Guide*, Webb and Bower Publishers Ltd/The Countryside Commission, 1987

Unit 6
John Ardagh, *Rural Germany*, A & C Black (Publishers) Ltd, 1990
Sir Winston S. Churchill Estate, for material from a speech to the House of Commons, 28 September 1944, Curtis Brown Group Ltd
Dana Facaros and Michael Pauls, *Cadogan Guides: Northeast Italy*, Cadogan Books, 1990
Nina Nelson, *The Netherlands*, B.T. Batsford, 1987
The Time Out Paris Guide, Time Out Publications, 1990
Alan Tucker (ed.), *The Penguin Guide to Spain*, Penguin Books, 1991
Nancy Van Italie (ed.), *Fodor's 93 Scandinavia*, Fodor's Travel Publications/Random House Inc., 1993

Unit 7
Andrew Adonis, *Parliament Today*, Manchester University Press, 1990
Rodney Brazier, *Constitutional Practice*, Oxford University Press, 1988 (2nd edn, 1994)
Bill Coxall and Lynton Robins, *Contemporary British Politics*, Macmillan, 1989
Bernard Crick, *The Reform of Parliament* (2nd edn) Weidenfeld & Nicholson, 1968
Andrew Reeve and Alan Ware, *Electoral Systems*, Routledge, 1992
Lynton Robins (ed.), *Political Institutions in Britain*, Longman Group Ltd, 1987

Unit 8
H.L.A. Hart, *Law, Liberty and Morality*, Oxford University Press, 1963
Simon Lee, *Law and Morals*, Oxford University Press, 1986
Calvin Pinchin, *Issues in Philosophy*, Macmillan Press Ltd, 1990
Jennifer Trusted, *Moral Principles and Social Values*, Routledge, 1987

Unit 9
Walter Allen, *The English Novel*, Penguin Books, 1958
Jane Austen, *Northanger Abbey*,
William Boyd, *Brazzaville Beach: A Novel*, Sinclair-Stevenson, 1990
Michel Butor, *Inventory: Essays*, Simon and Schuster, 1968
Margaret Drabble, 'A Very Personal Medium', in *The General Studies Review*, Vol. 1, No. 4, Philip Allan Publishers Ltd, 1993
Alice Thomas Ellis, 'Face to Face', in *The English Review*, Vol. 3 No. 4, Philip Allan Publishers Ltd, 1993
E.M. Forster, *Aspects of the Novel*, Edward Arnold, 1927
John Fowles, *The French Lieutenant's Woman*, Jonathan Cape, 1969 (Sheil Land)
B.S. Johnson, *Aren't You Rather Young to be Writing Your Memoirs?* Hutchinson, MBA Literary Agents Ltd, 1973

Unit 10
Graeme Burton, *More Than Meets The Eye*, Edward Arnold, 1990
James Curran and Jean Seaton, *Power without Responsibility* (4th edn), Routledge, 1991
D.H. Lawrence, 'Pornography and Obscenity' in *A Propos of Lady Chatterley's Lover*, Penguin, 1961
Simon Lee, *Law and Morals*, Oxford University Press, 1986

viii Acknowledgements

Roger Manwell, *This Age of Communication*, Blackie, 1966
Brian McNair, *News and Journalism in the UK*, Routledge, 1994
Neil Postman, *Amusing Ourselves to Death*, William Heinemann Ltd, 1986
Clive Ponting, 'Secrecy and Freedom of Information', in *Freedom of Information*, Macmillan Papermac,1987

Unit 11
Patrick Butler, *The Healing Handbook*, W. Foulsham and Co, 1990
Vernon Coleman, *Mindpower*, European Medical Journal, 1986 (new edn 1994)
Anya Gore, *Alternative Health: Reflexology*, Vermilion, 1990
Brent Hafen and Kathryn Frandsen, *An A–Z of Alternative Medicine*, Sheldon Press, 1984
Felix Mann, *Acupuncture: Cure of Many Diseases*, Butterworth-Heinemann Ltd, 1992
Roger Newman-Turner, *Naturopathic Medicine* (2nd edn), Thorsons, 1990
Brian Root, *Hypnosis: A Gateway to Better Health*, Weidenfeld and Nicholson, 1986

Unit 12
Neville Cardus, *Talking of Music*, William Collins, 1957
Aaron Copland, *Music and Imagination*, New American Library, 1959
Francis Davis, *Outcats*, Oxford University Press, 1990
Paul Griffiths, *Modern Music*, Thames and Hudson, 1978
Miles Kingston, *The Jazz Anthology*, HarperCollins*Publishers*, 1992
Constant Lambert, *Music Ho!* Faber and Faber Ltd, 1934
John Schaeffer, *New Sounds: The Virgin Guide to New Music*, W.H. Allen/Virgin Publishing Ltd, 1990

Unit 13
Kenneth Clark, *Civilization*, John Murray (Publishers) Ltd, 1969
William Gaunt, *The Observer's Book of Modern Art*, Frederick Warne, 1964
E.H. Gombrich, *The Story of Art* (12th edn), Phaidon, 1972
Hermann Leicht, *History of the World's Art*, Spring Books, 1963
Christopher Lloyd, *A Picture History of Art*, Phaidon, 1979
Andrew Sinclair, *The Need to Give: The Patrons and the Arts*, Sinclair-Stevenson, 1990
Peter Thoene, *Modern German Art*, Penguin Books, 1938

Unit 14
A.C. Ewing, *The Fundamental Questions of Philosophy*, Routledge, 1951
A.J. Ayer, *Language, Truth and Logic*, Victor Gollancz Ltd, 1936
Aristotle (ed. W.D. Ross), 'Metaphysics', in *Aristotle Selections*, Oxford University Press, 1927
R.W. Livingstone (ed.), *The Legacy of Greece*, Oxford University Press, 1922
Marx and Engels, (ed. C.J. Arthur), *The German Ideology*, Lawrence and Wishart, 1970
John Passmore, *A Hundred Years of Philosophy*, Gerald Duckworth and Co Ltd, 1957
Bertrand Russell, *History of Western Philosophy*, George Allen and Unwin, 1946
Bertrand Russell, *The Problems of Philosophy*, Oxford University Press, 1912
Ludwig Wittgenstein (trans G.E.M. Anscombe), *Philosophical Investigations* (2nd edn), Basil Blackwell, 1958

Unit 15
Margaret A. Boden, *Artificial Intelligence in Psychology*, MIT Press, 1989
Douglas R. Hofstadter and Daniel C. Dennell, *The Mind's I*, Harvester Wheatsheaf, 1981
John Hospers, *An Introduction to Philosophical Analysis*, Prentice Hall Inc., 1953
Aldous Huxley, *Brave New World*, HarperCollins*Publishers*, 1932
G. Jefferson, 'The Mind of Mechanical Man', in *British Medical Journal*, Vol. 1, 1949
Robert L. Nadeau, *Mind, Machines and Human Consciousness*, Contemporary Books, 1991
John Searle, 'Minds, Brains and Programs' in *The Behavioural and Brain Sciences*, Cambridge University Press, 1980
Alan Turing, 'Computing Machinery and Intelligence', in *Mind*, Vol. LIX, Oxford University Press, 1950
Joseph Weizenbaum, *Computer Power and Human Reason*, W.H. Freeman and Co., 1976

Unit 16
Don Cupitt, *The Sea of Faith*, BBC Books, 1984 (2nd edn 1994)
Albert Einstein, 'The Religious Spirit of Science', 1934, in A.P. French (ed.), *Einstein: A Centenary Volume*, Heinemann Publishers Ltd, 1979
William James, *The Varieties of Religious Experience*, Fontana, 1902
C.G. Jung, *Memories, Dreams, Reflections*, Collins, 1963
John A.T. Robinson, *Honest to God*, SCM Press,1963
Paul Tillich, *The Shaking of the Foundations*, SCM Press, 1949
A.N. Whitehead, *Science and the Modern World*, Penguin, 1925

Unit 17
Konrad Lorenz, *On Aggression*, Methuen and Co. Ltd, 1966
Henri Poincaré, 'Mathematical Creation', in *The Foundations of Science*, The Science Press, 1913
D.R. Newth, 'On Scientific Method', in *Science in its Context* (ed. J. Brierley)

Heinemann, 1964
J.J. Thomson, *Recollections and Reflections*, George Bell and Sons Ltd, 1936
Jacob Bronowski, *The Ascent of Man*, BBC Worldwide Ltd, 1973
W.I.B. Beveridge, *Seeds of Discovery*, Heinemann, 1980

Unit 18
Carol Buswell, *Women in Contemporary Society*, Macmillan Education, 1989
Jay J. Coakley, *Sport in Society: Issues and Controversies* (5th edn), Mosby Year Book Inc., 1994
Craig Donnelan, *Disabilities and Discrimination*, Independence Educational Publishers, 1992
John H. Goldthorpe, *Social Mobility and Class Structure in Modern Britain*, Oxford University Press, 1980
Charles Husband (ed.), *Race in Britain*, Unwin Hyman/Routledge, 1982
Dennis Kavanagh, *British Politics: Continuities and Change* (2nd edn), Oxford University Press, 1990
Heidi Safia Mirza, *Young, Female and Black*, Routledge, 1992
John R. Short, *Housing in Britain: The Post-War Experience*, London, Methuen, 1982
Pamela Abbott and Claire Wallace, *An Introduction to Sociology: Feminist Perspecitves*, Routledge, 1990

Unit 19
E.J. Bassey and P.H. Fentem, *Exercise: the Facts*, Oxford University Press, 1981
Frank L. Katch and W.D. McArdle, *Nutrition, Weight Control, and Exercise* (3rd edn), Lea and Febiger, 1988
Donald Norfolk, *Farewell to Fatigue*, Michael Joseph/MBA Literary Agents Ltd, 1985
Open University *et al.*, *The Good Health Guide*, Pan Books, 1980
Derek and Julie Parker, *Do It Yourself Health*, Thames and Hudson, 1982
Miriam Polunin (ed.), *The Health and Fitness Handbook*, Van Nostrand Reinhold, 1982
Brian J. Sharkey, *Physiology of Fitness* (3rd edn), Human Kinetics Publishers, 1990
John Stevenson, *Social Conditions in Britain between the Wars*, A.P. Watt Ltd, 1977
Miriam Stoppard, *Healthcare*, Weidenfeld and Nicolson, 1980

Unit 20
Ian Blair, *Taming the Atom*, IOP Publishing Ltd, 1983
John O.M. Bockris *et al.*, *Solar Hydrogen Energy*, Vermilion, 1991
Heinz Gartmann, *Science as History*, Hodder and Stoughton, 1960
Donald Hunt, *The Tunnel*, Images Publishing Ltd, 1994
Steve Jones, *The Language of the Genes*, HarperCollins*Publishers*, 1993
Steve Lambert and Suzanne Ropiequet (eds), *CD ROM – The New Papyrus* (Foreword William H. Gates), Microsoft Press, 1986
Stuart Gordon Macdonald, *Down the Drain*, Little Brown and Co, 1989
Fred Pearce, *The Dammed*, The Bodley Head, 1992
Graham Wright, *Mastering Computers* (3rd edn) Macmillan, 1988

Unit 21
Philippe de la Cotardière (ed.), *Larousse Astronomy*, Hamlyn, 1987
John D. Barrow and Joseph Silk, *The Left Hand of Creation*, Basic Books, 1984
John Gribbin, *Our Changing Universe: The New Astronomy*, Macmillan, 1976
Fred Hoyle, *Astronomy Today*, Heinemann, 1975
William J. Kaufmann and Frank D. Drake, 'Extraterrestrial Life' in *Universe*, W.H. Freeman and Co, 1968
Jayant Narlikar, *The Structure of the Universe*, Oxford University Press, 1977
Carole Stott and George Philip, *The Greenwich Guide to Astronomy in Action*, George Philip, 1989

Unit 22
Guy Arnold, *Aid and the Third World: The North/South Divide*, Robert Royce Ltd, 1985
Michael Barke (ed.), *Case Studies of the Third World*, Oliver and Boyd, 1991
Maggie Black, *A Cause for Our Times: Oxfam, the first fifty years*, Oxfam, 1992
Peter Donaldson, *Worlds Apart* (2nd edn), BBC Publications, 1986
R.J. Johnston and P.J. Taylor (eds), *A World in Crisis?* Basil Blackwell, 1989
John Lea, *Tourism and Development in the Third World*, Routledge, 1988
Harold Lever and Christopher Huhne, *Debt and Danger: The World Financial Crisis*, A.D. Peters and Co Ltd, 1985
John Madeley *et al*, *Who Runs the World?*, Christian Aid, 1994
Barbara Ward, *The Home of Man*, André Deutsch, 1976

Introduction

General Studies is an odd subject. It is not a subject at all; and it is all subjects. A course in General Studies is thought either to be worthless (by students, teachers and admissions tutors alike), or to be valuable as the one that makes sense of all the others. In some schools and colleges it is pursued as a non-examination course in the interests of 'breadth' and 'roundedness'; in others, candidates are entered for a General-Studies examination as an 'incentive', or with a view to scoring 'points'. Most people know what History is and why it is a valid subject of study; but there would be less agreement about the place of General Studies in the 16–19 curriculum – and still less about what a suitable syllabus for General Studies should look like.

It is not surprising that the syllabuses offered by examining boards are so diverse. By far the most popular is the NEAB syllabus. This includes reading comprehension, foreign language, spatial and mechanical, mathematical and general-knowledge exercises, all of which use questions of the multiple-choice kind; and require essays on the arts, sciences and social sciences. Thus, knowledge and skills are tested from right across the curriculum. The comprehensiveness of the NEAB syllabus is both its chief strength, and its chief weakness.

The London (ULEAC) AS syllabus contains most of the above items (with the conspicuous omission of a foreign-language exercise), but questions invite 'short answers' rather than offering multiple-choice alternatives. The Cambridge (UCLES) syllabus (at both A and AS level) makes the further omission of mathematics, but does include a 'data-response' question on Paper 1, an English comprehension and short-answer general-knowledge questions. Papers 2 and 3 call for essay-answers to questions on 'Humanities and Culture', and 'Science and Technology', respectively.

Coursework is an option on the NEAB and UCLES syllabuses, but is a compulsory component of the AEB syllabus. The focus of attention in this syllabus is not, say, 'history' or 'science'; it is 'conflict', 'leisure' or 'power' viewed historically and scientifically. Thus the study of each of three 'themes' is a General Studies syllabus in itself, calling for the writing of short, argumentative essays on 'contemporary issues'.

This book has been compiled with all of these syllabuses in mind; but it may also underpin any course issuing from no particular syllabus, or leading to no examination at all. It may serve as a teaching resource; it may supply fuel for class debate; or it may be the basis for open-learning work, where the student is partly, or entirely independent of a course tutor. Only the title of the book defines its readership in any way.

Each subject-unit has five parts: Parts 1 and 2 present information diagrammatically. These are teaching pages – but to each part is appended a set of review questions of a multiple-choice, or open-ended kind. Part 3 is a passage of up to 400 words of the sort chosen for the exercise of reading comprehension. Here, it relates to the subject in hand, and the questions attached to it invite discussion or take the form of a comprehension exercise. Part 4 comprises six or eight quotations from published texts that are directly relevant to the subject, and that might serve (in a manner explained in the section entitled: 'The All-Purpose Essay Plan') as raw material for an essay. Part 5 is a similar anthology of views, this time, the non-expert views of the man or woman in the street or the corridor.

Interspersed among the 22 subject-units, there are 'Items' of a teaching and testing kind in mathematics, French, English Language, and general knowledge. Finally, answers are given to all the 'closed' questions posed throughout the book and the final component is a comprehensive index.

The All-Purpose Essay Plan

A-Level students used to be told that essays should be in three parts: they should have an Introduction, a Main Body, and a Conclusion. It was fairly obvious what the Introduction and the Conclusion were for; it was the Main Body that was the problem. The advice begged all the important questions about 'structure' and 'line of argument'. It may be more helpful to think of an essay as having two parts:

CONTENT

COMMENT

These should be in something like the ratio: 2 parts Content to 1 part Comment.

There is no time for an Introduction one extended-paragraph long, in an examination essay. The most that is needed is:

(a) a definition of the key term(s) in the title; and

(b) a statement of what you intend to cover (and, perhaps, what you intend to leave out).

The danger in writing a more developed Introduction is that you may state your position too soon, and you find yourself not just into the essay, but out the other side before you know it. You've shot your bolt – and that is when panic sets in.

In the first two thirds of the essay you demonstrate knowledge and understanding of the part of the syllabus that the question is intended to call to mind.

An essay is about an issue, and any issue arousing interest has a conflict at the heart of it – a difference between two points of view, two angles, two emphases. The Content, therefore, is best divided in two: A and B.

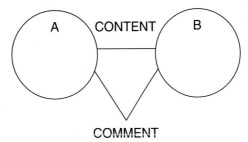

These two positions, theories, alternatives or arguments should be presented in turn. They may contradict, or complement each other. They may be the past and present views of an issue; advantages and disadvantages; two states, or two stages. The important thing is that there is more than one position; there would be no question to answer if there were not.

As an example, consider this question: **How far do the media, in your view, help or hinder the public understanding of science?**

All that you need to write by way of Introduction here would be something like this: 'The media are taken to include cinema, recorded music, radio and magazine and book publishing. I shall confine myself here to a consideration of the so-called 'mass media': television and the press.'

Your A position might be that the 'quality media' (i.e. broadsheet newspapers, and their television equivalents) have science correspondents who keep the public in touch with important medical breakthroughs, astronomical discoveries and the politics and economics of 'big science'. Then your B position might be that the 'popular' media trivialize, sensationalize and personalize science – or, for better or worse, neglect it altogether, because it isn't sexy.

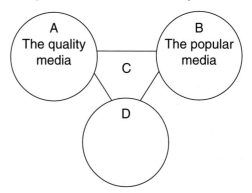

The C stands for case-study. A really telling illustration lifts an essay off the page – and an argument must contain at least one relevant example, chosen so as to reinforce your case and lead to your conclusion.

The title above asks for 'your view', as any title will – whether explicitly or implicitly. The D, therefore, stands for discussion. This is the place for a considered judgement that is yours, or that you have made yours.

Here is a second essay title: **We speak of progress in science and technology. Does it make sense to speak of progress in the arts?**

It may be that you (and most other commentators) take the view that to speak of progress in the arts is preposterous; in which case your A and B positions might be two different reasons for holding this view. Your 'plan' for such an essay would, perhaps, look something like this:

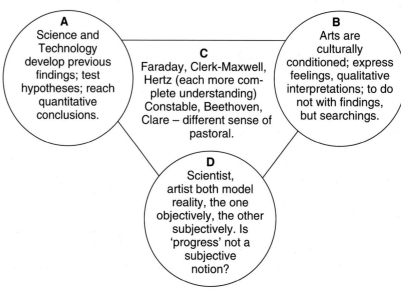

Part 4 of each chapter in this book is a page of quotations. These are intended to serve as the raw materials for an essay. Here is a typical Part 4, using eight quotations that may be of use in answer to this question: **'The poor you will have with you always' (John 12.8). Is it inevitable, in your view, that there will always be rich and poor?**

1
If you wish to be perfect, sell your possessions and give to the poor, and then you will have riches in heaven; and come follow me.' When the young man heard this, he went away with a heavy heart, for he was a man of great wealth. Jesus said to his disciples, 'I tell you this; a rich man will find it hard to enter the kingdom of heaven. I repeat, it is easier for a camel to pass through the eye of a needle than for a rich man to enter the kingdom of God.

Matthew 19:21–4

2
The world has always been divided into two classes – those who have saved, and those who have spent – the thrifty and the extravagant. The building of all the houses, the mills, the bridges, and the ships, and the accomplishment of all other great works which have rendered man civilized and happy, has been done by the savers, the thrifty; and those who have wasted their resources have always been their slaves.

(Richard Cobden, from a speech to working men in Huddersfield)

3
That there should be a class of men who live by their daily labour in every state is the ordinance of God; and doubtless it is a wise and righteous one; but that this class should be otherwise than frugal, contented, intelligent, and happy is not the design of Providence, but springs solely from the weakness, self-indulgence, and perverseness of man himself.

(Samuel Smiles, *Self-Help*, 1866)

4
We are concerned about development because we are concerned about the poor. The purpose of development should be to reduce poverty, if we can to eliminate poverty. Therefore in any rational thinking about development, the poor man should be rated as fifty times more important to us than the rich man – not the other way round. To say there should be equal rating is not enough because we are concerned about poverty.

(Hans Singer, 'Why do we need new approaches?' in *The Rich and The Poor*, 1974)

5
Just as the propertied classes of yesteryear opposed every reform and predicted imminent economic disaster if eight-year olds could no longer work in the mills, so today those groups that profit from the poverty that keeps people hungry are attempting to maintain the status quo between the rich and poor worlds.

(Susan George, *How the Other Half Dies*, 1976)

6
The fact that the opportunities open to the poor in a competitive society are much more restricted than those open to the rich does not make it less true that in such a society the poor are much more free than a person commanding much greater material comfort in a different type of society .... There are no absolute impediments, no dangers to bodily security and freedom that confine (the poor man) to the task and the environment to which a superior has assigned him.

(F.A. Hayek, *The Road to Serfdom* (1976 edn), 1944)

7
The whims and enthusiasms of rich individuals have given Britain much of its character. Abolish the rich and who would build country houses, breed racehorses, publish *The Times*? Who would finance plays and concerts rejected by committees, back festivals, save lost causes? Who would bother to restore fine buildings and antique furniture?

(William Davis, *It's No Sin to be Rich*, 1976)

8
Why do we in the western world allow families to live in sub-standard housing side by side with building workers for whom we are told there is no work? .... For what reason are we expected to accept the co-existence of unmet needs, unemployed people and unused financial resources? Our economic system was not ordained by God.

(Tony Benn, *Arguments for Socialism*, 1979)

It is unlikely that your notes (whether made in class, dictated, copied from the board, or made in the course of reading) will take the form of eight such extended quotations; but they are quite likely to derive from a number of different sources, and to represent a number of different viewpoints. Whether you are planning a coursework essay, or reviewing and re-organizing your notes prior to an examination, you could do worse than to cast the material into something like the following triangle.

A
A society that believed in God, and in God's plan, thought that rich and poor were part of the natural order of things. This applied to 1st century Palestine (John) and to Victorian England (Cobden/Smiles). The ill-disposed thought the poor should be 'contented' with their lot; readers of Matthew 19. should have been more charitable.

C
It may indeed be that the rich have built big houses, bridges, ships (Cobden), have bred racehorses and restored antiques (Davis), but they have done these things (and built many a folly) to their own greater glory. It was Hayek's (and Mrs Thatcher's) view that wealth would 'trickle down' to the poor, like champagne poured into the topmost glass of a pyramid of glasses.

B
God did not ordain that there should be rich and poor – man did (Benn). Reduction of poverty is not enough; it must be eliminated (Prof. Singer). Nor is it enough to change things in this country: two worlds are no more acceptable than two nations (George). There has to be positive discrimination in favour of the poor (Singer).

D
Little of the champagne seems to reach the glasses at the bottom. The poor seem to go on getting relatively, and absolutely, poorer in Hayek's 'competitive society'. Is it better to be free and starving, or not free and fed? This is not a question that the rich can answer. They may say that some poverty is inevitable. The poor will answer the question very differently.

The obvious A position is that there will always be rich and poor; likewise the obvious B position is that there is nothing inevitable about this – and nothing just.

Part 5 of each of the units in this book is also a page of quotations – but they represent the opinions of non-experts. These are intended to serve as starting points for discussion or essay-writing. The eight quotations below might be drawn on in answer to the following question: **Is the Information Superhighway all pluses, or are there minuses, too?**

1 It's so depersonalizing. Are relationships to be reduced to long-distance exchanges of bits, or bytes? The idea of doing your shopping, studying or borrowing library-books at a computer terminal – and never actually meeting anybody – is an awful prospect.

2 You can have unlimited communication with hundreds of thousands of people all over the world on the Internet, for the price of a local phone call. The flat-rate charge means wide-open access at the user's convenience – and, what's more, in English.

3 The educational potential of networking is immense. Schools can communicate with each other across the globe; curriculum materials can be downloaded; people can join on-line discussion groups, and have access to an enormous range of information-rich databases.

4 E.M. Forster's story *The Machine Stops* was prophetic: everybody staring at a screen, helpless when the computer crashes, or viruses multiply. If we let ourselves become dependent on high technology, we'll be unable to cope with machine failure when it comes – and Sod's Law says it will.

5 Networking is an essentially rather élitist sort of activity, for – mostly young, male technofreaks, and jargonauts, living in a kind of virtual reality cyberspace. It excludes a whole global underclass of computer illiterates – and that's most of us. It empowers technocrats at everybody else's expense. They speak in a language that's all their own, like children in playground code.

6 As the network gets overcrowded, so access will be rationed. The highway will be road-priced; and it'll be the money men, the media tycoons and telephone companies who will decide what's available. More will almost certainly mean worse as it has done with other media.

7 Travelling the I-way, or 'Infobahn', is an absorbing pastime in itself. It's tremendously satisfying to be in touch with like-minded strangers. People who are quite shy in company learn social skills and are, perhaps, empowered for the first time in their lives. The Internet is a real force for global democracy and individual self-expression.

8 The Superhighway will make most other media obsolete. Whole libraries become available, a database holding the full text of 16 national newspapers will be updated daily, making CD-ROMs look quaint; we'll download art galleries … the possibilities are endless.

The average person in the street is unlikely to voice such sentiments in quite such a considered way, but comparable views may be heard on Radio 4, or read on the correspondence and review pages of broadsheet newspapers.

The essay title suggests an obvious division into A and B positions. Few innovations are all pluses: the likelihood is that your C and D positions will seek to establish a balance. This is how the eight opinions might be incorporated into an essay-answer.

A
It must be a good thing to facilitate global communication. The more we know each other the more we are likely to understand – and the low cost is a decided plus (2). A generation of young people is growing up for whom travelling the Infobahn is no more complicated than exploring TV channels. The implications for education are far-reaching (3).

C
Still, if the 'highway' analogy applies, it cannot be said that any one group enjoys a monopoly of our roads (6). And as – literally – the roads become more and more congested, it may be no bad thing if some people do some of their shopping by E-mail (1), and more present-day commuters work from home.

B
The vision of us all becoming solitary screen-watchers, not going out and inter-acting with flesh-and-blood people is pretty ghastly (1), and certainly there are dangers of over-dependence, addiction even (4), as there are with most things. These dangers may be especially real among young, withdrawn, cerebral males (5).

D
We must harvest the benefits of the Information Superhighway (8) for the maximum number of people. Indeed, it could provide a channel for democratic participation (7). Perhaps the exploitation of networking in education (3) is our best guarantee against more meaning worse (6).

Part One
Classical

Classical architecture has its origins in the Greece of the 5th Century BC. The Romans took over many of the lines of Greek buildings, but to more monumental effect. The Greeks contributed the simple principle of post and lintel, which grew into the fully articulated colonnade. The Romans contributed the round-headed arch, and the line of arches (the arcade) that grew into the viaduct. (Note: the division of the triumphal arch into three, horizontally and vertically was a tripartism which came to be a regular feature of classical buildings.) Below is a composite classical building: that is, it contains elements of the classical style, but it is not any building in particular.

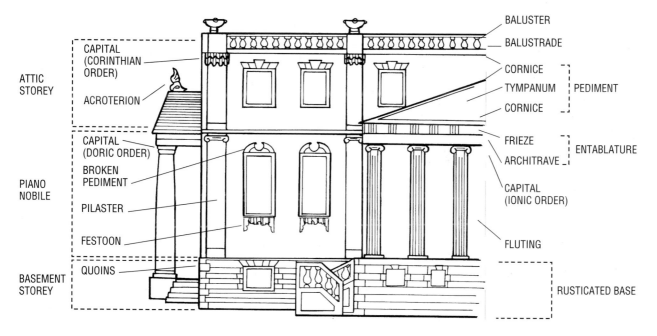

Classical architecture in Britain passed through five distinct, but overlapping, stages from the Renaissance onwards:

1 The **Palladian** period, from around 1615, when Inigo Jones introduced the restrained, symmetrical style of Andreas Palladio from Italy. His villas featured pedimented windows and porticoes.
2 The **Baroque** period, from around 1670, when Wren, Vanbrugh, Hawksmoor and others built houses and churches in a massive style featuring giant-order columns, domes, and heavy sculpting.
3 The **Georgian** period, from around 1750, when the Woods laid out Bath, and Adam planned squares, terraces, and circuses in Edinburgh and London: mass-produced, yet elegant.

4 The **Regency** period, from around 1810, when Nash (in particular) designed the Regent's Park terraces, and town houses were built in spas, finished in painted stucco, and wrought-iron balconies.
5 The **Greek Revival** period, from around 1820, when Barry and Smirke (and the architects of New England) returned to an uncluttered, Doric and Ionic Greek style.

A **Which is which below?**
B **Locate and identify each of the features labelled on the composite classical building, on a building or buildings, near you.**
C **Name one building of each of the five periods.**

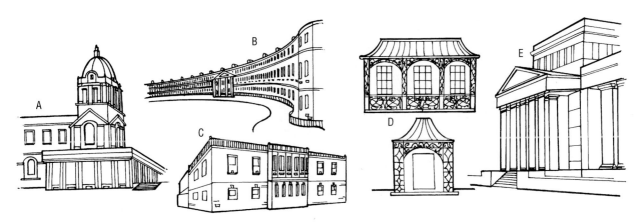

Part Two
Gothic

The Saxons were builders, not architects. Their buildings were crude in comparison with those of the classical period. The Normans re-introduced a neo-Roman ('Romanesque') style of architecture into Britain. It was a style characterized by the round-headed arch, the massive, round pillar and the barrel vault. There was a limit to how high a building could be, until (in the early 1100s), the pointed arch was introduced. The Gothic trend was towards increasing height as well as lightness (in both senses of the word): stonework was less weighty, more slender and more finely decorated; and (as glass became more available) the size of windows grew. From around 1200 until the English Renaissance of the 1500s, Gothic architecture took three distinctive forms. The style was revived in the 19th Century, giving us four 'periods':

1200–1300
Early English
Windows were tall and thin (resembling those in castles); but they came to be clustered in twos and threes. Buttresses strengthened exterior walls; flying buttresses were devised to reinforce upper storeys.

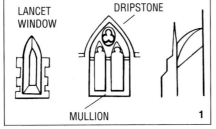

1400–1500
Perpendicular
Arches flattened over doors and windows. Horizontal bars (transoms) came to be as important as mullions. Vaulting was flattened in the celebrated 'fan' style.

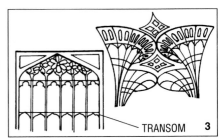

1300–1400
Decorated
Windows grew wider, with more delicate tracery. Plain geometry gave way to subtlety, with the ogee shape, and the carving of foliage in, for example, the rose window. Vaulting sprang more daringly from columns, soaring ever higher.

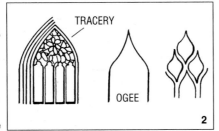

1800s
Gothic Revival (or 'Victorian Gothick')
This was a by-product of Romanticism. Though the buildings themselves were utilitarian (colleges, banks, stations), and the material was often brick, buildings aspired to be medieval in spirit. Notable architects were Pugin, Barry and Butterfield.

To which of these four periods does each of the ten features (A–J) belong?

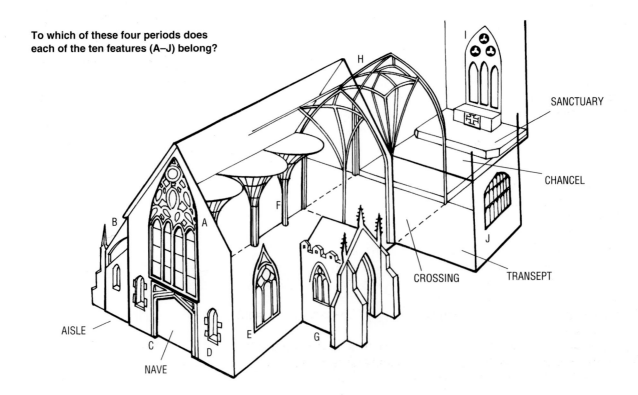

Part Three
Concerning Space

Sir Banister Fletcher, in his *History of Architecture* of 1896, called architecture the 'Mother of the Arts' in that it provides an opportunity for expression through painting, sculpture and the decorative arts. Nikolaus Pevsner went further, and claimed that architecture is superior to all the other arts and that they seek independence from architecture at their peril.

A bicycle shed is a building; Lincoln Cathedral is a piece of architecture. Nearly everything that encloses space on a scale sufficient for a human being to move in is a building; the term architecture applies only to buildings designed with a view to aesthetic appeal. 5 Now aesthetic sensations may be caused by a building in three different ways. First, they may be produced by the treatment of walls, proportions of windows, the relation of wall-space to window-space, of one storey to another, of ornamentation such as the tracery of a fourteenth-century window, or the leaf and fruit garlands of a Wren 10 porch. Secondly, the treatment of the exterior of a building as a whole is aesthetically significant, its contrasts of block against block, the effect of a pitched or flat roof or a dome, the rhythm of projections and recessions. Thirdly, there is the effect on our senses of the treatment of the interior, the sequence of rooms, the widening out of 15 a nave at the crossing, the stately movement of a Baroque staircase. The first of these three ways is two-dimensional; it is the painter's way. The second is three-dimensional, and as it treats the building as volume, as a plastic unit, it is the sculptor's way. The third is three-dimensional too, but it concerns space; it is the architect's own 20 way more than the others. What distinguishes architecture from painting and sculpture is its spatial quality ….

But architecture, though primarily spatial, is not exclusively spatial. In every building, besides enclosing space, the architect models volume and plans surface, i.e. designs an exterior and sets 25 out individual walls. That means that the good architect requires the sculptor's and the painter's modes of vision in addition to his own spatial imagination. Thus architecture is the most comprehensive of all visual arts and has a right to claim superiority over the others. 30

This aesthetic superiority is, moreover, supplemented by a social superiority. Neither sculpture nor painting, although both are rooted in elementary creative and imitative instincts, surrounds us to the same extent as architecture, acts upon us so incessantly and so ubiquitously. We can avoid intercourse with what people call the 35 Fine Arts, but we cannot escape buildings and the subtle but penetrating effects of their character, noble or mean, restrained or ostentatious, genuine or meretricious.

(Nikolaus Pevsner, *An Outline of European Architecture*, 1943)

1 Replace the following words and phrases with ones of your own:
   (a) 'aesthetic appeal'; (line 4)
   (b) 'projections'; (line 13)
   (c) 'a plastic unit'; (line 18)
   (d) 'so incessantly and so ubiquitously'. (lines 33–4)
2 What would you expect an 'ostentatious' building to be like (as opposed to a 'restrained' one); and a 'meretricious' building (as opposed to one that is 'genuine')?
3 What do you understand Pevsner to mean by 'the stately movement of a Baroque staircase'?
4 Do you accept his distinction between 'building' and 'architecture'?
5 Do you accept his grounds for the claim that architecture is 'superior' to other forms of visual arts?

Part Four
Modern Muddle

Modernism, Brutalism, Post-Modernism, Community Architecture .... It seems there has never been a greater distance between professional and public tastes than there is today. Using any of the quotations below, answer this question: **Are modern buildings a blot on the landscape?**

1
In [the 1920s and 1930s], the crusaders of a rational architecture, the followers of Le Corbusier, Gropius, Mies and the other heroes of the Modern movement ..., were lined up against the ... defenders of traditional, imitative styles. ... the men of the new architecture attacked and routed the enemy. But strangely enough, the aftermath of their victory looks like a gigantic architectural muddle. Most human beings are still living in substandard conditions, the homeless are increasing in number, the cities have turned into uncontrollable problems.

(P.M. Bardi, *Architecture*, 1972)

2
We have modified our historic townscapes to suit financially speculative building activities without being able to generate a new and valid environment. We have accorded priority to motor traffic and relegated the pedestrian above or below ground.

(Reinhard Gieselman, *Contemporary Church Architecture*, 1972)

3
Technology has come late to the construction industry, replacing craft-based processes with factory-made components assembled on the site. Prefabrication brings to architects the magic of repetition, the capacity to multiply a single thought in enormous quantity and at a scale surpassing all previous mass production. ... Each building is a thoroughly foreseen collection of standard parts, unrelated to tradition, or to the place, incapable of subtleties of grouping or articulation.

(Theo Crosby, *How to Play the Environment Game*, 1973)

4
No revolutionary change in the basic form or location of housing seems likely. The possibility that the majority of English people might in future be housed either in city tower blocks or in new towns seems remote, and it is more likely that urban renewal will continue to locate most people in existing towns and in fairly traditional types of housing.

(John Burnett, *A Social History of Housing 1815–1970*, 1978)

5
The pressure to preserve everything has led to the preservation of mediocre buildings while fine buildings occupying more valuable sites have ... been wantonly destroyed. Increasing restrictions are being imposed on architects which are so inhibiting as to destroy at the outset any chance of successful architecture, yet economic power has been able to force through appalling desecrations of historic town-centres. It would almost be better to have a free-for-all.

(Michael Raeburn, *Architecture of the Modern World*, 1980)

6
Very tall buildings have a unique capacity to create an identity for institutions, cities, and even countries. But by the end of the 1970s, possibly because of the prevailing lack of belief in architectural theory, skyscrapers even in America had become vapid, without the power to communicate or symbolize. Their owners after all had very little to believe in, beyond bland corporate efficiency.

(Deyan Sudjic, *Norman Frost, Richard Rogers, James Stirling*, 1986)

7
Given the unpopularity of most Modern architecture built in the 1960s and early 1970s, perhaps it is surprising that architects continued to work in the idiom for so long. In fact, the reason was rooted deep in the architect's consciousness. Modern architecture was as much a moral crusade as a way of building. It was seen as naturally good because it told no lies ... no self-respecting modern architect would pretend that one material was another.

(Jonathan Glancey, *New British Architecture*, 1989)

8
The best buildings of the future will interact dynamically with the climate in order better to meet the users' needs and make optimum use of energy. More like robots than temples, these apparitions with their chameleon-like surfaces insist that we re-think yet again the art of building. Architecture will no longer be a question of mass and volume but of lightweight structures whose superimposed transparent layers will create form so that constructions will become dematerialized.

(Richard Rogers, *Architecture: A Modern View*, 1990)

Part Five
Beauty and the Brutish

The buildings in and among which we live and work have a significant effect on us. Their size and shape and height and texture seem to matter to our well-being. Answer this question in the light of any of the opinions expressed below: **How do we judge whether or not a building is beautiful?**

1   It's a question of scale: massive buildings, whatever their style, are intimidating. Tower-blocks are inhuman; they make us feel tiny and insignificant. Beauty is a matter of proportion. Tower-blocks are out of proportion because their single defining feature is verticality.

2   Good architecture has nothing to do with fluted columns or pilasters or any other bits and pieces of *appliqué*. Classical or gothic knick-knacks add nothing to buildings that don't work in architectural terms. Beauty is about form following function; about appropriateness; about honesty.

3   Modern buildings are soulless. There's no art or craft in them. They're all engineering. There's nothing to catch the eye, no detail, no ornament. They're purely functional. Success is measured in terms of rental per square foot, not in terms of whether it's gracious or good to look at and has integrity as a work of art.

4   Modern art, modern music – these can be as outrageous as they like. You don't have to go to the gallery, and you don't have to listen to music that you don't like; but you have no choice when it comes to architecture. You can't help but confront it daily – so it needs to be a thing of beauty, and good design.

5   Environmentalists say they want to conserve the buildings of the past, yet there is nothing 'green' about old buildings. The materials – stone, hardwood, marble – are expensive and in short supply; and they waste energy. Modern buildings are better insulated, and are built of more environmentally-friendly materials. Like everything else, architecture has to be sustainable.

6   The most beautiful buildings are the plainest and simplest: the Parthenon; a Norman church, the Crystal Palace. The modern equivalents of these buildings are London's Centre Point and the Seagram Building on Fifth Avenue. These are the buildings our descendants will slap preservation orders on.

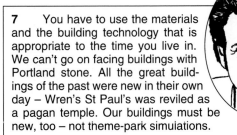

7   You have to use the materials and the building technology that is appropriate to the time you live in. We can't go on facing buildings with Portland stone. All the great buildings of the past were new in their own day – Wren's St Paul's was reviled as a pagan temple. Our buildings must be new, too – not theme-park simulations.

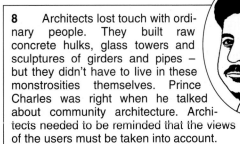

8   Architects lost touch with ordinary people. They built raw concrete hulks, glass towers and sculptures of girders and pipes – but they didn't have to live in these monstrosities themselves. Prince Charles was right when he talked about community architecture. Architects needed to be reminded that the views of the users must be taken into account.

Inventors

Here is a list of inventors, together with their birth and death dates, and a list of inventions. Match each inventor with the relevant invention.

1 Richard Arkwright (1732–92)

2 Charles Babbage (1792–1871)

3 Leo Hendrick Baekeland (1863–1944)

4 John Logie Baird (1888–1946)

5 Alexander Graham Bell (1847–1922)

6 Henry Bessemer (1813–98)

7 Clarence Birdseye (1886–1956)

8 Louis Braille (1809–52)

9 Werner Von Braun (1912–74)

10 Chester F. Carlson (1906–68)

11 Wallace Hume Carothers (1896–1937)

12 Christopher Cockerell (b. 1910)

13 Jacques-Yves Cousteau (b. 1910)

14 Louis Daguerre (1789–1851)

15 Gottlieb Daimler (1834–1900)

16 Abraham Darby (1678–1717)

17 John Boyd Dunlop (1840–1921)

18 George Eastman (1854–1932)

19 Thomas Alva Edison (1847–1931)

20 Willem Einthoven (1860–1927)

21 Robert Fulton (1765–1815)

22 Johannes Gutenberg (1400–68)

23 James Hargreaves (1722–78)

24 Christiaan Huygens (1629–95)

25 Friedrich König (1774–1832)

26 Etienne Lenoir (1822–1900)

27 Auguste and Louis Lumiere (1862–1954)

28 Guglielmo Marconi (1874–1937)

29 Samuel Morse (1791–1872)

30 William Murdock (1754–1839)

31 Thomas Newcomen (1663–1729)

32 Charles Parsons (1854–1931)

33 Isaac Pitman (1813–97)

34 Igor Sikorsky (1889–1972)

35 George Stephenson (1781–1848)

36 Joseph Swan (1828–1914)

37 Evangelista Torricelli (1608–47)

38 Alessandro Volta (1745–1827)

39 Robert Watson-Watt (1892–1973)

40 James Watt (1736–1819)

41 Eli Whitney (1765–1825)

42 Frank Whittle (b. 1907)

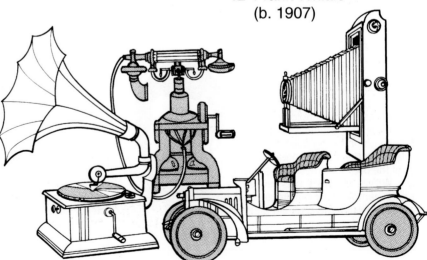

ITEM

A

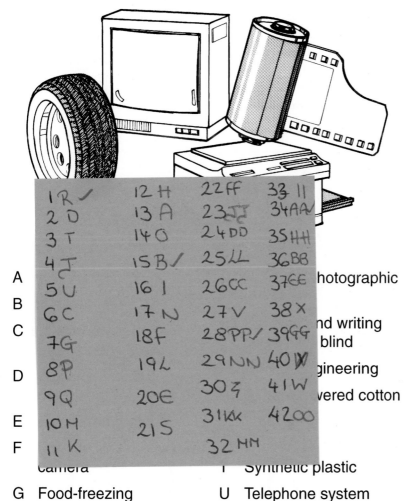

Handwritten note:
1 R ✓   12 H   22 FF   33 II
2 D   13 A   23 JJ   34 AA
3 T   14 O   24 DD   35 HH
4 J   15 B ✓ 25 LL   36 BB
5 U   16 I   26 CC   37 EE
6 C   17 N   27 V   38 X
7 G   18 F   28 PP ✓ 39 GG
8 P   19 L   29 NN   40 M
9 Q   20 E   30 Z   41 W
10 H   21 S   31 KK   42 OO
11 K   32 MM

A
B
C
D
E
F ...hotographic camera

G Food-freezing techniques

H Hovercraft

I Iron-smelting using coke

J Live television transmission

K Nylon – first all-synthetic fibre

L Phonograph – first gramophone

M Photocopying machine

N Pneumatic tyre

...nd writing ...blind

...gineering

...vered cotton

T Synthetic plastic

U Telephone system

V Cinema film camera and projector

W Cotton gin

X   Electric battery

Y   Fuel-efficient steam engine

Z   Gas lighting

AA Helicopter

BB Incandescent light

CC Internal combustion engine

DD Mechanical clock

EE Mercury barometer

FF Printing from movable type

GG Radar scanning system

HH Railway engine

II   Shorthand system

JJ   Spinning jenny

KK Steam-driven piston engine

LL Steam-driven printing press

MM Steam turbine

NN Telegraph and code

OO Turbojet engine

PP Wireless telegraphy

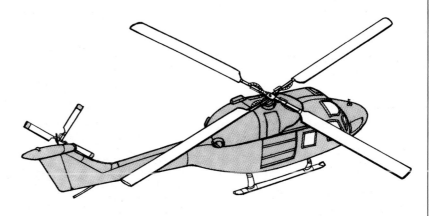

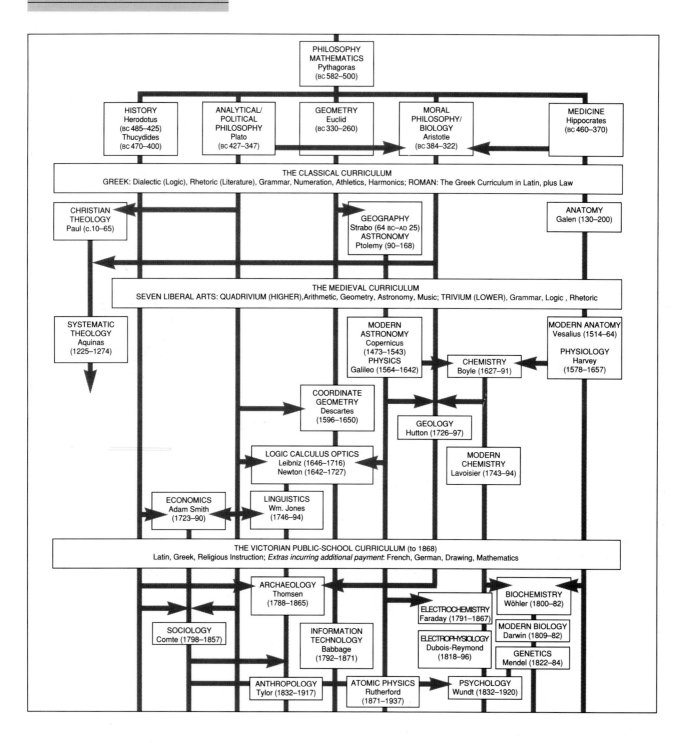

Part One
The Division of Knowledge

'Philosophy' means the love of wisdom or learning. It is where systematic 'knowledge' began; all academic subjects are the fruits of Philosophy. No new subject has been inspired by one person only, but the following were all pioneers who took learning along important new paths.

A Which old or new paths of knowledge do you think are most likely to be the most heavily trodden in the future?

B Who did which?

1 Expounded the view that erosion leads to sedimentation.
2 Discovered the statistical laws of transmission of hereditary factors.
3 Proved that it is possible to synthesize organic compounds.
4 Demonstrated the importance of oxygen to the maintenance of life.
5 Showed that the mind can be studied scientifically and objectively.
6 Devised laws concerning the passage of electricity through a solution.

A FARADAY
B HUTTON
C LAVOISIER
D MENDEL
E WOHLER
F WUNDT

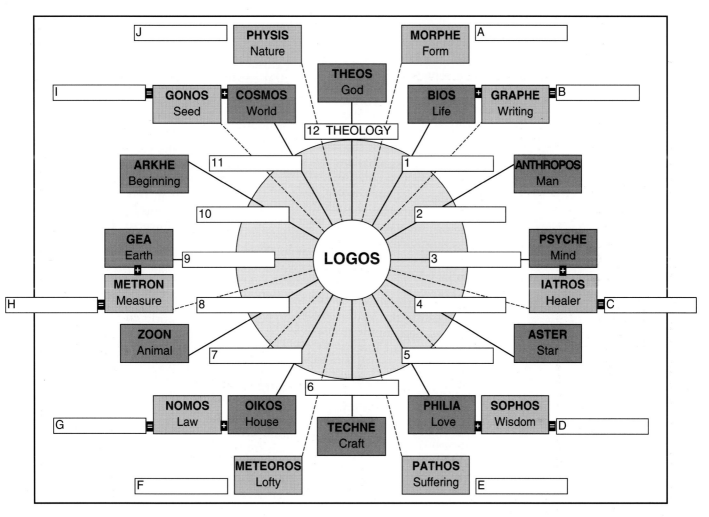

Part Two
Subject Names

In the clock diagram below, each of the 'hours' is a Greek root. At the centre of the clock is the Greek word 'logos', meaning 'word' or 'reason'. We attach this in its English form to each of the 12 roots shown here – as well as to many others – to give us the names of subjects of study, not all of which are on the academic curriculum.

1 Insert the appropriate names in boxes 1–11. The box at 12 o'clock is already completed by way of example.
2 In addition, fill in the 'half-hour' boxes (A–J). Boxes A, E, F and J are also '–ologies'; boxes B, C, D, G, H and I are compounds each of two Greek roots. What does each one mean?
3 What subject names do these further combinations give us, and what do they mean?
   (a) GEA + MORPHE + LOGOS =
   (b) GEA + GRAPHE =
   (c) ASTER + NOMOS =
   (d) BIOS + TECHNE + LOGOS =
   (e) ZOON + GEA + GRAPHE =
4 Other subjects of academic study have other roots. Which is which?
   (a) The adjectival form of a Greek word for 'learning'.
   (b) A combination of the Greek for 'word' and the Latin for 'associate'.
   (c) The Arabic word for 'bone-setting' or 're-uniting'.
   (d) A noun from the Greek verb meaning 'to narrate'.
   (e) The craft (techne) belonging to the Greek Muses.
   (f) An Arabic reference to pouring fluids in Egypt.
   (g) An adjectival form of the Latin word for 'tongue'.
   (h) The Greek adjective from the word for a 'Citizen' (of a 'City').

A ALGEBRA
B CHEMISTRY
C HISTORY
D LINGUISTICS
E MATHEMATICS
F MUSIC
G POLITICS
H SOCIOLOGY

Part Three

Arts and Sciences

The following passage is an extract from a speech delivered by the biologist T.H. Huxley at the opening of a science college in Birmingham in 1880.

The representatives of the Humanists in the nineteenth century, take their stand upon classical education as the sole avenue to culture, as firmly as if we were still in the age of Renaissance. Yet, surely, the present intellectual relations of the modern and ancient worlds are profoundly different from those which obtained three centuries ago.

The distinctive character of our own times lies in the vast and constantly increasing part which is played by natural knowledge. Not only is our daily life shaped by it, not only does the prosperity of millions of men depend upon it, but our whole theory of life has long been influenced, consciously or unconsciously, by the general conceptions of the universe which have been forced upon us by physical science.

In fact, the most elementary acquaintance with the results of scientific investigation show us that they offer a broad and striking contradiction to the opinion so implicitly credited and taught in the Middle Ages.

The notions of the beginning and the end of the world entertained by our forefathers are no longer credible. It is very certain that the earth is not the chief body of the material universe, and that the world is not subordinated to man's use. It is even more certain that nature is the expression of a definite order with which nothing interferes, and that the chief business of mankind is to learn that order and govern themselves accordingly. Moreover this scientific 'criticism of life' presents itself to us with different credentials from any other. It appeals not to authority, nor to what anybody may have thought or said, but to nature. It admits that all our interpretations of natural fact are more or less imperfect and symbolic, and bids the learner seek for truth not among words but among things. It warns us that the assertion which outstrips evidence is not only a blunder but a crime.

1 What do you suppose Huxley meant by:
  (a) 'the representatives of the Humanists'; (line 1)
  (b) 'natural knowledge'; (line 8–9)
  (c) 'subordinated to man's use'; (line 21)
  (d) 'scientific "criticism of life"'? (line 25)
2 In what respects might it be said that science contradicts what was believed and taught in the Middle Ages?
3 To what extent has your own scientific education given you the certainty that 'nature is the expression of a definite order'?
4 How far do you agree with Huxley's statement that truth is to be found 'not among words but among things'?

Part Four
Broader Abroad

The English curriculum is unusual in that, for students aged 16, it narrows to two, three or four subjects. The student of 16–19 elsewhere commonly studies *more* subjects than before, not fewer. **State the case for either broadening the 16–19 curriculum, or for leaving it as it is.**

1

We attach great value to the English practice of Specialization. Equally, we attach great importance to those complementary elements in the sixth-form curriculum which are designed to develop the literacy of science specialists and the numeracy of arts specialists. ... [But it] is fairly clear that a 'subject-minded' pupil, as the best are at this age, is likely to resent anything that takes much of his attention from his main interests.

(Ministry of Education, *15–18 'The Crowther Report'*, 1959)

2

All pupils in the sixth form should follow broad courses of study that keep open the options (both for subjects of study in higher education and for eventual occupation) as late as possible in the individual's educational career. We see this as desirable for the student of the arts or social studies as well as for the potential scientist and technologist. In consequence, decisions for or against science and technology would be deferred to an age of greater maturity than is at present the case.

(Department of Education, *The Dainton Report*, 1968)

3

The crucial change was the growing number entering sixth forms who did not want or were unsuited to courses of the traditional kind. This was especially true in comprehensive schools, where by 1966 as many as half the sixth form might be taking no A-levels. ... Certainly there is almost total agreement on the need for change. 'Study in Depth' has had its triumphs. But it is unsuited to the needs of a growing proportion of sixth formers.

(A.D. Edwards, *The Changing Sixth Form in the Twentieth Century*, 1970)

4

Many young people will want to change direction during the 16–19 years, either because they find themselves unsuited to their first path or because they have changed their minds about their ultimate destination. The system must allow for such changes and young people must not be locked into particular routes on the basis of decisions taken at the age of 16 or earlier.

(DES/CLEA, *Education for 16–19 year olds* 'The Macfarlane Report', 1981)

5

In a consultative paper published in May 1984 the Secretaries of State set the objective of broadening the curriculum for A level students without diluting standards, and proposed the introduction of new examination courses to that end – Advanced Supplementary or AS levels – which students would be able to take alongside A level courses and which would require about half the amount of teaching time of an A level course.

(DES (Cmnd 9469), *Better Schools*, 1985)

6

In 1988, the Higginson Committee recommended a pattern of five 'leaner' A-levels. The Thatcher Government dismissed the Report:

AS levels are based on the proposition that an A-level can be cut in two without loss in quality. Paradoxically, a more modest paring of A-levels is viewed with suspicion by the same government. ... The difficulty with relying on a combination of the present A-levels and AS levels is that each A-level takes up too much time.

(Gordon Higginson, 'On the Wrong Track' in the *TES*, 17 June 1988)

7

In principle, there would seem to be seven possible approaches to bringing more breadth to A-level courses: supporting studies, re-cast General Studies, another qualification, GNVQ units, more subjects, a baccalaureate, core skills .... General Studies has been a particular approach to breadth, treating it as a separate examinable subject ..., it may be deflecting us from the hard questions: do we want more breadth and, if so, of what kind?

(Alan Smithers and Pamela Robinson, *General Studies: Breadth at A Level?*, 1993)

8

NVQs will be outcome-related and set agreed levels of competence in vocational areas. GNVQs, on the other hand, are aimed at developing achievements and competences of more general application in a number of fields of employment and will also be concerned with processes. A conflict between the two approaches seems inevitable. It epitomizes the unresolved question of the relative values of education and training.

(Jean McGinty and John Fish, *Further Education in the Market Place*, 1993)

Part Five
The National Curriculum

The government played no part in devising the curriculum in English schools until 1944, when Religious Education was prescribed. The ten-subject National Curriculum was defined in the Education Reform Act of 1988 to make schools more publicly accountable for what they taught. Use any or all of the following opinions to answer this question: **Should the government be the body to choose what is studied in school?**

1   The problem with the government legislating for the curriculum is that the government changes. Is there to be a Conservative curriculum, followed by a Labour Party curriculum at election time, and then back to square one five years later? Heaven forbid!

2   It's important that we all learn basically the same things. How should we achieve equality of opportunity otherwise? There can't be one curriculum for haves, and another one for have-nots, one for the inner-cities, and another for the shires. A National Curriculum is our guarantee of equal rights, and social cohesion.

3   Most countries have a curriculum that is more or less the same right across the country. In an age when people move about a great deal, you need to be sure that the curriculum is much the same in the school that they move to as it is in the one that they've come from.

4   If the government isn't going to decide on the curriculum, who is? The school curriculum is the medium through which we come to understand ourselves as a society – as a nation. It's the way we pass on our culture from one generation to the next. It has to be done on a national scale.

5   I'd rather the curriculum was decided on by elected ministers, kept informed by an educated civil service, than by individual – perhaps eccentric – headteachers, out-of-touch governors, or pushy parents. Something as important as the school curriculum has got to be planned by central government.

6   There was, in effect, a national curriculum long before the 1988 act. Schools all taught more or less the same things. You could even say – languages apart – that schools across Western Europe teach a common curriculum; a sort of de facto EU curriculum.

7   Obviously, we all need to learn to read and write in primary schools, and learn the four rules of arithmetic, but beyond that, there's no need for uniformity at all. Some people are bookish, others aren't. We don't all need to learn French any more than we all need to learn to play the violin. Let schools decide what they're good at, and let parents choose the schools.

8   The thought of the government deciding the curriculum is bad enough: the trouble is politicians think they can decide on syllabuses as well. Before you know where you are, they're choosing the textbooks and re-writing history. I'd rather leave that to Fascists and Communists.

ITEM

B

Affixes: Latin Forms

The meanings of many of the longer Latinate words encountered in English texts can be worked out by breaking them down. They will almost certainly consist of a root and one or more affixes. An **affix** is the name given to any speech element which can be added to a root word. We will consider two kinds of affix here.

A prefix is an affix added before the root – generally modifying its meaning (e.g. un in unhappy).

A suffix is an affix added after the root – generally modifying its part of speech (e.g. ness in softness).

The root word together with its affix can be a noun, an adjective, or a verb.

A noun is, effectively, any word that can fill this gap: The _____. (e.g. The rain.)

An adjective is, effectively, any word that can fill this gap: The _____ rain. (e.g. The heavy rain.)

A verb is, effectively, any word that can fill these gaps: to _____, or it _____. (e.g. to rain, or it is raining.)

A word's part of speech determines that word's job within a sentence.

So, for example, the root SPECT comes from the Latin 'spectare' (meaning 'to look'). The prefix PRO– (meaning 'for', or 'forward'), gives us PROSPECT, which is both a noun and a verb.

*There is little **prospect** of success.* (noun)

*He has gone to **prospect** for gold.* (verb)

Other prefixes that we could add to this root include:

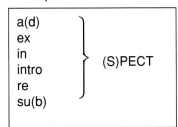

a(d)
ex
in
intro
re
su(b)
} (S)PECT

The suffixes –OR and –IVE give us PROSPECTOR, a noun, and PROSPECTIVE, an adjective.

*He is the **prospector** who found it.* (noun)

*We met the **prospective** wife.* (adjective)

We are going to be concerned mainly with prefixes. Here are seventeen of those most commonly used:

ad	= to	ob (op)	=	inverse
com (con)	= with	per	=	through
contra (o)	= against	pre	=	before
de	= from	pro	=	for, forward
di(s)	= away	re	=	again
e, ex	= out of	se	=	without
in (im)	= in (or, not)	sub	=	under
inter	= between	trans	=	across
intro	= into, inward			

ITEM B

In each of the ten boxes below is a root, preceded by six of the prefixes from page 13. It is followed by six verbs. Each of the verbs is a synonym of one of the prefixes plus the root. For example:

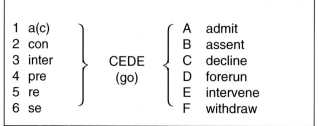

1	a(c)			A	admit
2	con			B	assent
3	inter	} CEDE	{	C	decline
4	pre	(go)		D	forerun
5	re			E	intervene
6	se			F	withdraw

The correct pairings are: 1–B; 2–A; 3–E; 4–D; 5–C; 6–F.

Now pair each prefix–plus–root with its appropriate synonym in each of the ten boxes below:

1

1	ad			A	cite
2	con			B	engender
3	de	} DUCE	{	C	entice
4	intro	(lead)		D	infer
5	pro			E	herald
6	se			F	tend

2

1	con			A	allude
2	de			B	award
3	o(f)	} FER	{	C	displace
4	re	(bring)		D	endure
5	su(f)			E	postpone
6	trans			F	tender

3

1	de			A	dispirit
2	e			B	enslave
3	inter	} JECT	{	C	expel
4	ob	(throw)		D	obtrude
5	re			E	protest
6	sub			F	spurn

4

1	com			A	allow
2	e			B	communicate
3	o(b)	} MIT	{	C	diffuse
4	per	(send)		D	engage
5	sub			E	exclude
6	trans			F	yield

5

1	com			A	banish
2	de			B	behave
3	im	} PORT	{	C	convey
4	re	(carry)		D	inform
5	su(p)			E	introduce
6	trans			F	sustain

6

1	com			A	arrange
2	de			B	counter
3	dis	} POSE	{	C	hypothesize
4	o(p)	(put)		D	incline
5	pro			E	suggest
6	su(p)			F	testify

7

1	com			A	lower
2	de			B	quell
3	ex	} PRESS	{	C	represent
4	o(p)	(press)		D	restrain
5	re			E	squeeze
6	su(p)			F	tyrannize

8

1	con			A	cease
2	de			B	comprise
3	in	} SIST	{	C	emphasize
4	per	(stand)		D	live
5	re			E	oppose
6	sub			F	persevere

9

1	a(t)			A	amuse
2	con			B	gain
3	enter*	} TAIN	{	C	hold
4	ob	(hold)		D	keep
5	per			E	procure
6	re			F	relate

10

1	con			A	change
2	contro			B	corrupt
3	di	} VERT	{	C	entertain
4	in	(turn)		D	oppose
5	per			E	overturn
6	sub			F	sabotage

* originally 'inter'

Part One
Economists

MERCANTILISM

17th and 18th Century theorists believed a nation's wealth consisted of the amount of **GOLD** it held in its treasury.

PHYSIOCRATS

Francois Quesnay (1694–1774) and other French thinkers thought that the wealth of a country is determined by the productive use made of **LAND** – its agriculture.

CLASSICAL ECONOMICS

Adam Smith (1723–90) held that a nation's wealth can be measured in terms of the **GOODS** that it produces.

In serving his own interests 'economic man' is guided by an 'unseen hand' to seek the public interest. That interest is enhanced by the division of labour, or specialization. Prices of goods reflect the **LABOUR** costs of their production.

MARXISM

Karl Marx (1818–1883) regarded labour as the basis of wealth. The capitalist makes a profit from 'surplus value', i.e. by paying less for labour than it is worth. The proletariat will need to seize control of the means of production to build a classless society.

David Ricardo (1772–1823) said that growing numbers of workers will compete for work and food. Bosses will pay them the minimum necessary for subsistence. This is the 'Iron Law' of wages. Profits will be spent, or saved and spent later, therefore consumption will never cease.

Thomas Malthus (1766–1834) rued the 'passion between the sexes' that caused populations to grow geometrically, while food grew only arithmetically. Profits will sometimes be spent and there will be prosperity; sometimes saved – then there will be depression.

SOCIAL MARKET

Alfred Marshall (1842–1924) denied the working of iron economic laws. What we suppose is the economic norm is not necessarily morally right. Economics is a *social* science.

LAISSEZ-FAIRE

Herbert Spencer (1820–1903) argued for laissez-faire, non-intervention by the state, in the interest of social and economic evolution, and the 'survival of the fittest'.

KEYNESIANISM

John Maynard Keynes (1883–1946) was convinced by the Depression that the government should borrow money and invest it in industry, to encourage output and employment. Government expenditure has a 'multiplier' effect on purchasing power. Society's aim should be full employment.

MONETARISM

Milton Friedman (1912–) argued for the minimum of public spending, a tight money supply, and the unfettered play of market forces. Government should only intervene to remove 'rigidities'.

J.K. Galbraith (1908–) believed in government planning to restrain unbridled pursuit of private gain, since this does not contribute to public wealth.

A Summarize in your own words the principal differences between Monetarism and Keynesianism.

B Who was most likely to argue for ...?

1 Public ownership of major manufacturing industries.
2 Setting prices for articles that mirror the work of producing them.
3 Leaving wages to the fair and free competition of the market.
4 An end to restrictive practices and closed shops.
5 Government intervention to inject purchasing power into the economy.
6 Harsh treatment of the poor to discourage unbridled breeding.

A　FRIEDMAN
B　KEYNES
C　MALTHUS
D　MARX
E　RICARDO
F　SMITH

Part Two
The Money-Go-Round

Below is a diagram illustrating some of the more significant money-movements between the public, household, industrial, financial and overseas sectors. Payments made outside the circle represent money-movements overseas.

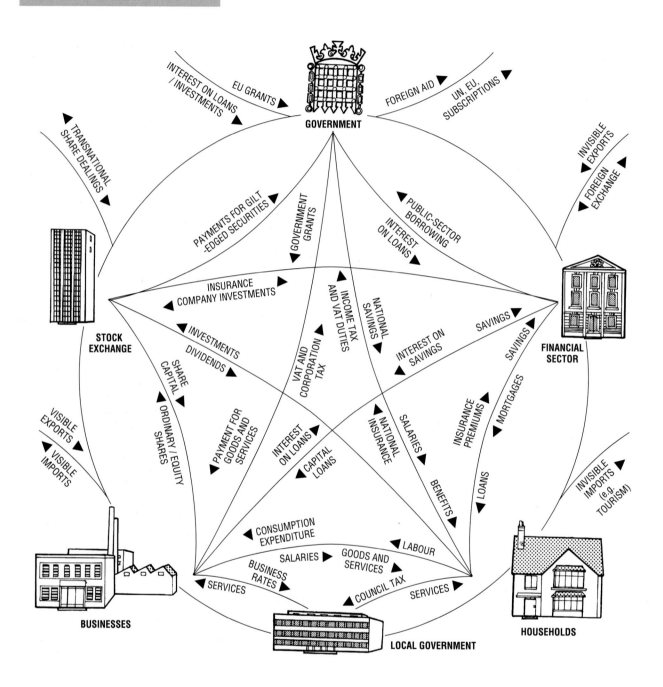

Which of the events in list 1–10 may add to circumstances in list A–J?

1   Marked balance of trade deficit.
2   Surge in demand for cars made in Britain.
3   Pressure on the pound on foreign exchanges.
4   Lowering of higher rates of income tax.
5   High demand for unskilled labour.
6   Buoyant company profits in successive years.
7   Rise in exports over imports.
8   Growth in consumption of Japanese equipment.
9   Fall in number of visitors to Britain.
10 Slump in private consumption expenditure.

A   More regressive taxation
B   A rise in UK interest rates
C   Low manual unemployment
D   More company bankruptcies
E   Surplus on balance of payments
F   A rise in visible imports
G   High share dividends
H   Growth in visible exports
I   Slump in invisible exports
J   Government borrowing overseas

Part Three
The Market

J.M. Keynes has been the defining economist of the twentieth century. Since the publication in 1935 of his *General Theory of Employment, Interest and Money*, economists have taken up positions for and against Keynesianism. Nobel Prize-winning economist Milton Friedman, of Chicago, has been the guru of 'post-Keynesian' monetarism. He identified market forces with freedom.

Adam Smith's 'invisible hand' is generally regarded as referring to purchases or sales of goods or services for money. But economic activity is by no means the only area of human life in which a complex and sophisticated structure arises as an unintended consequence of a large number of individuals   5
cooperating while each pursues his own interests.

Consider, for example, language. It is a complex structure that is continually changing and developing. It has a well-defined order, yet no central body planned it. No one decided what   10
words should be admitted into the language, what the rules of grammar should be, which words should be adjectives, which nouns ...

How did language develop? In much the same way as an economic order develops through the market – out of the voluntary   15
interaction of individuals, in this case seeking to trade ideas or information or gossip rather than goods and services with one another. One or another meaning was attributed to a word, or words were added as the need arose. Grammatical usages developed and were later codified into rules. Two parties who want to   20
communicate with one another both benefit from coming to a common agreement about the words they use. As a wider and wider circle of people find it advantageous to communicate with one another, a common usage spreads and is codified in dictionaries. At no point is there any coercion, any central planner   25
who has power to command, though in more recent times government school systems have played an important role in standardizing usage ...

Narrow preoccupation with the economic market has led to a narrow interpretation of self-interest as myopic selfishness, as ex-   30
clusive concern with immediate material rewards. Economics has been berated for allegedly drawing far-reaching conclusions from a wholly unrealistic 'economic man' who is little more than a calculation machine, responding only to monetary stimuli. That is a great mistake. Self-interest is not myopic selfishness. It   35
is whatever it is that interests the participants, whatever they value, whatever goals they pursue.

(Milton and Rose Friedman, *Free to Choose*, 1980)

1 Find words in the above similar in meaning to the following:
   (a) systematized;
   (b) refined;
   (c) reproached;
   (d) attached.
2 What is Adam Smith's 'invisible hand' supposed to have done?
3 In what important respect, according to the authors, is the development of an economic order comparable with the development of language?
4 What moral do they draw from the comparison?
5 In your view, are there matters of public 'interest' and 'value' which should not be left to the market to determine?

Part Four
Unemployment

Is unemployment an evil inseparable from capitalism, or is it inevitable where there is low inflation in a free society? This is an issue that divides economists and political parties alike. Make selective use of the following quotations to answer this question: **What can, and should, the government do about unemployment?**

1

[Lloyd George's] unemployment-insurance [scheme of 1920] retarded the shift of workers from declining to rising industries. On the other hand, it took the edge off discontent. Even when the unemployed rioted, this was to get higher rates of 'benefit', not to bring down a system which had made them unemployed. Once Labour had demanded 'the Right to Work'. Now it demanded 'Work or Maintenance', and the emphasis was on maintenance. Thanks to Lloyd George, barricades were not set up in English streets.

(A.J.P. Taylor, *English History 1914–1945*, 1965)

2

The Great Depression of the 1930s dispelled for ever the belief that the unaided free market would always restore full employment within an acceptable period of time. Those who believed that the free market did guarantee full employment were left to argue that, ... the market would ... restore it 'in the long run'. To those who waited from 1929 to 1937 for the problematical 'long run' to appear, Keynes provided the practical epitaph for their belief: 'Maybe you are right, but in the long run, we shall all be dead'.

(Richard G. Lipsey, *An Introduction to Positive Economics*, 2nd edn, 1966)

3

Unemployment is natural and desirable in technically advanced economies. The task of capitalist economies is not to fight unemployment at *any* cost, like the plague. Rather its objectives should be to make certain that normal technological unemployment falls upon those who can afford it, and to whom it should be the greatest of blessings.

(L. Kelso in David Howell, *Freedom and Capital*, 1981)

4

It is ironic that after the great technical achievements brought by the age of growth, all we are offered is a return to large-scale unemployment and poverty in the midst of plenty .... The modern economies had failed to develop the political and social institutions, at either domestic or international level, that are needed to make permanent full employment compatible with capitalism.

(Joan Robinson, *Contributions to Modern Economics*, 1978)

5

In a changing economy, it is important to match up the right people to the right jobs. Getting this match right allows society as a whole to produce more output ... The flow through the pool of unemployment is one of the mechanisms through which society reallocates people to more suitable jobs and increases total output in the long run.

(David Begg *et al.*, *Economics*, 1984)

6

We work partly in order to earn the wherewithal to enjoy not working – for leisure has come to mean spending money on the variety of goods and services offered by the rapidly growing 'leisure industry'. For most people, therefore, enforced idleness through unemployment is cruelly meaningless since it provides the opportunity to enjoy leisure while removing the means to do so.

(Peter Donaldson, *A Question of Economics*, 1985)

7

The very success of Keynesian full-employment policies carried within it the seeds of another intractable problem: inflation. Around the beginning of the 1970s the inflation rate, until then fairly stable, started to accelerate. This brought into question the long-term success of the Keynesian revolution itself, for accelerating inflation is an unsustainable condition; and if the price of full employment is accelerating inflation, then full employment cannot be maintained.

(Michael Stewart, *Keynes and After*, 3rd edn, 1986)

8

By the late 1970s and early 1980s, there was gloomy apprehension that unemployment in England was not only cyclical but structural – and that, whatever promises politicians might make, enhanced scientific and technical development would actually increase it.

(Asa Briggs, *A Social History of England*, 1982)

Part Five
Equality

The goals of equality (egalitarianism) and classlessness together lie at the heart of Marxian economics. Progressive, redistributive taxation is a prime tenet of socialism. **In a post-communist, post-socialist world is (precise or approximate) economic equality (still) a worthwhile ideal?**

1   A mother is about to share out a pie between her five children. Those five children want to see justice done. The presumption is of perfect equality. There must be very good reasons why the five pieces shouldn't be equal. Why is it different when we talk about a country's economy? Are there *good* reasons for the inequality that we permit?

2   Equality of income is a utopian idea. If you paid everyone the same no matter how much work they did or no matter how much skill they had, there would be no incentive to work harder, or to improve one's skills. No one would do more than they had to do to earn their wage – and most would do a good deal less.

3   We talk glibly about not over-taxing the rich because to do so would be a disincentive, and all the time the rich, as employers, pay their employees the minimum that will retain their labour. It's simply not true to say that those without capital – who have no means of building capital – have an equal chance to get rich as those who inherit wealth, or who elbow their way to get it.

4   We confuse equality of goods with equality of rights. Because the poor have seldom been granted equal rights, it's supposed that they would be granted them by being made richer. This is a fallacy: we can equalize rights tomorrow, without tinkering with people's incomes.

5   You can't legislate for equality. The economic distance between the élite and the masses in socialist countries was as great as that in any capitalist society. The free market is the surest means of achieving a standard of living that's high for all. A free society releases the energies and abilities of people to pursue their own objectives.

6   Improvement of economic conditions for the poor is one thing; equality is another. You don't have to make the rich give up their riches in order for the poor to enjoy a decent standard of living. The poor don't envy the rich; they simply want a better deal for themselves.

7   The stark difference between haves and have-nots is bad for democracy, and equality of opportunity. The consensus is for progressive taxation; indeed, without it, the government simply could not have raised the sums of money it has had to raise.

8   Those who say that, in a free market, all have an equal chance to acquire wealth, assume that there is an inexhaustible supply of goods to distribute. There isn't. The world's resources are finite. For this reason, if for no other, it simply isn't moral to let a few (relatively speaking) consume grotesquely more than their fair share of the resources available.

Maths 1: Introduction

Mathematics is an ancient subject. The oldest known mathematical artefact discovered by archaeologists is believed to be a small piece of the fibula of a baboon, marked with twenty-nine clearly defined notches. It has been dated to approximately 35,000 BC. The subject has thus had plenty of time to mature, unlike, for example, chemistry which only began to develop from Alchemy since the eighteenth century. What started as a means of recording data about storage of foodstuffs and the measurement of land developed into the disciplines of **arithmetic** and **geometry**, to which were added astronomy and music. For a long period, arithmetic remained very much the mathematics of everyday life but, in the Greek Classical period, geometry became increasingly abstract. Eventually, when it was codified in a textbook by **Euclid**, the *Elements*, in about 300 BC, it had become a subject to be studied for its own intrinsic beauty and for the training of logical minds. Even at this early stage, mathematics could be seen as a two-sided character which – like the god Janus – has one face turned towards the real world, looking for more and more ways to use mathematics to solve problems in everyday life, and the other face accepting increasing levels of logical complexity and abstraction.

Followers of **Pythagoras** were firm believers that mathematics held the key to knowledge of the truth of the universe. They were the ones to bring music into the subject with their discovery that harmony could be explained by arithmetical divisions of a plucked string. The attempt to understand the movement of the celestial spheres meant that astronomy, too, took its place as one of the four branches of the subject. Even today – although we no longer consider music and astronomy to be parts of mathematics – there is still a tendency to divide the subject into pure mathematics (with its abstract formulations) and applied mathematics (with its more practical approach).

The development of Arithmetic was held back by cumbersome numeration systems and an awkward collection of rules. Then, in the 12th Century, Europe was introduced to the Hindu invention of **zero**, and a system of numerals based on a place value. This led to the development of **Algebra**. In about 1850 **George Boole** applied algebraic techniques to the ancient subject of **Logic**. Logic had existed in Classical Greek times as an explicit collection of rules, codified by **Aristotle**, that were expressed in natural language. Boole, however, wanted to go further than this and so developed a purely symbolic system. This enabled Algebra to be free from Arithmetic.

In the same way, in the 17th century, **Newton** and **Leibniz** transformed the analytical ideas of **Archimedes** – which concerned ways of dealing with the volumes of shapes – into **calculus**, with its many techniques, such as differential equations and methods of integration.

Even geometry had been freed from earthly shape and form with the invention of new offspring such as **projective geometry** and **topology**, while earlier attempts to provide a rigorous framework for navigation and surveying had led to the development of **trigonometry**.

So we have a subject which, although providing a tremendous training for the mind in analytical and logical thought, has become increasingly remote from reality. Fortunately, many of these abstract ideas have proved to be useful for scientists attempting to make sense of their discoveries. To take one example, the apparently useless and imaginary idea of the square roots of negative numbers provided a vital link to enable **Maxwell** to explain the nature of **electromagnetic waves**.

As we have seen, mathematics has had time to develop an enormous collection of ideas to the point that it is one of the few subjects where it is possible for a British sixth-form student to study two A levels in the subject and still only scratch the surface of it. The average person is left feeling somewhat afraid of the subject, that the ideas are beyond normal comprehension and that mathematicians must be very peculiar people. Students of AS- or A-Level General Studies can feel threatened by the mathematics questions set in some of the papers, and may feel inclined to omit them or rush through them with a random guess at the answers. This would be a pity, especially as all students will have had some mathematical training for GCSE. It is not possible here to give a thorough overview of mathematics, but it is possible to demonstrate how a few ideas, mainly from geometry, taken from GCSE Mathematics can be extended to enable students to answer a few questions. One topic, percentages, will be looked at in some depth and be developed – in a way mirroring the history of mathematics – to embrace the use of algebraic techniques.

Q1: The speed of a body is given in metres per second. What do you need to multiply this by to obtain the speed in kilometres per hour?

Questions like this often crop up in A-Level General Studies examination papers. Knowledge of GCSE Mathematics should be sufficient to answer them. It would be worth your while to buy one of the many excellent revision texts and work through the exercises systematically. To answer this question, you need to know only the number of seconds in an hour and the number of metres in a kilometre. There are 60 seconds in a minute and 60 minutes in an hour, so to obtain the speed in metres per hour we need to multiply the speed in metres per second by 3,600 (60 × 60). We then need to divide that by 1,000 to get the speed in kilometres per hour. So, to convert the speed from metres per second to kilometres per hour we need to multiply by 3.6 (3,600 ÷ 1,000).

Exercise 1.1

1 Express a speed of 10 m/s in km/h.

2 Express a speed of 360 km/h in m/s.

3 A car driving at a constant speed covers a distance of 200 metres in 8 seconds. What is its speed?

4 The spacecraft Voyager II travelled at a constant speed of 80,000 km/h. How far did it travel in:

(a) 5 hours;

(b) 30 minutes;

(c) 1 second?

5 The speed of sound is 340 m/s (also referred to as 'Mach 1'). Work out the distance travelled in one minute by a jet flying at Mach 2 (i.e. twice the speed of sound).

Working through this exercise you will have seen how an apparently simple idea can quickly become more sophisticated. This theme is now taken up with examples from Geometry.

Q2: The perimeter of a square and the perimeter of an equilateral triangle are equal. The area of the square is 9 cm². What is the area of the equilateral triangle?

This might seem a straightforward question. GCSE Mathematics has taught us how to calculate the areas of squares, rectangles and triangles, etc. If the square has an area of 9 cm², then each side must be 3 cm long and the perimeter 12 cm. It then follows that each side of the equilateral triangle (all the sides being equal) is 4 cm.

It is here that the trouble starts. In exercises at GCSE you will have used the following formula:

$$\text{Area of triangle} = \frac{1}{2} (\text{base} \times \text{height})$$

It is fairly obvious that the base is 4 cm, but what is the height? To work this out we may resort to the use of Pythagoras' Theorem, again well known from GCSE Mathematics.

The square of the hypotenuse is equal to the sum of the squares of the other two sides.

This is one way of working, but we will continue here by looking at another method: the set-square triangles.

Set-square triangles

There are two set-square triangles, as shown below. One is an isosceles triangle, the other is half an equilateral triangle.

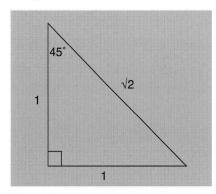

Figure 1

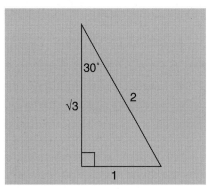

Figure 2

Note that the isosceles triangle (Figure 1) has √2 as the length of one of its sides, while the other (Figure 2) has √3. It follows then that if we are dealing with a question that has triangles with angles of 30°, 60° and 90°, then we can safely pick the answer with a √3 in it. On the other hand, if the question involves a triangle with two 45° angles in it, then it is fairly safe to pick the answer with a √2 in it.

In this example, the answers to choose from were:

A $\frac{81}{16}$ cm²

B   4√3 cm²

C $\frac{27}{4}$ cm²

D $\frac{16}{\sqrt{3}}$ cm²

E   9 cm²

We can reject A, C and E. Answer D looks a little dangerous, but B seems more likely and indeed B is the right answer. Our triangle is double the size of the one in Figure 2. The base is 4 cm and the height is 2√3. Multiply these two together and divide by two and we get our answer.

The same trick can be used in a number of questions, not just in those that are obviously about triangles. Hexagons, for example (Figure 3), consist of six equilateral triangles, so expect to see √3 incorporated in answers. Squares can be thought of either as two isosceles triangles or four (Figure 4).

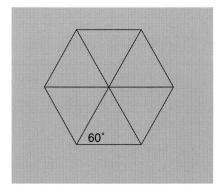

Figure 3

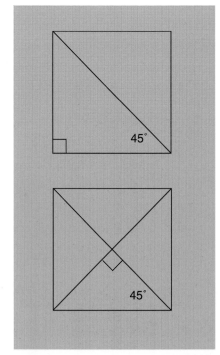

Figure 4

ITEM

The same idea appears in questions to do with trigonometry. In GCSE Mathematics you will have been introduced to the following formulae:

$$\sin \alpha = \frac{\text{opposite}}{\text{hypotenuse}}$$

$$\cos \alpha = \frac{\text{adjacent}}{\text{hypotenuse}}$$

$$\tan \alpha = \frac{\text{opposite}}{\text{adjacent}}$$

However, questions involving the set square angles are so common that it is a good idea to learn the following:

$$\sin 30° = \frac{1}{2}$$

$$\cos 30° = \frac{\sqrt{3}}{2}$$

$$\tan 30° = \frac{1}{\sqrt{3}} = \frac{\sqrt{3}}{3}$$

$$\sin 60° = \frac{\sqrt{3}}{2}$$

$$\cos 60° = \frac{1}{2}$$

$$\tan 60° = \sqrt{3}$$

$$\sin 45° = \cos 45° = \frac{1}{\sqrt{2}}$$

$$\tan 45° \quad 1$$

Q3: *ABCD* **is one face of a cube (Figure 6) with edges of length 2 units:** *O* **is the centre of the cube. What is the volume of the pyramid** *OABCD***?**

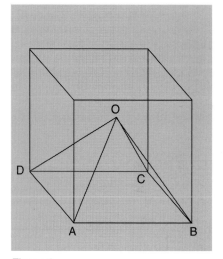

Figure 6

We are supposed to know that for objects that come up to a point, such as cones and pyramids, the formula is:

$$\text{Volume} = \frac{1}{3} (\text{base area} \times \text{height})$$

Even though it looks as if the question involves an angle of 45°, the answer does not involve $\sqrt{2}$ at all. The answer is $\frac{4}{3}$.

Exercise 1.2

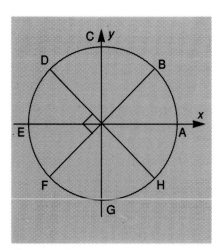

Figure 5

Figure 5 shows a circle of radius 2 units.
What are the coordinates of:

1 A
2 B
3 C
4 D
5 E
6 F
7 G
8 H

However, be careful.

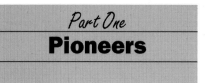

Part One
Pioneers

Muscle power – human and animal – was the primary energy source until the Industrial Revolution. Wind and water had been harnessed to drive pumping and grinding machinery; but something more was needed to raise water from deep mines. The steam engine met the need. Steam still drives turbines in the 'conventional' thermal power station, for the generation of electricity. The nuclear power station uses another fuel-source altogether.

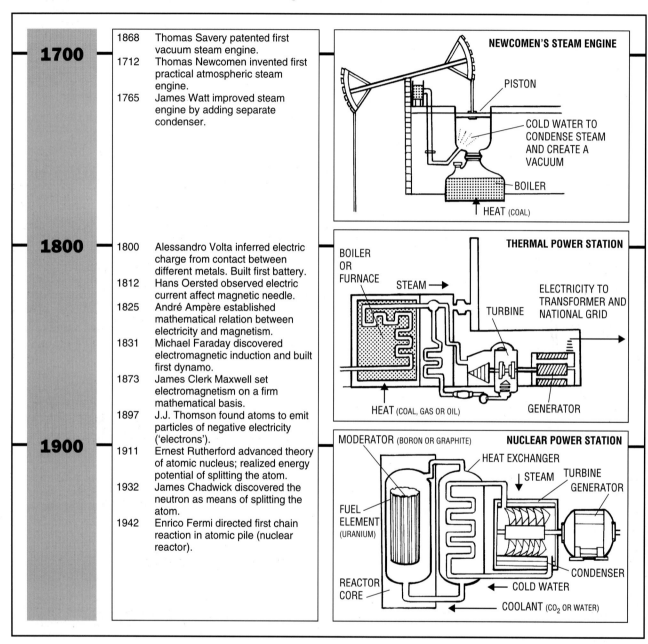

1700

1868	Thomas Savery patented first vacuum steam engine.
1712	Thomas Newcomen invented first practical atmospheric steam engine.
1765	James Watt improved steam engine by adding separate condenser.

1800

1800	Alessandro Volta inferred electric charge from contact between different metals. Built first battery.
1812	Hans Oersted observed electric current affect magnetic needle.
1825	André Ampère established mathematical relation between electricity and magnetism.
1831	Michael Faraday discovered electromagnetic induction and built first dynamo.
1873	James Clerk Maxwell set electromagnetism on a firm mathematical basis.
1897	J.J. Thomson found atoms to emit particles of negative electricity ('electrons').

1900

1911	Ernest Rutherford advanced theory of atomic nucleus; realized energy potential of splitting the atom.
1932	James Chadwick discovered the neutron as means of splitting the atom.
1942	Enrico Fermi directed first chain reaction in atomic pile (nuclear reactor).

NEWCOMEN'S STEAM ENGINE
PISTON
COLD WATER TO CONDENSE STEAM AND CREATE A VACUUM
BOILER
HEAT (COAL)

THERMAL POWER STATION
BOILER OR FURNACE
STEAM →
ELECTRICITY TO TRANSFORMER AND NATIONAL GRID
TURBINE
HEAT (COAL, GAS OR OIL)
GENERATOR

NUCLEAR POWER STATION
MODERATOR (BORON OR GRAPHITE)
HEAT EXCHANGER
STEAM
TURBINE GENERATOR
FUEL ELEMENT (URANIUM)
CONDENSER
REACTOR CORE
COLD WATER
COOLANT (CO$_2$ OR WATER)

Which is which?

1 Container for uranium fuel rods and moderating agent.
2 Heat-absorbing fluid for removing heat from nuclear reactor.
3 Copper windings on shaft rotated within 'shroud' at high speed.
4 Chamber in which steam is converted back to water.
5 Blades on a shaft turned by steam at high pressure.
6 Container in which water is heated to produce steam.
7 Apparatus for increasing electrical voltage for transmission to grid.
8 Chamber in which water is converted to steam in nuclear power station.
9 Metal can containing uranium fuel and fission product.
10 Rods of material to absorb neutrons and control nuclear reaction.

A BOILER
B CONDENSER
C COOLANT
D FUEL ELEMENT
E GENERATOR
F HEAT EXCHANGER
G MODERATOR
H REACTOR
I TRANSFORMER
J TURBINE

Part Two
Alternatives

We are consuming finite, fossil-fuel resources (coal, oil and natural gas) at an increasing rate. The hope that nuclear energy would replace these fuel sources has been dimmed (see Part Five). There has been rather little investment in the six renewable energy options below, although interest is growing.

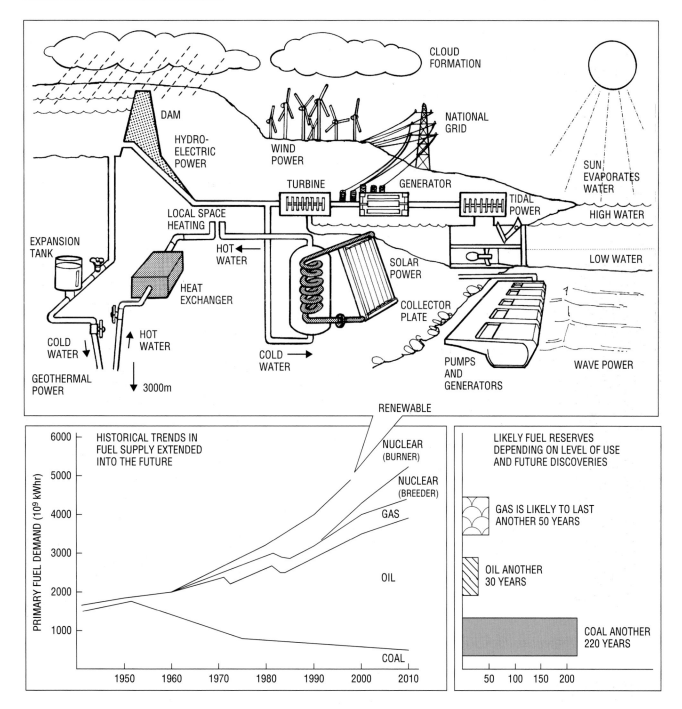

Evaluate the advantages and disadvantages of each of the six renewable sources of energy (1–6), on a 3-point scale, in terms of the six criteria, A–F:

			NEGATIVE	NEUTRAL	POSITIVE
1	Geothermal power	A Availability of suitable sites	1	2	3
2	Hydro-Electric power	B Ecological effects	1	2	3
3	Solar power	C Design and cost implications	1	2	3
4	Tidal power	D Environmental appearance	1	2	3
5	Wave power	E Predictability of supply	1	2	3
6	Wind power	F Amount of energy yield	1	2	3

Part Three
The Power Concept

The relationship between energy and power can best be explained by analogy with the relationship between distance and speed. **Speed** is defined as the distance travelled per unit time; **power** is defined as the energy converted per unit time. Similarly the total **distance** travelled is the average speed multiplied by the time spent travelling; the total **energy** converted is the average power multiplied by the time of operation.

This analogy can be extended to explain why the power of a machine is usually more important that its energy capacity. The point is that most machines can handle an infinitely large amount of energy but only at a finite rate. Left operating long enough a 100 watt light bulb could consume all the fuel resources of the world. But that is not the interesting thing about light bulbs …

The concept of power can be put into focus by noting the range of power ratings that exist in the world. If I sit quite still my body has to convert food energy at a finite rate simply to keep me warm and alive. Under these conditions my power rating is about 0.02 kW. If I run upstairs as fast as I can, my body is working hard and my body has a power of about 0.1 kW. Some very fit athletes have achieved a peak output of 0.5 kW, but this can only be sustained for a second or two. Classically a horse has a power output of one 'horse-power', equal to 0.75 kW, but in practice most work horses achieve higher power output than this. A simple machine like an electric drill has a power rating of 0.25 kW, and power tools, of the type used in light manufacturing industry, have power ratings between 1 and 10 kW. A motor-car engine has a power rating of about 100 kW, but only a fraction of this is available for propelling the car along the road. Railway locomotives have power ratings of several hundred kilowatts and an aircraft like Concorde has a power rating of 10,000 kW. The very largest machines are those used in electricity generating stations where a single turbine can have a power rating as high as 500,000 kW. This last number is equivalent to the combined power output of five million men working very hard!

(Peter Chapman, *Fuel's Paradise: Energy Options for Britain*, 1979)

1 **(a)** What are you doing if you argue 'by analogy'? (line 8)
   (b) Explain what energy 'conversion' means in this context. (line 6)
   (c) What is a 'finite rate'? (line 17)
   (d) What is the force of the word 'classically' here? (line 22)
2 What is 'the interesting thing about light bulbs'? (lines 13–14)
3 If power is defined as 'the energy converted per unit time', how should we express fully the measurement of power rating?
4 How might a 100-watt light bulb 'consume all the fuel resources of the world'? (lines 12–13)
5 Why do you suppose we make use of 'horse-power' as a classical unit of power?
6 How might the information in the third paragraph be expressed graphically? Try to draw it.

Part Four
Energy Policy

Fossil-fuel resources are running out; nuclear energy is under suspicion; alternative sources are diffuse and difficult to exploit. What about energy conservation? What about sustainability? Use some or all of the following quotations in an essay entitled: **Outline and evaluate an energy policy for the 21st Century**.

1

Wind, wave and tides all suffer from the fact that they are variable sources of power output. For example, there will be times when due to windless days or calm seas – and both can occur for periods of several days even in the winter time – they are producing little or no power. Insofar as this shortfall has to be made up by electricity from conventional power stations these newer energy sources would not necessarily reduce the installed capacity of such conventional stations needed to meet the total demand on windless or even calm days. What the newer sources will do is to save fuel that would otherwise be burned in conventional power stations.

(F.T.P. Clarke in a lecture given to the BAAS, 1977)

2

Over the past few years I have come to see the politics and social implications of energy policy as most important. My current understanding points to several non-technical issues which appear to me to be crucial. The four most important issues are: the constraints of political power; the role of competition in distorting information; the social significance of fear and blame; and finally the persistent focus on technical issues instead of the important human aspects .... The social and political implications of energy are enormous. They are usually not discussed because those in a position of power would like to stay there.

(Peter Chapman, *Fuel's Paradise: Energy Options for Britain*, 1979)

3

It was envisaged that North Sea Oil would begin to tail off in the 1980s and that nuclear power would have to be expanded to meet a growing demand for electricity. The main debate centred round the choice of a nuclear reactor model and the possible introduction of power from nuclear fusion and unlimited energy. Atoms for peace with continuous energy generated without the need for atmospheric pollution and the risks to life of mining and oil exploration give an attractive vision of the future. Why can't we have reactors purring away underground in isolated places giving us cheap electricity and freeing us from toil? What has led many people to see technology and particularly nuclear power as a threat to humanity rather than a boon?

(Mike Wild, *Energy in the 80s*, 1980)

4

Advocates of alternative energy technologies do not claim that any one will provide for all requirements. They say rather that a mix of different sources, matching demand in quality as well as quantity, is feasible and achievable within present constraints of finances, resources and time .... If even a modicum of the available research and development effort were redirected into the alternatives [to nuclear energy], they feel that the nuclear option would soon appear neither the only option nor the best. Others disagree: in their view only the rapid development of nuclear technology will supply the energy needed by the people of the earth.

(Walter C. Patterson, *Nuclear Power*, 2nd edn, 1983)

5

With two or three exceptions, Ultramar's attempts at diversification have not been particularly successful. The expertise and dynamism that management brought to the oil business over several decades have not been easily diverted into other fields. However, since by most standards, the oil industry is no longer a growth industry and will very gradually phase out, the arguments for diversification are still strong. ... There is no pressure for immediate action because management believes that Ultramar has many decades of vigorous life ahead within the oil industry.

(R.S. Atterbury, ed., *A Golden Adventure: The First 50 Years of Ultramar*, 1985)

6

In 1985 the Community put forward a series of objectives to be achieved by 1995 for energy use. A review in 1988 showed that these aims would be only partly met ... The depressing conclusion of the 1988 review was that the Community's total energy consumption by 1995 would rise by between 70 and 110 million tonnes of oil equivalent more than the target set in 1985.

(S.F. Goodman, *The European Community*, 2nd edn, 1993)

Part Five
The Nuclear Option

Refer to any or all of the more or less knowledgeable opinions expressed below in answer to this question: **Much was hoped for from nuclear energy in the 1970s and 1980s. To what extent, in your view, is such hope still justified?**

1 The problem with nuclear-power stations is where to put them. Where do you locate 40 giant 2,000 mW stations: We're running out of coastal sites and public opinion won't accept nuclear installations near centres of population. The transport of radioactive materials is an associated hazard.

2 The great advantage of nuclear energy over coal, oil, and gas-powered stations is that nuclear-powered stations don't release carbon dioxide and other greenhouse gases into the atmosphere, so they don't contribute to the problem of global warming.

3 We've only just begun to ask the really important questions about the long-term genetic effects of radioactive contamination. It's true that most radioactivity is natural; but we still need convincing answers to the incidence of leukaemia, infertility and other pathogen clusters already identified.

4 As coal ceases to be mined and supplies of oil and natural gas run out, nuclear power must take up the slack. There are adequate reserves of Uranium for the foreseeable future; and supplies are multiplied when we convert U238 into Plutonium. Fast-breeder reactors can extract 50–60 times more energy than ordinary Uranium reactors.

5 We can never rule out the possibility of nuclear accidents, due to human error. Windscale in 1957, Three Mile Island in 1979, Chernobyl in 1986 all resulted from one oversight or another. Fast-breeder reactors are more difficult to control than their predecessors because of the higher energy densities and toxicity of the fuel.

6 It's all very well talking about wind power, tidal power, solar power and so on, but these energy sources can only deliver supplies at the margin. And tidal barrages and wind farms carry ecological and environmental costs that mustn't be underestimated.

7 We're accumulating millions of hectolitres of waste, all of it highly toxic, and radioactive for hundreds of years. Disposal at sea is ruled out, so we have to bury it. But where? No one wants to live near a nuclear waste dump. Then we have to decommission the power stations. What a legacy to leave to our children!

8 The potential of nuclear fusion is much too great to break faith with nuclear energy. Whether or not we manage controlled fusion at low temperatures, the huge advantages of fusion are that supplies of the fuel (hydrogen) are abundant, and the only by-product (helium) is non-radioactive.

French Idioms

We drop a lot of French words and phrases in (educated) English – though one would be unfortunate indeed to meet 35 of them in as many lines. Match the French borrowings in the passage below with their English equivalents.

French Idioms

1 entente cordiale
2 contretemps
3 malentendu
4 penchant
5 ensemble
6 entourage
7 communiqué
8 liaison
9 sang froid
10 passé
11 je ne sais quoi
12 savoir-faire
13 connoisseur
14 gourmet
15 raison d'être
16 bon vivant
17 hauteur
18 manqué
19 frisson
20 soi-disant
21 faux pas
22 mélange
23 nouvelle cuisine
24 soupçon
25 nuance
26 chic
27 milieu
28 bête noire
29 raconteur
30 mot juste
31 par exellence
32 double entendre
33 poseur
34 jeu de mots
35 exposé

A BAS LA DIFFERENCE

The **entente cordiale** is nearly a century old. There has been the odd **contretemps**, as there always is between neighbours, but it is remarkable that there has not been a more serious **malentendu**, given the differences between the Englishman and the Frenchman, and our **penchant** for insularity. The wonder is that, **ensemble**, at meetings, our leaders – each with his **entourage** of native-language speakers – manage to understand each other, and to issue a **communiqué** which appears to reinforce the **liaison**, in spite of the Englishman's reputation for **sang froid**, and the Frenchman's for dalliance.

Perhaps it is **passé** to speak of differences when a tunnel joins us: but there is a **je ne sais quoi** about the Frenchman, a certain **savoir-faire**, in the face of which the average Englishman is at a disadvantage. He believes every Frenchman to be a **connoisseur** of fine wine and great art, a **gourmet** for whom five-star food is his very **raison d'être** – in short, a man of the world, a **bon vivant**, in whose company the Englishman feels boorish. It is not just the **hauteur** with which the Frenchman (and every Frenchman, we are told, is a master-chef **manqué**) regards English and American cooking that is intimidating; his **frisson** of distaste at much **soi-disant** 'fast food' is understandable. What worries the English host, or hostess, is that they should commit a **faux pas** by serving a meal that, to the Frenchman, is a **mélange** of tastes that he would prefer to keep separate – as in **nouvelle cuisine**, where the rule is to present a **soupçon** here, and then, to cleanse the palate, the merest **nuance** of a contrasting taste there. It is the sophistication, the **chic** attention to detail, that gives the Frenchman the social edge.

The edge is sharper still in the linguistic **milieu.** Language-learning is, of course, the Englishman's **bête noire**; but the problem here concerns how language is used. The French writer, or **raconteur**, takes care to choose the **mot juste**. His tongue discriminates between words and idioms as keenly as it does between tastes, so that he achieves, **par excellence**, a subtlety of meaning – or perhaps a **double entendre** – that may elude the transatlantic speaker. The latter will think the Frenchman a **poseur** who delights in a **jeu de mots**, an over-refined expression, so accustomed is the Anglo-Saxon to journalism that is all 'plain speaking' and **exposé**.

English Equivalents

A adroitness
B attitudinizer
C bugbear
D certain something
E connection
F context
G difference of opinion
H disdain
I double meaning
J eminently
K epicure

L error
M expert
N friendly argument
O hint
P man about town
Q misunderstanding
R mixture
S morsel
T narrator
U new cookery
V out of date
W play on words

X precise word
Y predilection
Z purpose
AA reserve
BB retinue
CC shudder
DD smart
EE so called
FF statement
GG together
HH unmasking
II unrealized

Since the last ice age (some 10,000 years ago), the world's mean temperature has risen about 4°C. It has risen by about 0.5°C in the last one hundred years. It is thought likely that it will rise by another 1.5°C in the next fifty years.

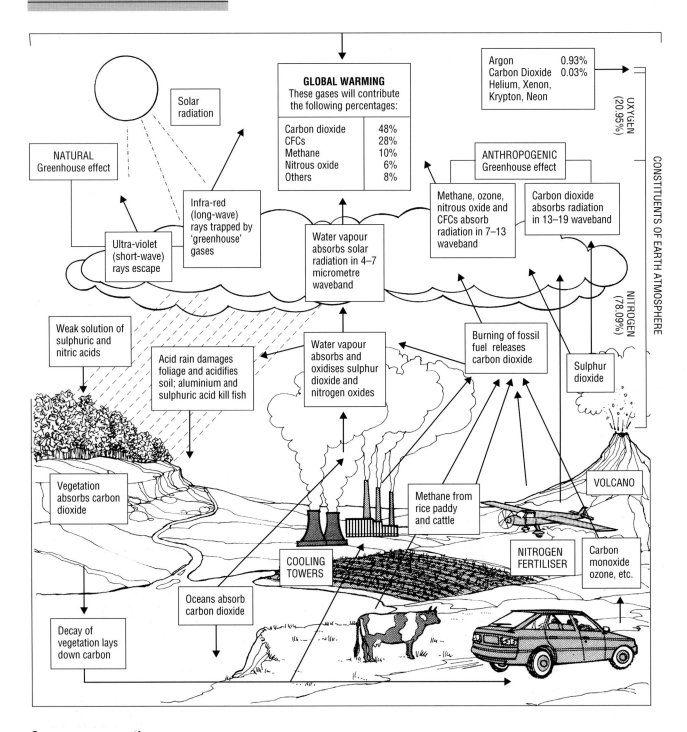

Some open questions

1 Describe in a few sentences:
   (a) the natural 'greenhouse' effect;
   (b) the problem of global warming;
   (c) the formation of acid rain.
2 What is meant by the 'carbon cycle'?
3 What might be the consequences of a rise in global temperature of 1.5°C? Refer to two such consequences.
4 What steps might be taken to stabilize (if not reverse) the man-made contribution to global warming?

Part Two
UK Land Use

The map and the pie-charts below indicate the multiple uses to which United Kingdom land is put; some of the pressures upon it; and some of the measures taken to resist those pressures.

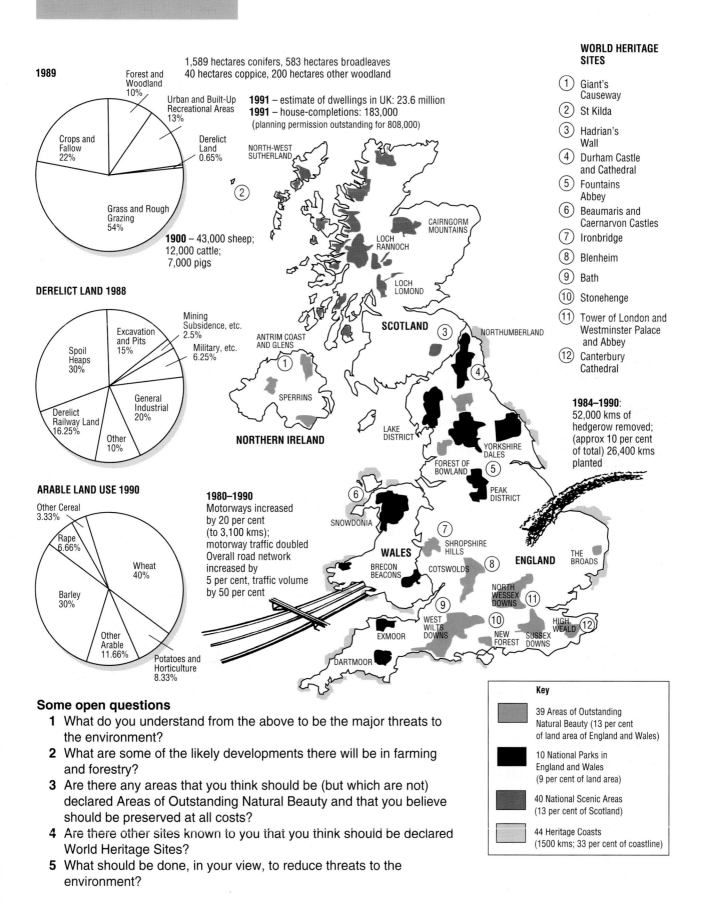

1989

1,589 hectares conifers, 583 hectares broadleaves
40 hectares coppice, 200 hectares other woodland

Forest and Woodland 10%
Urban and Built-Up Recreational Areas 13%
Crops and Fallow 22%
Derelict Land 0.65%
Grass and Rough Grazing 54%

1991 – estimate of dwellings in UK: 23.6 million
1991 – house-completions: 183,000
(planning permission outstanding for 808,000)

1900 – 43,000 sheep;
12,000 cattle;
7,000 pigs

DERELICT LAND 1988

Mining Subsidence, etc. 2.5%
Excavation and Pits 15%
Military, etc. 6.25%
Spoil Heaps 30%
General Industrial 20%
Derelict Railway Land 16.25%
Other 10%

ARABLE LAND USE 1990

Other Cereal 3.33%
Rape 6.66%
Wheat 40%
Barley 30%
Other Arable 11.66%
Potatoes and Horticulture 8.33%

1980–1990
Motorways increased by 20 per cent
(to 3,100 kms);
motorway traffic doubled
Overall road network increased by 5 per cent, traffic volume by 50 per cent

NORTH-WEST SUTHERLAND
CAIRNGORM MOUNTAINS
LOCH RANNOCH
LOCH LOMOND
SCOTLAND
NORTHUMBERLAND
ANTRIM COAST AND GLENS
SPERRINS
NORTHERN IRELAND
LAKE DISTRICT
YORKSHIRE DALES
FOREST OF BOWLAND
PEAK DISTRICT
SNOWDONIA
SHROPSHIRE HILLS
WALES
BRECON BEACONS
COTSWOLDS
ENGLAND
THE BROADS
NORTH WESSEX DOWNS
WEST WILTS DOWNS
NEW FOREST
SUSSEX DOWNS
HIGH WEALD
EXMOOR
DARTMOOR

WORLD HERITAGE SITES

1. Giant's Causeway
2. St Kilda
3. Hadrian's Wall
4. Durham Castle and Cathedral
5. Fountains Abbey
6. Beaumaris and Caernarvon Castles
7. Ironbridge
8. Blenheim
9. Bath
10. Stonehenge
11. Tower of London and Westminster Palace and Abbey
12. Canterbury Cathedral

1984–1990:
52,000 kms of hedgerow removed;
(approx 10 per cent of total) 26,400 kms planted

Key

▦	39 Areas of Outstanding Natural Beauty (13 per cent of land area of England and Wales)
■	10 National Parks in England and Wales (9 per cent of land area)
▨	40 National Scenic Areas (13 per cent of Scotland)
▢	44 Heritage Coasts (1500 kms; 33 per cent of coastline)

Some open questions

1. What do you understand from the above to be the major threats to the environment?
2. What are some of the likely developments there will be in farming and forestry?
3. Are there any areas that you think should be (but which are not) declared Areas of Outstanding Natural Beauty and that you believe should be preserved at all costs?
4. Are there other sites known to you that you think should be declared World Heritage Sites?
5. What should be done, in your view, to reduce threats to the environment?

Part Three
Green Belts

The environment rose to prominence as an issue in the late 1960s. Edward Heath established a new Department of the Environment (DoE), and many books were written on the subject. Tony Aldous was Environment Correspondent on the London Times.

The impact of housing development on the countryside makes itself felt most sharply in two main circumstances – new towns and development proposals in 'green belt' areas on the fringes of our towns and cities. Green belts, originally in the case of London the product of an inter-war initiative by the [London County Council] and the home counties and extended to other large and sometimes not so large towns (e.g. Gloucester/Cheltenham) under the Town and Country Planning Acts, are sometimes misunderstood and have of late come in for some criticism. The original purpose was to prevent the sort of urban sprawl to which much of the old county of Middlesex had by then succumbed.

Green belts throw a cordon round the built-up areas and in effect tell the developer: 'Thus far and no farther'. They do not, however, as such do anything to ensure or facilitate public access or recreational use of land thus restricted, though they often include large open spaces which are traditionally or, as a result of acquisition, open to public use, as well as public footpath systems. From the farmer's or land-owner's point of view, however, green belt designation may be far from a blessing. He may have to cope with the trespass, damage and hooliganism which tends to occur in farmland near a town's edges, without being able to sell up and reap the benefit of development values.

Another weakness of the green belt is that development tends to leapfrog to the country towns beyond, leading to more mass, long-distance commuting, which it may be argued is undesirable socially in terms of individual working and family lives, and economically in so far as imbalance of railway operation and demand for extra road provision result.

Broadly, however, green belts have served their prime purpose of limiting sprawl and providing an attractive and healthy setting for many of the post-war new towns, and politicians and civil servants at the DoE show every intention of continuing to uphold them, even in the face of acute demand for building land. They are not, however, inflexible; and it is in a way a testimony to green belt status and reputation that whenever a minister decides to remove a few acres from this designation and allows homes to be built there, there is a great outcry.

5

10

15

20

25

30

35

(Tony Aldous, *Battle for the Environment*, 1972)

1 What do you understand by the term 'home counties'? (line 6)
2 What do you gather had happened to Middlesex before green-belt legislation was passed?
3 What impact or effect does the word 'cordon' have (line 12) that the word 'belt' may not have?
4 In your view, is it green-belt designation that is responsible for the farmers' problems referred to in the second paragraph?
5 What evidence is there in the passage that green-belt policy is not 'inflexible'? (line 34)
6 On the strength of what you have read (and of experience that you might have had) would you say that green belts were, on balance, a 'good' idea or a 'bad' one?

Part Four
Access to the Land

Who owns the land, and who has a right of access to it? Refer to any of the following quotations to answer this question: **How can the rights of farmers, tourists, foresters, ramblers and others be reconciled, so that all might have access to the land?**

1

To many of us, the term 'national park' signifies the freedom of the open hills, and the liberty to wander where we will ... of course, on land actually owned by the park such freedom is implicit, for the authority has a duty to provide access 'for the enjoyment of the public'. Elsewhere, however, there are restrictions. While much of the upland scenery is classed as common land, this does not necessarily mean that it is 'common' to all. Contrary to many town-dwellers' conceptions, common land is not ownerless, with unrestricted access.

(J.M. Brereton, *The Brecon Beacons National Park*, 1990)

2

Many residents were tourists themselves once – and they are the worst when it comes to considering tourism in the future. They don't want any more. They want customs barriers set up on the boundaries, the roads closed and trains halted and every outsider turned back. I did see one letter in a local paper which wanted all cars stopped at the National Parks boundary and only those with proper climbing gear allowed in.

(Hunter Davies, *A Walk around the Lakes*, 1993)

3

Nowadays the sheep walks of the Wolds have given way to prairie farms of heavily subsidized wheat, and ramblers are obliged to cling to a narrow track, the Wolds Way, an anathema to the majority of the landed gentry who own fields of five hundred acres or more. Yet few, surely, can contest the proposition that monoculture is a depressing sight to those who are not making a fortune out of it.

(John Hillaby, *John Hillaby's Yorkshire*, 1986)

4

Roads have now been widened and motorways built. You can cruise up from London in four or five hours, you can zip by the Lakes on broad fast routes. Hotels, camping and caravan sites, hostels and second homes have made it accessible to all sorts of people. There are drawbacks: complaints that local people are being driven out because of the high price of property; complaints that the broad routes to the familiar peaks are now so trodden that they have become an eyesore.

(Melvyn Bragg, *Land of the Lakes*, 1990)

5

The Three Peaks Race takes place normally at the end of April. ... The Race has not been popular with farmers. The runners used to map their own route, and often kept it a secret from others; they were not too careful about which fields they crossed. Spectators could be worse, climbing on or over walls to get a good view or a good photograph. And they left gates open.

(Harry Reé and Caroline Forbes, *The Three Peaks of Yorkshire*, 1983)

6

The trouble with Dovedale is that too many people go there expecting too much and cannot avoid one another because the place is so cramped. Imagine the human contents of Terminal 3 at Heathrow transferred into a lovely natural environment and you will appreciate that going to Dovedale cannot be construed as getting away from it all. The rest of us can tramp through Dovedale at dawn or dusk or outside the holiday season.

(Rex Bellamy, *The Peak District Companion*, 1980)

7

One of the gravest problems in the countryside is that so many of the leisure pursuits competing for a foothold are totally incompatible. Fishermen could enjoy their quiet, contemplative sport if speedboaters did not insist on shattering the silence. ... Bird watchers wish to observe the same birds the sportsmen come to shoot, and walkers wallow knee-deep in mud where pony trekkers trek or motor-cyclists scramble.

(Phil Drabble, *A Voice in the Wilderness*, 1991)

8

The highest tor, Yes Tor, where it is still the custom to watch the sunrise on Easter Sunday in the hope of seeing the device of a lamb in the disc, has two military huts built on it. A large compound has grown up on moorland at Okehampton Camp, and a tarmac road for military vehicles penetrates a third of the way towards the centre of the northern plateau.

(John Weir, ed., *Dartmoor National Park; Official Guide*, 1987)

Part Five

On the Road

Roads both unite and divide us. We love the car, and we loathe it. Write an essay based on any or all of the following opinions, under the title: **Make a case either for improvement of the road system, or for measures to curb car-use**.

1   A direct correlation has been shown between the amount of traffic passing your house and your state of health. Up to 15 million people suffer headaches, ear infections, and respiratory illnesses. Double the number of vehicles on our roads, which is what the motor manufacturers want, and you'll double the illnesses.

2   The CBI has estimated that congestion is costing £15 billion a year. A number of British businesses are relocating to Northern France where there are only 35 vehicles per kilometre, to our 63. This is in spite of the fact that there's more traffic in France – more traffic, and more roads. It's madness to cut back on the road-building programme.

3   How do most of us choose to travel? We go by car, because it's the quickest and most convenient way to travel. Are we to say: you mustn't go by car? In a free country, you have to give people the choice. For young people, learning to drive and having their own car is a part of growing up, and achieving freedom and independence.

4   We talk about freedom of choice, but what choice do school children, the poor and the old have? We deregulate the buses and run down the railways, and we talk about choice! One third of families don't have cars in this country- which is just as well. Imagine the chaos if they did.

5   Roads have devastated areas of outstanding beauty, sites of special scientific interest (SSSIs), and historic towns. Ask the people of Winchester, Wanstead and North West Manchester what they think of motorways. No community is safe from bisection by six or eight lanes of tarmac, lights and noise. The roads programme simply isn't sustainable.

6   An awful lot of jobs depend on motor manufacture, components, motorway building and maintenance, petrol stations and service areas. The effect of cutbacks in the motor industry and the road-building programme would be devastating for employment across whole regions.

7   We can't go on pumping carbon monoxide, nitrogen dioxide and ozone into the air we breathe. We know the consequences of global warming and plant depletion that this pollution causes. We've got to stop if we want there to be a tomorrow.

8   Talk to people who live in towns and villages that are plagued by through traffic: they'll tell you they want a by-pass. It isn't an option *not* to build new roads, when lives are endangered, and old buildings are being shaken to pieces. A by-pass is life-enhancing.

ITEM

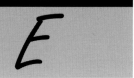

Similes

A simile is a simple likeness – a comparison of one thing with another.
Below are listed fifty similes in which an (unnamed) object is described
adjectivally in terms of another, named object (a noun or noun phrase).
Many of these are drawn from the same pre-industrial background as the
Proverbs in Item L (see page 86). Some of these similes have been used
so frequently that they have lost their freshness, and their impact as
figures of speech, and they have become clichés.
Match one half of the simile with the other.

1	As black as …	A	your arm
2	As blind as …	B	a barn door
3	As bold as …	C	a bat
4	As bright as …	D	a bee
5	As busy as …	E	a beetroot
6	As clean as …	F	a bell
7	As clear as …	G	a board
8	As cool as …	H	brass
9	As cunning as …	I	a brush
10	As daft as …	J	a button
11	As dark as …	K	a cucumber
12	As dead as …	L	the day is long
13	As deaf as …	M	a die
14	As drunk as …	N	ditchwater
15	As dull as …	O	a dodo
16	As fit as …	P	an eel
17	As flat as …	Q	a feather
18	As good as …	R	a fiddle
19	As green as …	S	a fox
20	As happy as …	T	gold
21	As hard as …	U	grass
22	As heavy as …	V	a hatter
23	As honest as …	W	the hills
24	As large as …	X	houses
25	As light as …	Y	lead
26	As long as …	Z	life
27	As mad as …	AA	lightning
28	As neat as …	BB	a lord
29	As old as …	CC	a mule
30	As plain as …	DD	nails
31	As pleased as …	EE	a new pin
32	As pretty as …	FF	night
33	As proud as …	GG	old boots
34	As quick as …	HH	a pancake
35	As red as …	II	a peacock
36	As right as …	JJ	a picture
37	As safe as …	KK	a pikestaff
38	As slippery as …	LL	a post
39	As solid as …	MM	Punch
40	As stiff as …	NN	rain
41	As straight as …	OO	a rake
42	As stubborn as …	PP	a rock
43	As thick as …	QQ	a sandboy
44	As thin as …	RR	a sheet
45	As tough as …	SS	sin
46	As ugly as …	TT	Solomon
47	As warm as …	UU	soot
48	As white as …	VV	toast
49	As wide as …	WW	two short planks
50	As wise as …	XX	a whistle

Can you think of further similes to add to this list?
Can you think of alternative similes, using the same adjectives as above?
In particular, can you think of other common similes than the one having
the form: 'as black as ….'?

Part One
Past and Place

Here is an exercise in both history and geography. Events have been chosen for their intrinsic importance, and for their distribution across the map.

What happened where?

336 BC	Alexander the Great made ruler of Greece.
AD 410	Visigoths under Alaric plunder the city.
AD 732	Charles Martel halts Moorish advance.
1066	William of Normandy declared King.
1295	Marco Polo returns home from China.
1453	Ottoman Turks capture Byzantium.
1492	Moors expelled from European mainland.
1517	Martin Luther protests against Roman Church.
1523	Gustavus Vasa drives Danes from Sweden.
1541	Calvin sets up theocratic state.
1579	William the Silent unites the United Provinces against Spain.
1588	Spanish Armada sets sail.
1642	Charles I calls royalists to arms.
1690	Protestant William of Orange defeats Catholic James II.
1769	Napoleon Bonaparte is born.
1789	The fall of the Bastille ushers in revolution.
1801	Nelson destroys Danish fleet.

1812	Napoleon retreats from a burning city.
1812	Congress to settle European borders after collapse of Napoleon's empire.
1855	Russians surrender to Britain and France in the Crimea.
1860	Victor Emmanuel becomes King of (new) Italy.
1871	New capital of Kaiser Wilhelm and Chancellor Bismarck.
1914	Assassination of heir to Austrian throne.
1917	Revolution of Bolsheviks against Tsar.
1937	Blitzkrieg by German Luftwaffe.
1938	Chamberlain makes pact with Hitler.
1955	Eastern Bloc military pact.
1956	Russian suppression of uprising.
1968	Russians invade and put a stop to Dubcek's 'Socialism with a human face'.
1975	Conference on Security and Cooperation in Europe.
1986	Explosion of nuclear reactor at Chernobyl.
1989	Fall of dictator Ceaucescu.

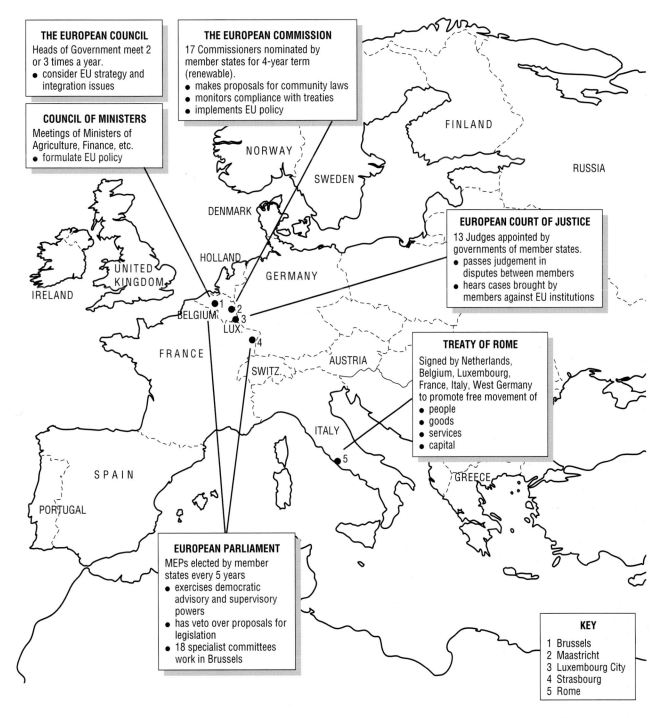

Part Two
EU Institutions

The European Union (EU) has evolved through a number of stages. First there was the European Economic Community (EEC), or 'Common Market', of six states. Then there was the European Community (EC) of 12 states; and now there is the EU, working out the implications of the Maastricht Treaty. Austria, Finland and Sweden (but not Norway) voted to join the EU in 1994. Below are the current major decision-making bodies of the EU.

THE EUROPEAN COUNCIL

Heads of Government meet 2 or 3 times a year.
- consider EU strategy and integration issues

COUNCIL OF MINISTERS

Meetings of Ministers of Agriculture, Finance, etc.
- formulate EU policy

THE EUROPEAN COMMISSION

17 Commissioners nominated by member states for 4-year term (renewable).
- makes proposals for community laws
- monitors compliance with treaties
- implements EU policy

EUROPEAN COURT OF JUSTICE

13 Judges appointed by governments of member states.
- passes judgement in disputes between members
- hears cases brought by members against EU institutions

TREATY OF ROME

Signed by Netherlands, Belgium, Luxembourg, France, Italy, West Germany to promote free movement of
- people
- goods
- services
- capital

EUROPEAN PARLIAMENT

MEPs elected by member states every 5 years
- exercises democratic advisory and supervisory powers
- has veto over proposals for legislation
- 18 specialist committees work in Brussels

KEY

1 Brussels
2 Maastricht
3 Luxembourg City
4 Strasbourg
5 Rome

Which is which?

1 Agreement to promote economic and political union of members.
2 Measure for protection of 'fundamental' rights of employees.
3 Support mechanism to maintain prices of foodstuffs.
4 Decisions to be made as close to point of impact as possible.
5 Device for bringing about currency stability.
6 Mechanism for the promotion of European monetary union.
7 Designed to accelerate achievement of internal market.
8 Legislature whose members are directly elected by voters.

A Common Agricultural Policy
B European Monetary System
C European Parliament
D Exchange Rate Mechanism
E Maastricht Treaty (1992)
F Single European Act (1986)
G Social Charter
H Subsidiarity Principle

Part Three
War and Peace

We in this Island and throughout our Empire who drew the sword against mighty Germany, we who are the only great unconquered nation which declared war on Germany on account of her aggression against Poland, have sentiments and duties towards Poland which deeply stir the British race. Everything in our power has been and will be done to achieve, both in the letter and in the spirit, the declared purposes towards Poland of the three great Allies.

... We must never lose sight of our prime and overwhelming duty, namely, to bring about the speediest possible destruction of the Nazi power. We owe this to the soldiers who are shedding their blood and giving their lives in the cause at this moment. They are shedding their blood in the effort to bring this fearful struggle in Europe to a close; and that must be our paramount task. Every problem – and there are many; they are as legion; they crop up in vast array – which now faces the nations of the world will present itself in a far easier and more adaptable form once the cannons have ceased to thunder in Europe, and once the victorious Allies gather round the table of armistice or peace. I have every hope that wise and harmonious settlements will be made, in confidence and amity, between the great Powers, thus affording the foundations upon which to raise a lasting structure of European and world peace. I say these words on the Polish situation, and I am sure that our friends on both sides will realize how long and anxious has been the study which the Cabinet have given to this matter, how constantly we see representatives of the Poles, how frequent and intimate our correspondence is with Russia on this subject.

I cannot conceive that it is not possible to make a good solution whereby Russia gets the security which she is entitled to have, and which I am resolved that we will do our utmost to secure for her, on her Western Frontier, and, at the same time, the Polish Nation have restored to them that national sovereignty and independence for which, across centuries of oppression and struggle, they have never ceased to strive. ...

The future of the whole world, and certainly the future of Europe, perhaps for several generations, depends upon the cordial, trustful and comprehending association of the British Empire, the United States and Soviet Russia, and no pains must be spared and no patience grudged which are necessary to bring that supreme hope to fruition.

(From a speech to the House of Commons, 28 September 1944, in *The Dawn of Liberation: Winston Churchill's War Speeches*, 1945)

1 **(a)** Who were the 'three great Allies'? (line 7)
  (b) What does Churchill mean by the phrase, 'they are as legion'? (line 14)
  (c) Suggest a synonym of 'amity'. (line 19)
  (d) What is a 'cordial' association? (line 35)
2 What does it mean to achieve a purpose 'both in the letter and in the spirit'? (line 6–7)
3 Why was so much importance being attached to the future status of Poland, even before the war was over?
4 What signs are there of Churchillian optimism in this speech, and what signs of pessimism?
5 What appear to be Churchill's priorities here, where victory is almost certain?

Part Four
Neighbours

What do we think of our fellow Europeans? How different are they from us? Is there more than a channel dividing us from our neighbours? Either: (a) **Assess our chances of overcoming our differences with our European partners**; or (b) **Write about the British as a European guidebook might write about us.**

1

Have you ever noticed how many pharmacies, pâtisseries and book-shops there are in Paris? The French are health-obsessed and will take any pill that is offered yet stubbornly refuse to admit the dangers of cholesterol, which lie in wait in the form of sweet, eggy delights greedily indulged in at goûter time. Guiltily, they repair to a bookshop to feed the intellect. The literary scene, however, is low-key, despite the fact that more people watch Apostrophes – the book programme hosted by the popular Bernard Pivot – than any of the other dull offerings on French TV.

(*The Time Out Paris Guide*, 1990)

2

There is no exact Spanish equivalent to English words such as to eavesdrop or to overhear. In Spain it is impossible to eavesdrop in the usual sly sense of the word because people simply speak too loudly. The noise level in Madrid, as in all of Spain, is several points above what might be acceptable elsewhere. Everything is convivial and loud, and that applies to acquaintances meeting on a street corner as well as to groups gathered in a bar and to drivers honking their horns in gridlocked traffic.

(Alan Tucker, *The Penguin Guide to Spain*, 1991)

3

Many Germans have powerful cars and the macho executive type tends to be an aggressive driver: so, unless your car goes fast and you like fast driving, it might be advisable to keep off the fast lane of an Autobahn where the big Mercs, Audi 200s and BMW 700s go pulsating along at speeds of up to 250 kph, impatiently flashing their headlights behind you if you dare to cruise at a mere 150 kph or so. This, for me, is the single most unattractive feature of touring in Germany. But apart from this, on lesser roads, the Germans are well-disciplined drivers, even pedantically so. In or out of a car they tend to like minding their neighbours' business, so that if you park where you shouldn't, or have your lights on wrongly, or make a turning where you shouldn't, they will seize an opportunity to tell you so.

(John Ardagh, *Exploring Rural Germany*, 1990)

4

You simply cannot overdress in Italy; whatever grand strides Italian designers have made on the international fashion merry-go-round, most of their clothes are purchased domestically, prices be damned. Now whether or not you want to keep up with the natives is your own affair .... It's not that the Italians are very formal; they simply like to dress up with a gorgeousness that adorns their cities just as much as those old Renaissance Churches and palaces ... Italian Customs are usually benign, though how the frontier police manage to recruit such ugly, mean-looking characters to hold the submachine guns and drug-sniffing dogs from such a good-looking population is a mystery; but they'll let you be if you don't look suspicious.

(Dana Facaros & Michael Pauls, *Cadogan Guides: Northeast Italy*, 1990)

5

There is a saying that 'The Lord made heaven and earth, but the Dutch made Holland'. Certainly they take their unrelenting struggle with the ocean as a matter of course ... Such stupendous undertakings have left an indelible mark on the Dutch character. They are a practical, efficient, but cautious people. One of their maxims, 'Don't go on the ice after one night's frost', typifies their caution.

(Nina Nelson, *The Netherlands*, 1987)

6

There is still much truth in the myth of the taciturn Scandinavian. A story tells of the two Danes, two Norwegians and two Swedes who were marooned on a desert island. When a rescue party arrived six months later, they found that the two Danes had started a co-operative, and the two Norwegians had founded a local chapter of the patriotic society Sons of Norway. The two Swedes were waiting to be introduced.

(Nancy Van Italie, *Fodor's 93 Scandinavia*, 1993)

Part Five
United States of Europe

Is a United States of Europe feasible, in your view, and if so, is it desirable? Base your answer to this question on any or all of the following opinions.

1   There will be no United States of Europe as long as you all continue to speak different languages. The USA only holds together because we all speak English. Every new American had to learn it.

2   The village, the city, the principality, the nation, have each been the dominant political unit. The historical trend is from smaller to bigger units. As long as it is based on consent, the bigger the unit, the better its chance of survival.

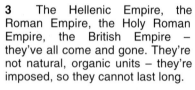

3   The Hellenic Empire, the Roman Empire, the Holy Roman Empire, the British Empire – they've all come and gone. They're not natural, organic units – they're imposed, so they cannot last long.

4   The British people will never agree to federation. They'll never sink their identity in a political mishmash. We fought and won two world wars to defend what it means to be British. Nicholas Ridley was right: the Germans would dominate a federal Europe.

5   The United States of Europe doesn't have to be like the United States of America. We don't have to think of it as one country, with one government. It's an effective trading bloc – and this is all it will be at first. It may well grow into something more later.

6   It simply wouldn't work. The Soviet Union didn't work; Yugoslavia didn't work; pre-Partition India didn't work. Cultural differences can only be glossed over for a time. If they're suppressed, they will only break out more violently later when the pressure is off.

7   It's feasible, yes, as long as it isn't forced. We have too many interests in common to be at each other's throats. There's strength in unity. It's got to be desirable if it prevents another European war.

8   The United States of Europe was Winston Churchill's idea. Bertrand Russell went further: he said there would never be real stability until we had a world government. I agree.

Maths 2: Simple Percentages

Q1: What is 10% of £40?

Most of us can see that the answer to this is £4 without doing any calculations. It is a pity that questions in the examination are not this easy. Let us try something a little more difficult.

Q2: What is 17½% of £240?

This is a little harder. It is relevant too. It could be the VAT on something that costs £240 before tax. The usual method goes something like this:

$$17\frac{1}{2}\% \text{ of } £240 = \frac{17\frac{1}{2}}{100} \times £240 = £42.$$

How can we develop this idea so that we can answer questions that are more complicated?

Look at this example:

$$22\% \text{ of } £500 = \frac{22}{100} \times £500$$

$$= 0.22 \times £500 = £110.$$

Notice how the percentage 22% can be replaced by the decimal fraction 0.22. This is a simple idea and very useful. 22% means 22 out of 100; 0.22 is 22 hundredths. We shall develop this idea so it is worth mastering it if you haven't already done so: 6% is the same as 0.06; 12½% is 0.125. So working out 12½% of £240 becomes a simple matter of multiplying 240 by 0.125.

Exercise 2.1

Express the following percentages as decimal fractions:

(a)	50%	(b)	10%
(c)	43%	(d)	73%
(e)	15%	(f)	7%
(g)	17½%	(h)	8½%
(i)	0.1%	(j)	0.01%

Exercise 2.2

Work out:

(a) 50% of $60
(b) 10% of £200

(c) 43% of $120
(d) 73% of £24
(e) 15% of £8
(f) 7% of 240 cm
(g) 17½% of £8
(h) 8½% of £650
(i) 0.1% of 5 km
(j) 0.01% of $3200

Question 2.2(g) asked for the VAT on £8. The answer is £1.40. Consider the following question:

Q3: VAT at 17½% is introduced on an item that originally cost £8. What is the new price including VAT?

The answer is, of course, £9.40. Note that if you multiply 8 by 1.175, you get 9.40. This method saves a lot of time, which is very precious in an examination. It is an idea that we shall develop further.

Exercise 2.3

Increasing something by 13% can be calculated by multiplying by 1.13. Increasing something by 9% can be calculated by multiplying by 1.09. What should numbers be multiplied by to increase them by:

(a)	10%	(b)	12%
(c)	17½%	(d)	30%
(e)	5%	(f)	75%
(g)	6½%	(h)	8¼%
(i)	5¾%	(j)	0.1%

The same idea can be used for decreasing quantities, such as for calculating discounts or amounts of depreciation. The amount remaining after reducing something by 10% can be calculated by multiplying by 0.90; reducing by 12½% will be calculated by multiplying by 0.0875

$$(100 - 12\frac{1}{2} = 87\frac{1}{2}).$$

Exercise 2.4

What should numbers be multiplied by to calculate a reduction by:

(a) 12%
(b) 15%
(c) 90%
(d) 17½%
(e) 30%

Part One
Left and Right in British Politics (1650–1950)

The notions of 'left-wing' and 'right-wing' date from the French Revolution; but the labels can loosely be applied to two traditions in British Politics since around 1650.

LEFT	EVENTS	RIGHT
Parliamentarians (Roundheads)	**English Civil War** 1642–48	**Royalists** (Cavaliers)
1650 **WHIGS** (from Scots for 'Rustler')	**Restoration of Charles II (Stuart)** 1660	**TORIES** (from Irish for 'Bandit')
Earl of Shaftesbury Led campaign against Catholic James II.	**Glorious Revolution.** Parliament offered crown to Protestant William of Orange, and wife Mary Stuart. 1689	Early supporters of James, but anti-Catholic
Moneyed interest Tolerance of religious dissent, anti-Jacobite.		Landed interest, strong Anglicanism, pro-Stuart (Jacobite).
1700	**Accession of George I (Hanover)** 1714	Tories in eclipse during Hanoverian succession.
Robert Walpole 1st 'Prime Minister' (1721–42) Long Whig ascendancy	**Failure of Jacobite uprisings** 1715 and 1745	
William Pitt the Elder (Chatham) (PM 1756–61) and	**Reign of George III** 1760–1820	
1800 **William Pitt the Younger** (PM 1783–1806) Parties still informal groupings. Father and son nominally whigs, but demands for reform and the American and French Revolutions polarized parliamentary politics.	**Trafalgar** 1805 **Waterloo** 1815 **Reform Bill** 1832	**William Pitt** Took Britain to war against Napoleonic France; repressed radicals at home. **CONSERVATIVES**
Charles James Fox Represented reform and opposition to crown; abolition of slavery and religious toleration.	**Accession of Victoria** 1837	**Robert Peel** (PM 1834–5; 1841–6) Economist whose Repeal of Corn Laws split the party for a generation.
Lord Grey (PM 1830–34)	**LIBERALS**	**Benjamin Disraeli** (PM 1868, 1874–80)
Lord Melbourne (PM 1835–44)	**W.E. Gladstone** (PM 1868–74, 80–85, 1886, 1892–94) Stood for constitutional reform, free trade, nonconformists' rights and Irish home rule.	Loyalty to Church, crown; imperialism.
Lord Palmerston (PM 1855–65)	**H.H. Asquith** (P.M. 1908–16)	**Lord Salisbury** (PM 1885–6, 86–92, 95–1902) Opposition to Irish home rule.
		Arthur Balfour (PM 1902–05)
1900 **LABOUR**	**Lloyd George** (PM 1916–22) Trade Union legislation, Social Security and parliamentary reform.	**Stanley Baldwin** (PM 1923–4, 24–29, 35–37)
Keir Hardie, Founder and sole MP 1892–95. Trade unionism, social reform, nationalization.	**Landslide Liberal win** 1906	
Ramsay MacDonald (PM 1924, 1929–31)	**Second World War** 1939–45	**Winston Churchill** (PM 1940–45, 1951–55)
Clement Atlee **1950** (PM 1945–50) Welfare state, redistribution of wealth.		Domestic consumption, denationalization.

A Bring the chart up to date by identifying political developments between 1950 and 1995, or 2000.

B Whose policy is whose (Labour, Liberal, or Conservative)?

1 Less government
2 Comprehensive schools
3 Deregulation
4 Proportional Representation
5 Public Ownership
6 Worker Participation
7 Privatization
8 Nuclear Energy
9 Universal Benefits
10 Community Politics

Part Two
The Houses of Parliament

Below is a diagram showing the passage of a bill through Parliament. Some bills are introduced in the Lords; but most government bills begin life in the Commons. The diagram assumes a bill that is an important piece of government policy.

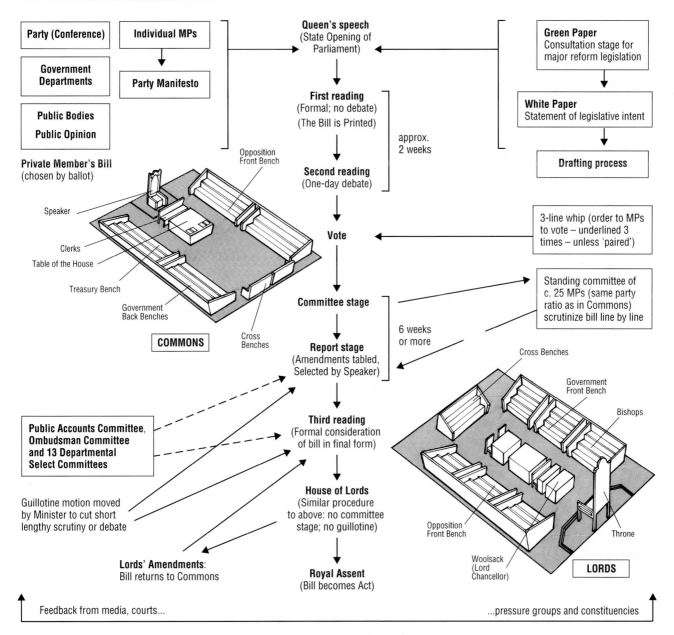

Party (Conference)	Individual MPs
Government Departments	Party Manifesto
Public Bodies / Public Opinion	

Private Member's Bill (chosen by ballot)

Queen's speech (State Opening of Parliament)

First reading (Formal; no debate) (The Bill is Printed)

approx. 2 weeks

Second reading (One-day debate)

Green Paper Consultation stage for major reform legislation

White Paper Statement of legislative intent

Drafting process

Vote

3-line whip (order to MPs to vote – underlined 3 times – unless 'paired')

COMMONS

Speaker / Clerks / Table of the House / Treasury Bench / Government Back Benches / Opposition Front Bench / Cross Benches

Committee stage

6 weeks or more

Standing committee of c. 25 MPs (same party ratio as in Commons) scrutinize bill line by line

Report stage (Amendments tabled, Selected by Speaker)

Public Accounts Committee, Ombudsman Committee and 13 Departmental Select Committees

Third reading (Formal consideration of bill in final form)

Guillotine motion moved by Minister to cut short lengthy scrutiny or debate

House of Lords (Similar procedure to above: no committee stage; no guillotine)

Cross Benches / Government Front Bench / Bishops / Opposition Front Bench / Throne / Woolsack (Lord Chancellor)

LORDS

Lords' Amendments: Bill returns to Commons

Royal Assent (Bill becomes Act)

Feedback from media, courts...   ...pressure groups and constituencies

A **Assess the importance or otherwise of the contribution of the general public to the above legislative process.**

B **Who does which job?**

1 Cabinet minister who ensures efficient management of the Commons.
2 Peers who do not sit with government or opposition peers.
3 Head of judiciary, speaker in the Lords, and cabinet minister.
4 Head of security in the Lords who summons the Commons at the State Opening.
5 Party managers responsible for ensuring healthy voting figures.
6 Leader of governing party on front bench; the prime minister.
7 Group of opposition MPs with counterpart responsibilities to ministers.
8 Senior permanent official, and adviser to the Speaker in the Commons.
9 An MP who chairs debates and regulates proceedings in the Commons.
10 Appointee who investigates MPs' complaints of maladministration.

A BLACK ROD
B CLERK TO THE HOUSE
C CROSS BENCHERS
D FIRST LORD OF THE TREASURY
E LEADER OF THE HOUSE
F LORD CHANCELLOR
G OMBUDSMAN
H SHADOW CABINET
I SPEAKER
J WHIPS

Part Three
Cabinet Government

Walter Bagehot's *The English Constitution* was published in 1867, the year of the Second Reform Act. Much has changed since then (there are women in Parliament for one thing), but much remains the same.

The efficient secret of the English Constitution may be described as the close union, the nearly complete fusion, of the executive and legislative powers. No doubt by the traditional theory, as it exists in all the books, the goodness of our constitution consists in the entire separation of the legislative and executive authorities, but in truth its merit consists in their singular approximation. The connecting link is the cabinet. By that we mean a committee of the legislative body selected to be the executive body. The legislature has many committees, but this is the greatest. It chooses for this, its main committee, the men in whom it has most confidence. It does not, it is true, choose them directly; but it is nearly omnipotent in choosing them indirectly. ...

There is nearly always some one man plainly selected by the voice of the predominant party in the predominant house of the legislature to head that party, and consequently to rule the nation. We have in England an elective first magistrate as truly as the Americans have an elective first magistrate. The Queen is only at the head of the dignified part of the constitution. The Prime Minister is at the head of the efficient part. The Crown is, according to the saying, the 'fountain of honour' but the Treasury is the spring of business. Nevertheless our first magistrate differs from the American. He is not elected directly by the people; he is elected by the representatives of the people. He is an example of 'double election'. The legislature chosen, in name, to make laws, in fact finds its principal business in making and in keeping an executive.

The leading minister so selected has to choose his associates, but he only chooses among a charmed circle. The position of most men in parliament forbids their being invited to the cabinet; the position of a few men ensures their being invited. Between the compulsory list whom he must take, and the impossible list whom he cannot take, a Prime Minister's independent choice in the formation of a cabinet is not very large; it extends rather to the division of the cabinet offices than to the choice of cabinet ministers.

1 **(a)** What is the difference between the 'executive' and the 'legislative' powers? (line 3)
   (b) What does it mean to describe anything as 'omnipotent'? (line 12)
   (c) What does Bagehot mean by the 'dignified' part of the constitution? (line 18)
   (d) What does he mean by its 'efficient' part? (line 19)
2 How does the legislature come to choose the members of the cabinet, according to Bagehot?
3 In what sense is the British Prime Minister chosen as the result of an 'elective' process?
4 What is the relevance here of the reference (line 20) to the Treasury?
5 Which 'few men' do you suppose are on the 'compulsory list' of potential cabinet members?

Part Four
Reform

Answer the following question, basing your response on a selection of quotations from those below: **Which aspect(s) of the political process stand(s) most in need of reform, in your view?**

1

Britain today suffers under the burden of three native curses: that of amateurism, that of 'inner circle' secrecy, and that of snobbery. All three serve to debase both the quality of political life and the energy of economic activity. The unreformed Parliament is more than a symbol of these things: it helps to perpetuate them by the most effective of all forces in politics and society – example. If Parliament is reformed, the whole climate of expectations could change, much of the sweet fog we muddle through might lift.

(Bernard Crick, *The Reform of Parliament*, 1968)

2

Reforms canvassed, and finding some support among MPs, have included morning sittings of the House, a fixed parliamentary year, more Estimates Days, greater powers for Select Committees (e.g. the power to compel the attendance of ministers), and a reform of the procedures for the scrutiny of delegated legislation.

(Lynton Robins, *Political Institutions in Britain*, 1987)

3

The institutions of British central government have proved chronically resistant to change throughout this century. Since 1945 Britain has lost an empire, ceased to play in the international first division and [has] been compelled by its economic and strategic predicament to enter the European community; yet its core political infrastructure remains substantially unchanged from that in place on the resignation of Lloyd George in 1922. Even today's party system, constrained by an electoral system long abandoned by the rest of Europe, bears a striking resemblance to that of the mid-1920s.

(Andrew Adonis, *Parliament Today*, 1990)

4

Supporters of the present British ('first-past-the-post') system defend it largely because it tends to produce single-party governments. Proponents of PR argue that the present system under-represents important minority views and can give unlimited political power to a party which has a Parliamentary majority based on considerably less than 50 per cent of the popular vote. From much of the debate we might imagine that there were only two main types of possible electoral systems and we must choose either one or the other. But ... there is an infinite variety of electoral systems.

(Andrew Reeve & Alan Ware, *Electoral Systems*, 1992)

5

The possible efficiency of a unicameral parliament [one with a single legislative chamber] based on the Commons may be strongly doubted: that House has shown itself to be slow in reforming its procedures so as to be either efficient or a real check on the government ... Whatever may be in future party manifestos, it is difficult to foresee House of Lords reform or abolition being considered so important to a future government as to justify the parliamentary time and trouble involved in achieving it against the wishes of the opposition parties. Radical reform of that House may be as far off as such reform of the House of Commons.

(Rodney Brazier, *Constitutional Practice*, 1988)

6

Despite the occasional defeat, the Government still gets by far the greater part of its legislation through in the form it wants. On the whole, moreover, it is right that it should. To call for an extension of the power of parliament is to advocate the defeat of policies on which governments have been elected, by shifting and ideologically incoherent coalitions of opposition and government back-benchers. The reformers' goal, if achieved, would work against the grain of the political system whose central principle is the production of a majority government secure enough to govern effectively by virtue of reliable party support.

(Bill Coxall and Lynton Robins, *Contemporary British Politics*, 1989)

Part Five
Politicians and the People

There is a danger, even in a supposed democracy, that politicians will lose touch with the people whom they are paid to represent. Politics becomes a way of life, conferring power which MPs learn to enjoy. Below are some opinions on which you might base an answer to this question: **Are there grounds for the complaint that politicians are too remote from the people who elect them to office?**

1   Politicians have only themselves to blame if the public perception of them is at an all-time low. You only have to watch them on television at Prime Minister's Question Time to see what a bunch of schoolboys they are. All they seem to be interested in is scoring points and facing down their opponents. Does government have to be run in this adversarial way?

2   We expect too much of our politicians. Why should they be any more moral or selfless than the voters who elect them? Today, more than ever before, they're under the glare of the TV lights all the time, and the press is more intrusive and less deferential. Their constituents expect them to be experts in everything with the help of one part-time research assistant, if they're lucky.

3   It's the corruption that undermines public confidence in the system. Chancellor of the Exchequer one minute, a non-executive director at a merchant bank the next; an ex-Minister of Transport doubles as transport spokesman in the Lords, and Chairman of a private motorway company. They collect directorships faster than most of us go through toothbrushes.

4   It's not fair to claim that politicians are remote. They're much more involved in constituency matters than they used to be. They're under tremendous media pressure to act on this issue, and campaign on that one. They have to attend weekly surgeries, be in the House to vote on major bills, and deal with mountains of correspondence. They're at everyone's beck and call all the time.

5   Frankly, being in politics is a pretty thankless task. The average backbencher works in pretty squalid conditions; sittings go on till late at night; and an MP often lives miles away from his or her family, only seeing them at weekends. One's outgoings are quite high in spite of expense allowances, and there's very little job security, especially in a marginal constituency.

6   Politics, public relations, advertising – they're all the same game. They're all about image: sharp suits, caring smiles and soothing voices. They're all slogan-mongers, – freedom of choice, the feel-good factor, brand loyalty. People are taken in – at least at elections, when the 'Bargain Sale' sign goes up. The disappointment follows when you get the goods home.

7   Power does corrupt – but our own politicians are better than most. In certain countries they control the press and the army, and amass huge personal wealth. An unfettered opposition, a free press and television prevent that sort of concentration of power in this country. British MPs are only human, but they're no more, and no less, honest than the rest of us.

8   The problem is that MPs in safe seats become complacent; and governments with big majorities grow careless of public opinion. More frequent elections, and a more proportional representation of the voters, would ensure that politicians behaved as they should: like our servants, and not our masters.

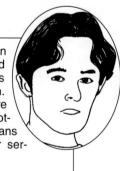

ITEM

G

French: Texts and Titles

A common exercise in reading comprehension is to match short pieces of text with suitable 'titles' that summarize their meaning. The object of this exercise is to identify keywords in the text that echo words in the title and so to match each title with its corresponding passage. Here is an example in which a number of words have been ringed. These words are either key words, directly related to the appropriate title, or they may be difficult words which require explanation. The titles are all figurative, rather than literal descriptions. Here, the answers are provided.

A La Cathédrale de Notre Dame et la Conciergerie se trouvent sur l'Ile de la Cité. Ce sont les deux **édifices** de l'Ile les plus riches en souvenirs du passé, symbolisant **deux tendances** essentielles de l'histoire de France: le Christianisme, et le rationalisme.

buildings

two tendencies, trends, features

have suffered

B De nombreux villages de France **ont souffert** une mort lente … partout les jeunes quittent **leur pays natal** et **s'en vont chercher un emploi** dans les centres commerciaux et administratifs. Certaines régions **ont subi** un véritable dépeuplement.

the country of their birth

go in search of work

have undergone

C La première ligne du **Chemin de Fer** Métropolitain (le Métro d'aujourd'hui) a été ouverte au public le 19 juillet 1900. Un système de chemin de fer **souterrain** semblable **existait depuis déja** plusieurs années dans d'autres capitales.

railway

underground

had already existed

original statutes, rules

D L'Académie française date de plus de trois cents ans. Le suivant est un des **statuts originaux**. 'La principale fonction de l'Académie sera de travailler à donner des règles à notre **langue**'. De nos jours, cette institution se croit la **gardienne** de la pureté de la langue.

tongue, language

keeper, holder

Which passage invites which title?

1	The late-arriving train	C
2	Twin pillars of the state	A
3	Holding our tongue	D
4	Country mice go for cheese	B

Here is another batch of four brief passages on the same themes as above. Again, certain words and phrases are ringed and translated, and again the titles are figurative. (Note that the words which are ringed may not necessarily be the key words.) This time the answers are not given. Match the passage with its appropriate title from the list given below.

thousands

seasonal

a wave

E Chaque jour des **milliers** de Parisiens traversent l'Ile de la Cité, par le Pont Saint Michel, le Pont au Change, le Pont Neuf, en se rendant à leur travail. Une **vague saisonnière** de touristes **déferle** dans ses places et sur ses quais; et n'oublions pas que les **ruelles** de l'Ile ont des habitants.

spreads (literally breaks)

little streets

F Le métro présente certaines particularités. Les lignes souterraines – et beaucoup ne le sont pas – sont construites assez près de **la chaussée:** cela réduit la nécessité d'escaliers mécaniques et d'ascenseurs, **sans parler** des long **couloirs** que l'on trouve fréquemment à Londres.

the roadway

not to mention

corridors

48

ITEM

G

any ——————

far from being ——————

lend ——————

are expressed ——————

rather than ——————

at the same time ——————

fate ——————

G L'Académie n'exerce **aucune** influence directe; mais le rôle indirect qu'elle joue dans le développement du français est **loin d'être** négligeable. De nombreux écrivains qui sont académiciens **prêtent** un prestige incalulable à cette institution.

H La Picardie, la Provence, et bien d'autres provinces anciennes ont chacune leurs traditions et leur identité qui **s'expriment** par des différences dans leurs villages **plutôt que** dans leurs villes. **En même temps,** le **sort** de tous ces villages offre de grandes ressemblances.

Which passage invites which title?

5 The power of the pen
6 A short step from the street
7 A thousand visit; a thousand visits
8 Variations on a pastoral theme

A large number of French words are similar to their English counterparts, and much of the meaning of the passages can be inferred from these words. Here, finally, are four passages on different themes, unsupported by marginal notes. Work out which words are key words and, again, choose the appropriate title for each passage.

I Il est dangereux de géneraliser lorsqu'on parle de la jeunesse. Mais il va sans dire que chaque génération de parents estime que les jeunes travaillent moins, sont moins sérieux, et s'amusent trop – bref, que la jeunesse a perdu maintes qualités depuis leur temps, et néglige les devoirs d'autrefois.

J On voit nettement l'influence puissante des médias sur la langue. La presse surtout, avec son énorme tirage, fait connaître au grand public les mots nouveaux – mots techniques, par exemple – et les emprunts aux langues étrangères. L'influence de la télévision et de la radio est importante dans le domaine de la prononciation.

K Le peuple français, tout comme la plupart des nations, est un mélange de races. Dès l'aube de l'histoire, la France a vu l'immigration de communautés étrangères qui, chassées par révolution et misère, et trouvant en France asile et foyer, y ont pris racine de façon permanente.

L Tout après la deuxième guerre mondiale, la France s'est engagé dans un programme conséquent de recherche qui lui a permis de prévoir la construction d'un réseau de centrales nucléaires. C'était un programme ambitieux qui a exigé des moyens financiers importants, et la formation d'équipes de techniciens spécialisés.

Which passage invites which title?

9 Word-smiths at large
10 Routes and roots
11 Teenagers now and then
12 Ambition, energy, expense

Part One
The English Legal System

There are a number of sources of laws in England and Wales, of which Parliament is (increasingly) the most important. Many countries (e.g. the USA) have a written constitution which supplies the ultimate framework for law. Others (e.g. France) have a Code offering legal guidelines. Britain has neither.

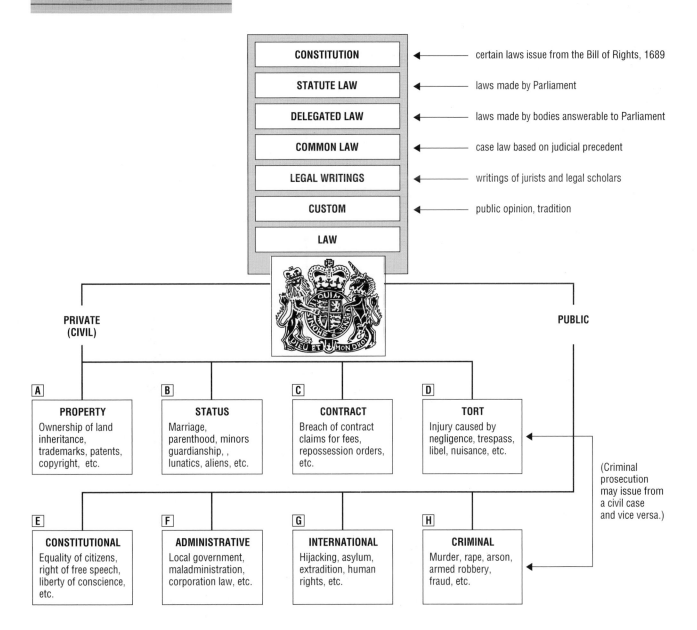

CONSTITUTION	← certain laws issue from the Bill of Rights, 1689
STATUTE LAW	← laws made by Parliament
DELEGATED LAW	← laws made by bodies answerable to Parliament
COMMON LAW	← case law based on judicial precedent
LEGAL WRITINGS	← writings of jurists and legal scholars
CUSTOM	← public opinion, tradition
LAW	

PRIVATE (CIVIL)   **PUBLIC**

A — PROPERTY
Ownership of land inheritance, trademarks, patents, copyright, etc.

B — STATUS
Marriage, parenthood, minors guardianship, , lunatics, aliens, etc.

C — CONTRACT
Breach of contract claims for fees, repossession orders, etc.

D — TORT
Injury caused by negligence, trespass, libel, nuisance, etc.

(Criminal prosecution may issue from a civil case and vice versa.)

E — CONSTITUTIONAL
Equality of citizens, right of free speech, liberty of conscience, etc.

F — ADMINISTRATIVE
Local government, maladministration, corporation law, etc.

G — INTERNATIONAL
Hijacking, asylum, extradition, human rights, etc.

H — CRIMINAL
Murder, rape, arson, armed robbery, fraud, etc.

Assuming a charge is brought, under which branch of the law would the following cases be heard?

1 An intruder gains access to the Queen's bedroom, but does no damage.
2 A playwright is sued for alleged breach of copyright.
3 A peer accuses a European airline of overcharging him.
4 A civil servant leaks information about the government's conduct of the Falklands War.
5 A 12-year-old is made a ward of court following family breakdown.
6 Five people are charged with false imprisonment of a 16-year-old girl.
7 A pop-singer sues a newspaper for false claims that she is bulimic.
8 A mayor invents a bogus election candidate to split the opposition vote.
9 A foreign vessel harasses a British trawler on the high seas.
10 A local council is accused of unreasonable behaviour in allocating school places.

A PROPERTY
B STATUS
C CONTRACT
D TORT
E CONSTITUTIONAL
F ADMINISTRATIVE
G INTERNATIONAL
H CRIMINAL

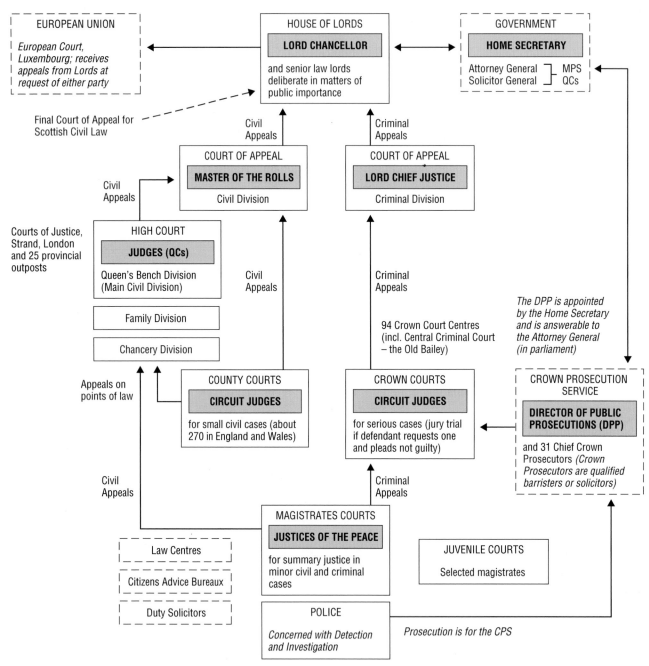

Part Two
The English Court System

The law in Scotland and Northern Ireland is different from that in England and Wales. Many European laws will override those of the United Kingdom in the future.

EUROPEAN UNION

European Court, Luxembourg; receives appeals from Lords at request of either party

HOUSE OF LORDS

LORD CHANCELLOR

and senior law lords deliberate in matters of public importance

GOVERNMENT

HOME SECRETARY

Attorney General ⎤ MPS
Solicitor General ⎦ QCs

Final Court of Appeal for Scottish Civil Law

Civil Appeals

Criminal Appeals

COURT OF APPEAL

MASTER OF THE ROLLS

Civil Division

Civil Appeals

COURT OF APPEAL

LORD CHIEF JUSTICE

Criminal Division

Courts of Justice, Strand, London and 25 provincial outposts

HIGH COURT

JUDGES (QCs)

Queen's Bench Division (Main Civil Division)

Family Division

Chancery Division

Civil Appeals

Criminal Appeals

94 Crown Court Centres (incl. Central Criminal Court – the Old Bailey)

The DPP is appointed by the Home Secretary and is answerable to the Attorney General (in parliament)

Appeals on points of law

COUNTY COURTS

CIRCUIT JUDGES

for small civil cases (about 270 in England and Wales)

CROWN COURTS

CIRCUIT JUDGES

for serious cases (jury trial if defendant requests one and pleads not guilty)

CROWN PROSECUTION SERVICE

DIRECTOR OF PUBLIC PROSECUTIONS (DPP)

and 31 Chief Crown Prosecutors *(Crown Prosecutors are qualified barristers or solicitors)*

Civil Appeals

Criminal Appeals

MAGISTRATES COURTS

JUSTICES OF THE PEACE

for summary justice in minor civil and criminal cases

JUVENILE COURTS

Selected magistrates

Law Centres

Citizens Advice Bureaux

Duty Solicitors

POLICE

Concerned with Detection and Investigation

Prosecution is for the CPS

Which is which?

1 A Justice of the Peace, either stipendiary (regularly paid) or unpaid; tries minor, local cases.
2 General-purpose lawyer; briefs a barrister to represent his client.
3 One who brings a criminal charge on behalf of the Crown.
4 The person who is charged in a civil court.
5 One who is called to give testimony in a court case.
6 A defendant who goes to appeal on his conviction or sentence.
7 One who brings a charge against someone in a civil court.
8 Lawyer called to the Bar who practises as an advocate.
9 Barrister who has 'taken silk' and is eligible to be a judge.
10 Elector chosen at random to help decide a verdict in a criminal case.

A APPELLANT
B BARRISTER
C DEFENDANT
D JUROR
E MAGISTRATE
F PLAINTIFF
G PROSECUTOR
H QUEEN'S COUNSEL
I SOLICITOR
J WITNESS

Part Three

Law and Justice

Antonio, the Merchant of Venice, is bonded to repay money borrowed from Shylock the money-lender, or to surrender a pound of his flesh. The bond was signed 'in merry sport'; but unforeseen circumstances prevent his honouring the debt. Shylock takes him to court, determined to have his pound of flesh. Portia is Bassanio's beloved, disguised here as a lawyer. Antonio is his friend.

Shylock:	... I would have my bond.	
Duke:	How shalt thou hope for mercy, rend'ring none?	
Shylock:	What judgment shall I dread, doing no wrong? ...	
	The pound of flesh which I demand of him	5
	Is dearly bought, 'tis mine, and I will have it.	
	If you deny me, fie upon your law! ...	
Portia:	Of a strange nature is the suit you follow;	
	Yet in such rule that the Venetian law	
	Cannot impugn you as you do proceed. ...	10
Bassanio:	... I beseech you,	
	Wrest once the law to your authority;	
	To do a great right do a little wrong,	
	And curb this cruel devil of his will.	
Portia:	It must not be; there is no power in Venice	15
	Can alter a decree established;	
	'Twill be recorded for a precedent,	
	And many an error, by the same example,	
	Will rush into the state; it cannot be. ...	
Antonio:	Most heartily I do beseech the court	20
	To give the judgment.	
Portia:	Why then, thus it is:	
	You must prepare your bosom for his knife. ...	
	Have by some surgeon, Shylock, on your charge,	
	To stop his wounds, lest he do bleed to death.	25
Shylock:	Is it so nominated in the bond?	
Portia:	It is not so express'd, but what of that?	
	'Twere good you do so much for charity.	
Shylock:	I cannot find it; 'tis not in the bond. ...	
Portia:	A pound of that same merchant's flesh is thine. ...	30
Shylock:	Most rightful judge!	
Portia:	And you must cut this flesh from off his breast. ...	
Shylock:	Most learned judge! A sentence! come, prepare.	
Portia:	Tarry a little; there is something else.	
	This bond doth give thee here no jot of blood:	35
	The words expressly are 'a pound of flesh'. ...	
	But, in the cutting it, if thou dost shed	
	One drop of Christian blood, thy lands and goods	
	Are, by the laws of Venice, confiscate.	

(Abridged from Shakespeare's *The Merchant of Venice* iv.i)

1 (a) How might 'I would have my bond' be interpreted in modern English? (line 1)
   (b) What is meant by 'suit' here? (line 7)
   (c) Substitute a word or phrase of your own, having a similar meaning, for 'impugn'(line 9)
   (d) What is a 'precedent'?(line 16)
2 What exactly is it that Bassanio urges Portia to do?
3 Why will she not do it?
4 What is the nature of Shylock's understanding of the law?
5 What is ironical about Portia's insistence that there be no blood shed?
6 How far does this passage justify the view either that law and justice are the same thing, or that they are bound to be different?

Part Four
The Law's Business

The Church used to be the monitor of public morals. The law was a compound of religious precepts and what was supposed to be the order of nature. With the decline of religion, the secular law has inherited a paternal responsibility for public morals. Base an answer to the following question on any or all of the opinions expressed below: **Is it the business of the law to interest itself in the private moral lives of citizens?**

1

The only purpose for which power can be rightfully exercised over any member of a civilized community, against his will, is to prevent harm to others. His own good, either physical or moral, is not a sufficient warrant. ... The only part of the conduct of anyone, for which he is amenable to society, is that which concerns others. In the part which merely concerns himself, his independence is, of right, absolute. Over himself, over his own body and mind, the individual is sovereign.

(John Stuart Mill, *On Liberty*, 1859)

2

The function of the criminal law is to preserve order and decency, to protect the citizens from what is offensive or injurious, and to provide sufficient safeguards against exploitation and aggravation of others, particularly those who are specially vulnerable because they are young, weak in body or mind, inexperienced .... It is not, in our view, the function of the law to intervene in the private lives of citizens.

(The Report of the Wolfenden Committee on Homosexual Offences and Prostitution, 1957)

3

'A recognized morality' is, in Lord Devlin's words, 'as necessary to society's existence as a recognized government'; ... one who is 'no menace to others' nonetheless may by his immoral conduct 'threaten one of the great moral principles on which society is based.' ... It is of course clear (and one of the eldest insights of political theory) that society could not exist without a morality which mirrored and supplemented the law's proscription of conduct injurious to others. But there is no evidence to support, and much to refute, the theory that those who deviate from conventional sexual morality are in other ways hostile to society.

(H.L.A. Hart, *Law, Liberty and Morality*, 1963)

4

Lord Devlin wrote in 1965, and censure of homosexuality, which seemed perhaps conservative but reasonable then, is out of place now. During the course of twenty years the laws allowing homosexuals to associate more freely and overtly have led to greater public tolerance and understanding; many, like Devlin ..., who opposed relaxation of the original restraining laws would not now support reimposition of the restraints.

(Jennifer Trusted, *Moral Principles and Social Values*, 1987)

5

On Mill's principle, if free consent and privacy obtain, then an act is to be tolerated. There are, however, acts which would not be tolerated even if these conditions were satisfied, for example, euthanasia and incest. Devlin holds that laws must reflect the moral views of the citizens. It is as much the business of the law to suppress vice as it is to suppress subversion. ... Hart argues that if an act is to be suppressed, then a group of experts must show that it is dangerous. The law should not prohibit an act because the community regards it as immoral.

(Calvin Pinchin, *Issues in Philosophy*, 1990)

6

Let us move on from preoccupation with alleged difference in approaching the redundant question whether the law should enforce morality, by accepting that of course the law does and should depend on moral values. Then we can concentrate on arguing about *which* values the law should accommodate and how much emphasis should be given, say, to the liberal moral values of tolerance and autonomy. ... Rather than regarding 'paternalism' as beyond the pale, we need to consider how 'parental paternalism' can help us to develop as autonomous beings, when that ought to stop, and when medical or legal paternalism (as in the case of discouraging the initial taking of heroin) can help even adults to lead their lives as autonomously as possible.

(Simon Lee, *Law and Morals*, 1986)

Part Five
Breaking the Law

Use any or all of the following opinions as the basis for an essay having this title: **'There are occasions when it is not only one's right, but it is one's duty to break the law.' Discuss.**

1 The law applies to everybody. If one group claims the right to break the law, what's to stop a second group breaking another law to thwart the first group? If everyone has the right to break the law (and in a democracy, it has to be everyone or no one) then you can no longer talk meaningfully of law.

2 Assassination is against the law, yet who in Britain, in 1944, would not have applauded an attempt on Hitler's life? Who in America would not have cheered if a smart bomb had 'taken out' Saddam Hussein, in the Gulf War? Is there one law for Hitler and another one for John F. Kennedy?

3 Rousseau's line was that law was the expression of the general will – the will of the people. The people didn't take the law into their own hands, therefore, when they 'broke it', it belonged in their hands.

4 Law is made by the dominant class in society. It is framed and enforced in the interests of this class. Law is the means by which the few sustain their power over the many. In keeping this law, the many resign themselves to powerlessness.

5 The suffragettes broke man-made laws to bring their cause to public attention. Poll-tax defaulters broke a Tory law. The 'customary' Sunday-trading law was changed only because the big stores openly flouted it. History will vindicate all three groups.

6 Government is a contract between ruler and ruled. In an open society it is equally binding on both parties. John Locke's view was that if the ruler breaks the contract, the people have the right – even the duty – to resist the ruler, and their rule.

7 Once you've conceded the right to break the law you've opened a Pandora's Box. 'Might' very soon becomes 'right'. In an anarchy, it's the strong who win, and the weak who get hurt.

8 There's nothing sacrosanct about the law: it's a social construct. It's being made and re-made, bent and interpreted all the time. It's organic, parts of it growing, parts of it dying – it's a natural process.

ITEM

Affixes: Greek Forms

We derive more of our vocabulary from Greek than might be supposed. While many of our borrowings came to us through Latin, the language of the Roman, western 'catholic' church, the New Testament was written in Greek and Greek was the language of the Byzantine, eastern 'orthodox' church. The schism between east and west did not occur until 1034 – well into the so-called medieval period.

When Byzantium/Constantinople fell to the Turks in 1453, a sizeable hoard of Greek manuscripts found refuge in Italy. The words we borrowed from these Greek texts were not words for ordinary objects: we had these in English already from the Jutes, Saxons and Normans. Rather, as it was scholars who read the manuscripts, the Greek words that gained currency were scholarly words. (See Unit 2: Curriculum, Part 2: Subject Names.)

As we saw in Item B (page 13), an affix is the name given to any speech element which can be added to a root word, and it is added normally as either a prefix or a suffix. The Greek word for 'eye' is ophthalmos. The word 'eye' is serviceable enough as a noun, but it is not a word that easily accommodates prefixes and suffixes. So we used the Greek root for the abstract nouns:

ophthalmia (an inflammation of the eye)
ophthalmology (study and therapy of the eye)
ophthalmologist (student and therapist of the eye)

Greek has been a rich source of roots for technical terms and we have also made use of a number of Greek prefixes, particularly for attachment to Greek roots. Here are sixteen of those in fairly common use:

a	=	without
anti	=	against
apo	=	from
dia	=	through
ek, ex	=	out of
en	=	in, on
epi	=	on
eu	=	good, well
hypo	=	below
mega	=	large
mono	=	one
para	=	beside
peri	=	round
poly	=	many
syn(m)	=	with
tele	=	far

The most common suffix comes straight from the Greek —IKOS, which gives us the following adjectival ending:

opthalm–ic
scept–ic–al
ecclesiast–ic–al

Here we shall confine ourselves to applying the above sixteen prefixes, and the one adjectival suffix.

For a brief guide to parts of speech, see Item B, page 13.

Below is a Greek root. Which of the sixteen prefixes listed above can be added to it to make a word meaning the same as the word or phrase in English?

_____ + lithos (stone) + ic = massy, imposing, dolmen-like

The answer is mega—, giving us the word 'megalithic'.

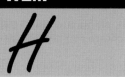

ITEM *H*

Now add an appropriate prefix to each of the following roots to make a word synonymous with the word or phrase in English. The prefixes are given below in an alphabetical list, for ease of reference.

1 _____ + metron (measure) + ical   = matching perfectly about an axis

2 _____ + sitos (food) + ic   = depending on another for one's livelihood

3 _____ + pathos (suffering) + ic   = knowing others' minds by other than sensory means

4 _____ + phēmē (speaking) + istic   = toned down for use in polite company

5 _____ + chrōma (colour) + tic   = in a single colour

6 _____ + gramma (letter) + tic(al)   = witty and very much to the point

7 _____ + thēsis (proposition) + tic(al)   = a statement counterposed to another

8 _____ + pateia (walking) + tic   = always on the move

9 _____ + morphē (shape) + ic   = having no fixed shape

10 _____ + kritēs (judge) + ic(al)   = pretending to be what one is not

11 _____ + phonē (voice) + ic   = consisting of many musical sounds

12 _____ + ergon (work) + etic   = lively, vigorous

13 _____ + gnōsis (knowledge) + tic   = inference from symptoms

14 _____ + logos (word, reason) + ethic   = defensive speech on one's own, or another's behalf

15 _____ + topos (place) + ic   = out of its proper place

A	a	=	without
B	anti	=	against
C	apo	=	from
D	dia	=	through
E	ek, ex	=	out of
F	en	=	in, on
G	epi	=	on
H	eu	=	good, well
I	hypo	=	below
J	mega	=	large
K	mono	=	one
L	para	=	beside
M	peri	=	round
N	poly	=	many
O	syn(m)	=	with
P	tele	=	far

Part One
English Literary Genres (to 1900)

A genre is a particular form, usually literary. The following classification is a not uncommon one. Each has been dominant at different times for different social-cultural reasons. Literary works are listed below under broad categories, and some works which are not easily categorized are included where important.

	1 NON-FICTION	2 POETRY	3 DRAMA	4 PROSE FICTION
	DARK AGES (from c. 700)			
A	RELIGIOUS WORKS IN LATIN (Aldhelm, Bede, etc.) *Anglo-Saxon Chronicle* (Alfred)	*Beowulf* (Anon) RELIGIOUS POEMS (Cynewulf, Caedmon, etc.)	LITURGICAL PLAYS IN LATIN	
	MIDDLE AGES (from c. 1200)			
B	MYSTICAL WRITINGS (Hilton, Rolle, Kempe, Juliana, etc.)	BALLADS ROMANCES *Canterbury Tales* (Chaucer) ALLEGORIES	MIRACLE/MYSTERY PLAYS MORALITY PLAYS *Everyman* (Anon)	*Morte D'Arthur* (Malory)
	RENAISSANCE (from c. 1500)			
C	CHRONICLES (Holinshed, etc.) *Book of Martyrs* (Foxe) *Essays* (Bacon)	SONNETS (Wyatt, Surrey, Sidney) *The Faerie Queene* (Spenser) BLANK VERSE	INTERLUDES COMEDIES, HISTORIES, TRAGEDIES (Kyd, Greene, Peele, Marlowe, Shakespeare)	*Arcadia* (Sidney) NARRATIVES (Deloney, Nashe, etc.)
	STUART PERIOD (from c. 1600)			
D	*King James Bible* SERMONS DIARIES (Pepys, Evelyn, etc.) PHILOSOPHY (Hobbes, Locke, etc.)	METAPHYSICAL POETRY (Donne, Herbert, Vaughan) CAVALIER POETRY (Lovelace, Carew, etc.) PURITAN POETRY (Milton, Marvell, etc.)	(… Shakespeare, Jonson) REVENGE TRAGEDY (Webster, Tourneur, etc.) RESTORATION COMEDY (Wycherley, Behn, Congreve, Vanbrugh, etc.)	*Oroonoko* (Behn) *Pilgrim's Progress* (Bunyan)
	AUGUSTAN AGE (c. 1700)			
E	JOURNALISM (Steele, Addison, Defoe) SATIRE (Swift, etc.) *Dictionary* (Johnson) HISTORY (Hume, Gibbon)	SATIRE (Pope, Johnson, Goldsmith) NATURE POETRY (Thomson, Gray, etc.) *John Gilpin* (Cowper)	SENTIMENTAL DRAMA (Steele, Lillo etc.) *She Stoops to Conquer* (Goldsmith) *The Rivals (etc.)* (Sheridan)	*Robinson Crusoe* (Defoe) *Pamela* (Richardson) PICARESQUE NOVELS (Fielding, Smollett, etc.) *Tristram Shandy* (Sterne)
	ROMANTICISM (from c. 1790)			
F	*Life of Johnson* (Boswell) ESSAYS (Lamb, Hazlitt, de Quincey) JOURNALISM (Jeffrey, Smith, Lockhart, etc.)	*Songs of Innocence and Experience* (Blake) ROMANTIC POETRY (Wordsworth, Coleridge, Keats, Byron, Shelley, etc.)	*The Cenci* (Shelley)	SENTIMENTAL NOVELS GOTHIC NOVELS (Walpole, Radcliffe, Lewis, Shelley, etc.) ROMANTIC NOVELS (Austen, Scott, etc.)
	VICTORIAN PERIOD (from c. 1840)			
G	HISTORY (Macaulay, Carlyle, etc.) *Apologia Pro Vita Sua* (Newman) CRITICISM (Ruskin, Arnold, Pater)	EPICS, LYRICS (Tennyson, Browning, Arnold, Rossetti, Swinburne, Morris, etc.) *The Rubaiyat of Omar Khayyam* (Fitzgerald)	MELODRAMA *The Second Mrs Tanqueray* (Pinero) COMEDIES (Wilde, Shaw)	*Wuthering Heights* (Brontë) CONDITION-OF-ENGLAND NOVELS (Dickens, Disraeli, Thackeray, Gaskell, Eliot, etc.) NOVELLA, SHORT STORY (James, Hardy, etc.)

There are 28 'cells' in the above table. Assign each of the following works to its appropriate cell (e.g. Beowulf A2).

1 PARADISE LOST
2 THE RAPE OF THE LOCK
3 VANITY FAIR
4 TROILUS AND CRISEYDE

5 DR FAUSTUS
6 A TALE OF A TUB
7 THE IMPORTANCE OF BEING EARNEST
8 KUBLA KHAN

9 THE HISTORY OF TOM JONES
10 PRIDE AND PREJUDICE
11 IN MEMORIAM
12 THE COUNTRY WIFE

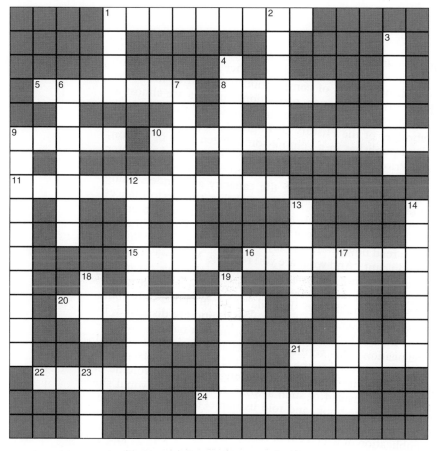

Part Two

Literary Terms

Read the clues and fill in the crossword with the appropriate words from the alphabetic list of literary terms.

A ALLITERATION
B ANALOGY
C BATHOS
D BURLESQUE
E EPIC
F EULOGY
G EUPHEMISM
H IDIOM
I IRONY
J MALAPROPISM
K METAPHOR
L METRE
M ODE
N ONOMATOPOEIA
O PARADOX
P PARONYM
Q PUN
R SARCASM
S SATIRE
T SIMILE
U SLANG
V SPOONERISM
W SYNONYM
X SYNTAX
Y TAUTOLOGY
Z TYPE

Clues Across
1 A mild description of something offensive.
5 A scornful jibe; bitter irony.
8 A characteristic form of expression.
9 Colloquial language; jargon.
10 Recurrence of a consonantal sound.
11 Formation of a word imitating the sound of the thing signified.
15 A prefiguring; a model.
16 The non-literal description of an object by reference to another.
20 An imitation which mocks its original by exaggeration.
21 The grammatical structure of a sentence.
22 Communication of meaning, in words that are literally opposite in meaning.
24 A word having the same meaning as another.

Clues Down
1 A long poem narrating heroic events.
2 The ridicule of folly or vice.
3 Descent from the elevated to the ridiculous; anti-climax.
4 Explicit comparison of one thing with another.
6 A parallel case, for illustration.
7 The wrong use of a word having a similarity with the right one.
9 Transference of initial consonants of spoken words.
12 Needless use of words having the same meaning.
13 The rhythm of stressed and unstressed syllables in verse.
14 An (apparent) self-contradicton.
17 A word having the same root or sound as another.
18 A play on words.
19 A song or speech of praise.
23 An elaborate lyric addressed to someone or something.

See also Item K, p.74, for examples of the terms.

Part Three
The Case for the Novel

In the following extract from *Northanger Abbey*, Jane Austen lays aside the story of Catherine Morland for a moment to defend the novel against its detractors. She not only berates 'reviewers', she blames 'novel-writers' themselves for patronizing their own heroines when they read 'only a novel'.

Although our productions have afforded more extensive and unaffected pleasure than those of any other literary corporation in the world, no species of composition has been so much decried. From pride, ignorance, or fashion, our foes are almost as many as our readers; and while the abilities of the nine-hundredth abridger of the History of England, or of the man who collects and publishes in a volume some dozen lines of Milton, Pope, and Prior, with a paper from The Spectator, and a chapter from Sterne, are eulogized by a thousand pens, there seems almost a general wish of decrying the capacity and undervaluing the labour of the novelist, and of slighting the performances which have only genius, wit, and taste to recommend them. 'I am no novel-reader – I seldom look into novels – Do not imagine that I often read novels – It is really very well for a novel.' Such is the common cant. 'And what are you reading, Miss —?' 'Oh! it is only a novel!' replies the young lady, while she lays down her book with affected indifference or momentary shame. 'It is only "Cecilia", or "Camilla" or "Belinda"', or, in short, only some work in which the greatest powers of the mind are displayed, in which the most thorough knowledge of human nature, the happiest delineation of its verities, the liveliest effusions of wit and humour, are conveyed to the world in the best-chosen language. Now, had the same young lady been engaged with a volume of The Spectator, instead of such a work, how proudly would she have produced the book, and told its name! though the chances must be against her being occupied by any part of that voluminous publication of which either the matter or manner would not disgust a young person of taste – the substance of its papers so often consisting in the statement of improbable circumstances, unnatural characters, and topics of conversation which no longer concern any one living.

5

10

15

20

25

30

1 **(a)** What would a reviewer do who 'eulogized' a work? (line 9)
   (b) What do you take to be the meaning of 'cant' (line 15)
   (c) What is 'affected' indifference? (line 17)
   (d) What does 'happiest' mean, in this context (line 20–1)?
2 In what spirit, and in what language, does Jane Austen speak of novels?
3 What does she appear to think it is the business of the novelist to do?
4 Why is it all too likely that the 'young lady' referred to in line 17 laid down her novel with 'momentary shame'?
5 In what tone does Austen speak of histories and essays?
6 What is so ironic about her reference to 'improbable circumstances' and 'unnatural characters' in the pages of *The Spectator*?

Part Four

Truth and Fiction

Is a novelist just a story-teller, or does a 'good' novelist aim to 'tell it like it is'? Base an answer to the following question on any or all of the views expressed below. **In what sense might a novel – a work of 'fiction' – be as 'true to life' as any non-fiction text?**

1 We cannot understand each other, except in a rough and ready way: we cannot reveal ourselves, even when we want to; what we call intimacy is only a makeshift; perfect knowledge is only an illusion. But in the novel we can know people perfectly, and, apart from the general pleasure of reading, we can find here a compensation for their dimness in life. In this direction fiction is truer than history, because it goes beyond the evidence ....

(E.M. Forster, *Aspects of the Novel*, 1927)

2 We know what the novelist sets out to do when he writes a novel. Like any other artist the novelist is a maker. He is making an imitation, an imitation of the life of man on earth. He is making, it might be said, a working model of life as he sees and feels it, his conclusions about it being expressed in the characters he invents, the situations in which he places them, and in the very words he chooses for those purposes .... The novelist is free to choose his material only in a limited sense, and his choice is governed by the deepest compulsions of his personality.

(Walter Allen, *The English Novel*, 1958)

3 If I meet a friend and he gives me some surprising piece of news, in order to convince me of its truth he can always resort to telling me that such and such people were also witnesses, that all I have to do is check the story with them. On the other hand, from the moment a writer puts the word novel on the cover of his book, he declares that it is useless to seek any kind of confirmation.

(Michel Butor, *Inventory: Essays*, 1968)

4 You may think novelists always have fixed plans to which they work, so that the future predicted in Chapter One is always inexorably the actuality of Chapter Thirteen. But novelists write for lots of reasons: for money, for fame, for reviewers, for parents, for friends, for loved ones, for vanity, for pride, for curiosity, for amusement .... Only one same reason is shared by all of us: we wish to create worlds as real as, but other than the world that is. Or was. That is why we cannot plan. We know a world is an organism, not a machine.

(John Fowles, *The French Lieutenant's Woman*, 1969)

5 I am not interested in telling lies in my own novels. A useful distinction between literature and other writing for me is that the former teaches one something true about life: and how can you convey truth in a vehicle of fiction? The two terms truth and fiction are opposites, and it must logically be impossible .... The novel is a form in the same sense that the sonnet is a form; within that form, one may write truth or fiction. I choose to write truth in the form of a novel.

(B.S. Johnson, *Aren't You Rather Young to be Writing Your Memoirs?* 1973)

6 It's the information boom that has really altered the way people write novels. Over the last ten years a lot of novelists have been writing with keen interest in fact: historical novels about today, as it were, because they are competing with the mass of information that we get every day on television. But we're aware that the news we see, and the news we read, is being manipulated all the time. We realize that the novel can be more truthful than the instant news media which are always telling you a story for a particular political purpose.

(Margaret Drabble, 'A Very Personal Medium', in *The General Studies Review*, 1993)

7 What I absolutely try to do is never, never tell a lie, and if I have a sort of aperçu, I do my best to put down exactly what I mean, to represent things truly in the way I have seen them. I really do try terribly hard to be honest, to be truthful. To say as precisely as I can what it is that I've seen or heard.

(Alice Thomas Ellis, 'Face to Face' in *The English Review*, 1993)

8 I am Hope Clearwater. She is Hope Clearwater. Everything is me, really. Try to remember that, though it might be a little confusing at first. Where shall I begin? In Africa, I think, yes, but far from Brazzaville Beach. A final note: the important factor in all this is honesty, otherwise there would be no point in beginning.

(William Boyd, *Brazzaville Beach: A Novel*, 1990)

Part Five
The Film of the Book

Novels are as often watched as read these days. They are serialized on television, or 'interpreted' by a film director for the cinema screen. Is the experience of watching the film version of a book altogether different from the experience of reading the original? Using a selection of the opinions expressed below, answer the following question: **What is gained, and what is lost, when a novel is filmed?**

1   A novel generally suffers, I think, when filmed. Relationships are often romanticized, and subtle nuances are lost. It's the novel of ideas that loses out most: you just can't capture in a film the play of metaphors; the language. A film's all dialogue, but there's much more than dialogue in a good novel.

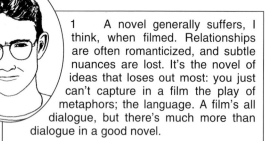

2   You simply can't do justice to a big novel on the small screen – I mean 'big' spatially, like *The Grapes of Wrath,* or *The Power and The Glory* or *Catch 22.* These are larger-than-life stories. A film version has to envelop you emotionally in a way only an epic cinema film version can do.

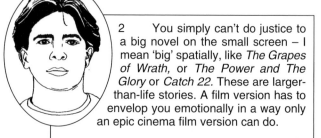

3   You can't easily film Lawrence – though all credit to directors like Ken Russell who have tried – because there's so much text. It's dense with references for you to consider and reflect upon in the imagination.

4   There have been films that have been better than the books they were based on. The Merchant-Ivory version of Ishiguro's *Remains of the Day*, for example, was a tremendous aesthetic experience: there was so much to look at. It didn't matter much that the story-line was perhaps inconsequential, whereas it did matter in the novel.

5   The experience of reading a novel is a rich one because the reader is spending time with the writer. As the novel develops, so the reader's thoughts develop and interact with the author's. The characters and context are being created together – it's not a one-way thing like it is with a film. A film is all over in a couple of hours and your senses are drenched.

6   The novels of Charles Dickens and George Eliot come over rather well on television. After all, Dickens delivered his novels in instalments in the first place. Each of them is a series of intimate scenes which is wholly appropriate to the small screen.

7   John Fowles is a bit of a trick writer, in a novel like *The French Lieutenant's Woman.* You can translate those sorts of tricks on to the cinema screen. Some writers, you feel, almost write with the cinema in mind. They adopt film techniques in the writing of their novels – panning, montage, etc. – so that reverse adaptation, if you like, is no problem.

8   E.M. Forster's *A Passage to India* is a fabulous novel; but then David Lean made a fabulous film of it. Forster's excellent at evoking the atmosphere of British India – but how many readers of the novel can experience the visual aspect of it: the pageant; the landscape – that Lean's film presented so well? You could feel the irritation exuding from the very soil.

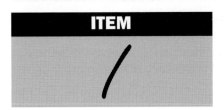

Maths 3: More Percentages

Q1: The old price of an item is £A before being increased by r% to £B. What is the formula for B in terms of A and r?

How do we do this? First of all, do not let the letters A, B and r upset you. Change them to numbers and see what happens. (As we have seen, questions involving algebra can sometimes be made much easier by the judicious substitution of numbers.) Let A be £100 and r be 7. The question then becomes:

Q2: The old price of an item is £100 before being increased by 7% to £B. What is the formula?

Well, B is obviously 107. The method is like this:

7% is $\frac{7}{100}$. Adding 7% of £100 is calculated like this: $100 + \frac{7}{100} \times 100$. Putting the letters A and r back in the right places we have:

$$B = A + \frac{r}{100} A = A(1 + \frac{r}{100})$$

Either of the two answers should correspond to the multiple choices on offer.

Q3: At the start of a year an item was worth £A but it depreciates at r% during the year. What was it worth at the end of the year?

This is the same as the previous question, except that the amount (the depreciation instead of the interest) is subtracted instead of being added. The formula becomes

$$B = A - \frac{r}{100} A = A(1 - \frac{r}{100})$$

Q4: A sum of money is invested for one year at 7% interest. This interest is subject to tax at 20%. What is the effective rate of interest?

One problem with answering this question is that we do not know how much money is involved. Do not let this worry you. Pick an arbitrary figure.

£100 will do. The normal method goes something like this:

7% of £100 is £7. This is subject to tax at 20%. 20% of £7 is £1.40. That leaves us with only £5.60. The *effective* rate of interest is therefore 5.6%.

Another way of looking at it is to consider that, if you are taxed at 20%, then you are left with 80%. This is equivalent to 0.80. 7% is 0.07. 0.07 x 0.80 = 0.056. This is 5.6%. That was not too difficult. Can we extend the idea?

Q5: The sum of money invested at 7% interest subject to tax at 20% is left in the account for five years. What is the effective rate of increase?

The effective rate of interest is 5.6% (from the previous question). We can work out how much the amount is increased by multiplying by 1.056 (using the technique of Exercise 3.1). This works for each year, so for five years we multiply by 1.056 five times:

$1.056 \times 1.056 \times 1.056 \times 1.056 \times 1.056 = 1.056^5 = 1.313165 \ldots$

Since this is the same as increasing something by just over 31%, this is the rate of increase over the five years.

Exercise 3.1

1 Calculate the effective rate of increase of the following rates of interest subject to the following tax rates:
   (a) 6% @ 20% tax
   (b) 10% @ 25% tax
   (c) 9.8% @ 22% tax
   (d) 11.2% @ 40% tax

2 Calculate the value of an investment at the following rates of interest over the periods indicated:

	Investment	Rate P.A.	Years
(a)	£2000	12%	5
(b)	£550	6%	10
(c)	£3000	5½%	25
(d)	£50	11½%	6
(e)	£2500	6¼%	4

Finally, we shall tackle this one:

Q6: £A is invested at r% for n years by which time it will have increased to £B. What is the formula for B in terms of A and r?

We have the formula for one year from a previous question. It is:

$$B = A(1 + \frac{r}{100})$$

The part in brackets is the multiplier giving the increase like the 1.056 of the previous question. Just as in the previous question this multiplier was raised to the power of 5, so in this question we substitute the letter n. The answer is therefore:

$$B = A(1 + \frac{r}{100})^n$$

Part One
A Map of the Media

The spoken word was first captured in the printed book before being freed again, with the transmission and recording of sound, to be heard by audiences in the mass. Communication reached its pinnacle in film and television broadcasting, presenting the immediacy of human experience.

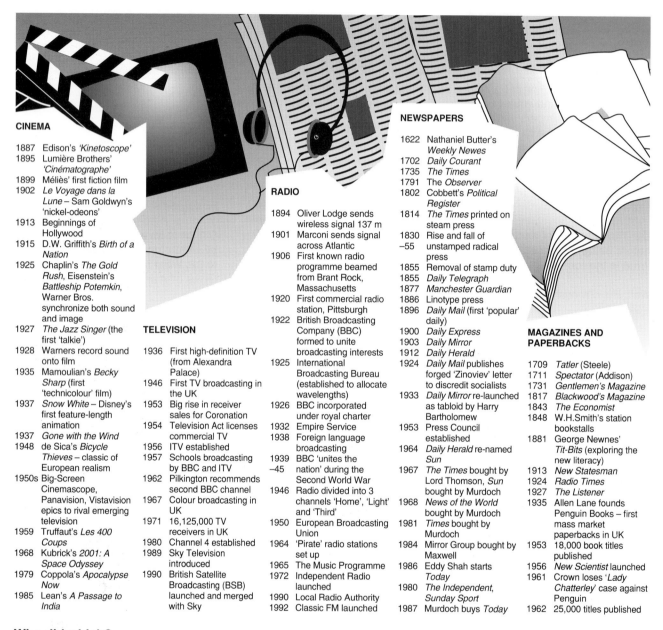

CINEMA

1887 Edison's *'Kinetoscope'*
1895 Lumière Brothers' *'Cinématographe'*
1899 Méliès' first fiction film
1902 *Le Voyage dans la Lune* – Sam Goldwyn's 'nickel-odeons'
1913 Beginnings of Hollywood
1915 D.W. Griffith's *Birth of a Nation*
1925 Chaplin's *The Gold Rush*, Eisenstein's *Battleship Potemkin*, Warner Bros. synchronize both sound and image
1927 *The Jazz Singer* (the first 'talkie')
1928 Warners record sound onto film
1935 Mamoulian's *Becky Sharp* (first 'technicolour' film)
1937 *Snow White* – Disney's first feature-length animation
1937 *Gone with the Wind*
1948 de Sica's *Bicycle Thieves* – classic of European realism
1950s Big-Screen Cinemascope, Panavision, Vistavision epics to rival emerging television
1959 Truffaut's *Les 400 Coups*
1968 Kubrick's *2001: A Space Odyssey*
1979 Coppola's *Apocalypse Now*
1985 Lean's *A Passage to India*

TELEVISION

1936 First high-definition TV (from Alexandra Palace)
1946 First TV broadcasting in the UK
1953 Big rise in receiver sales for Coronation
1954 Television Act licenses commercial TV
1956 ITV established
1957 Schools broadcasting by BBC and ITV
1962 Pilkington recommends second BBC channel
1967 Colour broadcasting in UK
1971 16,125,000 TV receivers in UK
1980 Channel 4 established
1989 Sky Television introduced
1990 British Satellite Broadcasting (BSB) launched and merged with Sky

RADIO

1894 Oliver Lodge sends wireless signal 137 m
1901 Marconi sends signal across Atlantic
1906 First known radio programme beamed from Brant Rock, Massachusetts
1920 First commercial radio station, Pittsburgh
1922 British Broadcasting Company (BBC) formed to unite broadcasting interests
1925 International Broadcasting Bureau (established to allocate wavelengths)
1926 BBC incorporated under royal charter
1932 Empire Service
1938 Foreign language broadcasting
1939 BBC 'unites the
–45 nation' during the Second World War
1946 Radio divided into 3 channels 'Home', 'Light' and 'Third'
1950 European Broadcasting Union
1964 'Pirate' radio stations set up
1965 The Music Programme
1972 Independent Radio launched
1990 Local Radio Authority
1992 Classic FM launched

NEWSPAPERS

1622 Nathaniel Butter's *Weekly Newes*
1702 *Daily Courant*
1735 *The Times*
1791 The *Observer*
1802 Cobbett's *Political Register*
1814 *The Times* printed on steam press
1830 Rise and fall of
–55 unstamped radical press
1855 Removal of stamp duty
1855 *Daily Telegraph*
1877 *Manchester Guardian*
1886 Linotype press
1896 *Daily Mail* (first 'popular' daily)
1900 *Daily Express*
1903 *Daily Mirror*
1912 *Daily Herald*
1924 *Daily Mail* publishes forged 'Zinoviev' letter to discredit socialists
1933 *Daily Mirror* re-launched as tabloid by Harry Bartholomew
1953 Press Council established
1964 *Daily Herald* re-named *Sun*
1967 *The Times* bought by Lord Thomson, *Sun* bought by Murdoch
1968 *News of the World* bought by Murdoch
1981 *Times* bought by Murdoch
1984 Mirror Group bought by Maxwell
1986 Eddy Shah starts *Today*
1980 *The Independent*, *Sunday Sport*
1987 Murdoch buys *Today*

MAGAZINES AND PAPERBACKS

1709 *Tatler* (Steele)
1711 *Spectator* (Addison)
1731 *Gentlemen's Magazine*
1817 *Blackwood's Magazine*
1843 *The Economist*
1848 W.H.Smith's station bookstalls
1881 George Newnes' *Tit-Bits* (exploring the new literacy)
1913 *New Statesman*
1924 *Radio Times*
1927 *The Listener*
1935 Allen Lane founds Penguin Books – first mass market paperbacks in UK
1953 18,000 book titles published
1956 *New Scientist* launched
1961 Crown loses '*Lady Chatterley*' case against Penguin
1962 25,000 titles published

Who did which?

1 Star of silent films who thrived also in the era of the 'talkies'.
2 Editor of the *Manchester Guardian* (1877–1929), later to be relaunched as the *Guardian*.
3 Politician and proprietor of the *Daily Express* (1919–1964).
4 British film director, master of suspense thrillers: *Psycho*, *Frenzy*, etc.
5 First Director General of the BBC, and lifelong advocate of public-service broadcasting.
6 American dancer who starred with Ginger Rogers in 1930s' musicals.
7 Film-star who founded United Artists (1919) with D.W. Griffith, Charlie Chaplin and Douglas Fairbanks.
8 Owner–Manager of ATV, one of the new (1950s) independent television companies.
9 Hollywood director of lavish, epic, often biblical films (e.g. *The Ten Commandments*, 1957).
10 Writer and radio broadcaster ('Postscripts') during the Second World War.

A LORD REITH
B FRED ASTAIRE
C MARY PICKFORD
D CECIL B. DE MILLE
E LORD BEAVERBROOK
F GRETA GARBO
G ALFRED HITCHCOCK
H C.P. SCOTT
I LEW GRADE
J J.B. PRIESTLEY

Part Two
Accountability

To which bodies do the media have to give an account of themselves? Who is in control? The government has legal and financial power; it has the power to commission enquiries, and to appoint the members of public watchdogs. These have the power of reproof. The power of the public would seem to be limited; yet consumers do have the power to purchase or not, as well as the power to press – or not to press – the OFF switch.

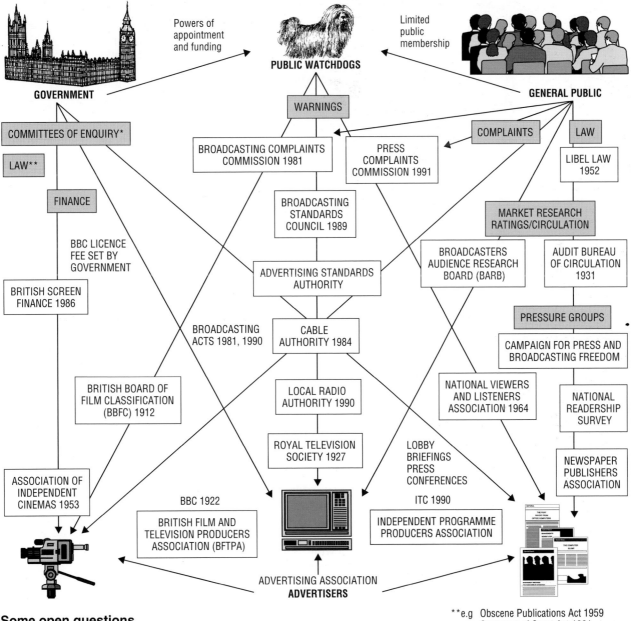

Some open questions

1 What influence, in your view, does the public have on:
   (a) the information that the media transmit, and;
   (b) the entertainment that they provide?
2 How could this influence be extended?
3 What examples can you think of (if any) where the freedom to sell has met with outside interference from:
   (a) broadcasting companies;
   (b) newspaper publishers?
4 What examples can you think of (if any) of the abuse of freedom on the part of:
   (a) a broadcasting company;
   (b) a newspaper?
5 Ought the watchdogs to be given sharper teeth, or ought they to be put to sleep?

**e.g Obscene Publications Act 1959
Contempt of Court Act 1981
Video Recording Act 1984
Official Secrets Act 1989

*e.g. PILKINGTON 1962   BROADCASTING
ANNAN 1977

CALCUTT 1990   PRESS

Part Three

TV Ads

Advertising is not a medium. The media are a vehicle for advertising; indeed commercial television and newspapers are dependent on advertising for their existence. The following passage concerns the impact of advertising on television.

The most important pressure on television scheduling and programme-making is that of advertising expenditure. If television companies sell audiences, what kinds of audiences do advertisers want, and how are they packaged to attract sales? Indeed how does the real purpose of producing audiences for advertisers affect the apparent purpose of producing programmes for audience consumption?

The American system of programme sponsorship, in which advertisers pay for individual programmes, was rejected when commercial television started in Britain on the grounds that it gave advertisers direct power over programme content. Instead, only 'spot advertising' was permitted. Advertisers could buy time slots only between or within programmes. At first, advertisements were limited to an average of six minutes per hour. Later, when it was seen that this led to an accumulation of advertisements in peak viewing times, which had above average amounts of advertising, it was decided to limit advertisements to no more that seven minutes in any one hour. The decision to adopt restricted spot advertising had been hailed as a victory for public service broadcasting. ... Spot advertisements were compared with newspaper advertising. They were seen as guaranteeing the independence of programme-making from the influence of advertisers: no rational person, it was argued, supposes that what newspapers publish in their editorial columns is determined by advertisers. Spot advertising would protect the editorial integrity of commercial television. ...

Sponsorship of all programmes except news and current events was finally permitted in 1988. However, on the ITV channels there continued to be a fierce battle about who could sponsor what – and considerable anxiety about potential commercial abuses of the authority of some programmes. Such niceties, of course, were not part of the satellite broadcasting regime. Here there were few restrictions on sponsorship and far more advertising was allowed. Indeed, one of the oddities of the intense political campaigns of the period was the BBC's failure to point out, in its own defence, that while the British public enjoys some adverts, repeated research has shown how irritating they find too many.

(James Curran and Jean Seaton, *Power without Responsibility*, 1991)

1 What is meant by the following:
   (a) 'scheduling'; (line 1)
   (b) 'public service broadcasting'; (line 19)
   (c) 'editorial integrity'; (line 25)
   (d) 'niceties' (line 30)?
2 In what sense do television companies 'sell audiences'?
3 What do you think the authors mean by the 'apparent purpose' of ITV broadcasters as opposed to their 'real purpose'?
4 In what ways can advertisements on television be compared with advertisements in newspapers?
5 Why were advertisers forbidden to sponsor programmes about current events?
6 Why would more advertising be allowed on satellite television?

Part Four
Censorship

Many would say that censorship is bad: most would agree that restraint is good. The problem is (as it always is in questions concerning law and morals) where to draw the line. Answer this question by reference to the quotations below: **In what circumstances, in your view, is it irresponsible to exercise 'freedom of expression'?**

1
Even I would rigorously censor genuine pornography. It would not be difficult. In the first place, genuine pornography is almost always underworld, it doesn't come into the open. Secondly, you can recognize it by the insult it offers, invariably, to sex and to the human spirit. Pornography is the attempt to insult sex, to do dirt on it. This is unpardonable.

(D.H.Lawrence, 'Pornography and Obscenity', in *A Propos of Lady Chatterley's Lover*, 1961)

2
The two matters about which the film censor is primarily concerned are sex and violence and, in particular, their possible effect on the younger members of the audience. The expression of sexual desire and the urge to violence are both part of human nature; both have been and remain prominent in the highest art .... What matters in the presentation of sexual feeling, as in any other emotional expression, is how far it reveals the truth about the characters; sexual exhibitionism by itself is dramatically meaningless, like eating and drinking.

(Roger Manvell, *This Age of Communication*, 1966)

3
The fight against censorship is a nineteenth-century issue which was largely won in the twentieth. What we are confronted with now is the problem posed by the economic and symbolic structure of television. Those who run television do not limit our access to information but in fact widen it. ... But what we watch is a medium which presents information in a form that renders it simplistic, nonsubstantive, nonhistorical and noncontextual; that is to say, information packaged as entertainment. We are never denied the opportunity to amuse ourselves.

(Neil Postman, *Amusing Ourselves to Death*, 1986)

4
One explanation for the emphasis placed on freedom of expression is that restrictions may stifle the emergence of the truth. Today's heresy may become tomorrow's orthodoxy but only if it is allowed expression. But it is difficult to imagine how pornography helps us to ascertain the truth.

(Simon Lee, *Law and Morals*, 1986)

5
The goal-posts tend to move according to judgements of the day. Gay News was successfully prosecuted by an MP invoking an old-fashioned notion of blasphemy as covered by the Obscene Publications Act for publishing a poem about Christ as a homosexual. But some other attempts to use this act have failed.

(Graeme Burton, *More Than Meets The Eye*, 1990)

6
Freedom of information is not a 'left–right issue' but one that affects all governments. As Sir John Hoskyns, head of the policy unit inside No.10 for Margaret Thatcher, has said; 'Open Government is not a fashionable option, but a precondition for any serious attempt to solve Britain's underlying problems. The Official Secrets Act, by hiding peacetime fiascos as though they were military disasters, protects Ministers and officials from embarrassment.'

(Clive Ponting, 'Secrecy & Freedom of Information' in *Freedom of Information*, 1987)

7
Pornography expresses anti-social attitudes, it is argued, that should be suppressed. It is inherently oppressive: it demeans with its constant suggestion of women's availability, and it fosters through the expression of scorn and contempt values that give rise to discriminatory acts against women. A parallel is sometimes made between pornography and incitement to racial hatred on the grounds that both detract from the status of the victim.

(James Curran and Jean Seaton, *Power without Responsibility*, 1991)

8
There have always been some legal constraints of course. Journalists are not allowed to defame individuals, or they are subject to libel actions (as many of the tabloids found to their cost in the 1980s). Nor are they allowed to breach the Official Secrets Act by revealing confidential official information. Incitement to racial hatred is prohibited under race relations legislation .... For the most part, however, newspapers have succeeded in keeping the law at a distance.

(Brian McNair, *News & Journalism in the UK*, 1994)

Part Five
The Press and Privacy

When does investigation become intrusion? The public has a right to know about corruption in high places: but does it have a right to know about the private lives of the royals and media personalities? **Should we set a watchdog on the press, or would this amount to censorship?** The following views may help you to answer this question.

1   It's really only the tabloids which can be said to give offence where individual privacy is concerned. Legislation against the sort of prying, offensive reporting that the tabloids go in for wouldn't interfere with the legitimate, responsible journalism of the quality newspapers. The tabloids have failed to put their own house in order, so the courts must do it for them.

2   To muzzle the press because of the excesses of the tabloids would be to discourage the exposure of wrong-doing by politicians and businessmen. A voluntary code of conduct that really works is what's wanted: a reader's representative on the paper, or a Press Complaints Commission that can levy significant fines.

3   Self-regulation has been tried and been found wanting. There is simply too much to be gained from door-stepping and cheque book journalism to expect papers, in competition with each other for 'exclusives' to refrain from invading individual privacy. The rich can invoke the libel laws; the rest of us need the protection of an ombudsman backed up by statute law.

4   People in public life do very nicely thank you out of all the publicity they receive. If they get caught in bed with someone else's wife, or with their fingers in the till, they have only themselves to blame if the press finds out, and splashes them all over the front page. They can't court publicity one moment, then cry foul the next. Power corrupts, and unexposed power corrupts absolutely.

5   The trouble is that we get not what we want, so much as what press-barons and editors who need to make their mark have to sell. They are capitalists for whom the news is what they say it is. It's a commodity for sale in the market; and sex and crime sell faster than political debate. They wield enormous power to mould public taste and opinion.

6   We may dislike some of the more blatant examples of press intrusion, but the fact is that the papers – dailies and Sunday papers – are only giving the readers what they want. If the *Sun* and *Sunday Sport* are offensive, and obsessed by the sex-lives of soap starlets, it's because the public lap it up. We get the press we deserve.

7   Censorship of any sort is a dangerous thing. Who is to be trusted to regulate the press? The government? Judges? A government-appointed quango of the 'great and the good'? God forbid! None of them would represent the general public. Stories in dubious taste are a small price to pay for free speech.

8   I've no doubt the public *is* interested in the private lives of the royals; but we've no *right* to know how they conduct themselves when they're not on duty. They have the same right as anyone else to protection from intrusion, from telephoto lenses, and from other trickery. You don't have to be a republican to find it all rather tasteless.

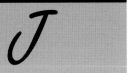

French: Inferring Meanings

A common way of testing a reader's understanding of written French is the 'cloze' test, where a passage is presented with a number of gaps in it. Short lists of words are provided, from which the reader has to choose the most suitable words to fill the gaps. It is not necessary to understand the whole passage – though, of course, this helps. What **is** necessary is that the insertions should make sense.

Here is a short example. The passage is about the French language. Many of the words in it are almost identical in English ('complètement', 'scientifiques', 'officielle'), and the meanings of others can be inferred, or guessed at (i.e. those that are ringed and annotated).

menaced — La langue française est (menacée.) Elle (recule) (quand elle n'est pas — recoils (is in retreat)

complètement ____1____) dans les (congrès) scientifiques et les — congresses (meetings)

decrease(s) — ____2____ politiques; et elle (décroit) même à la télévision, et dans

les cinémas. Elle reste, bien ____3____ , une langue officielle dans

councils — les (conseils) ____4____ , mais l'anglais l'emporte dans les — refectories (canteen)

____5____ et les (réfectoires)

1		2		3		4		5	
A	parlée	A	partis	A	entendu	A	américains	A	couloirs
B	oubliée	B	carrières	B	dit	B	britanniques	B	allées
C	rappelée	C	assemblées	C	pensé	C	français	C	stades
D	dévelopée	D	cours	D	élevé	D	européens	D	librairies

The correct choices here would be: 1–B; 2–C: 3–A; 4–D; 5–A. Here is a translation:

The French language is under threat. It is used less (when it isn't completely spoken/**forgotten**/remembered/developed) at scientific meetings and political parties/careers/**assemblies**/courses; and it is shrinking even on television, and at the cinema. It remains, of course, an official language in American/British/French/**European** councils, but English is triumphing over it in the **corridors**/alleys/stadiums/bookshops, and canteens.

— a word is wanted similar in meaning to 'meetings'

— French is one of the official EU languages

'bien entendu' is an idiom which you know or you don't

it has to be a word that makes sense alongside 'canteens'

Here is the remainder of the passage for you to complete.

C'est pour cette raison qu' ____1____ les langues arabe, arménienne, hébraïque, et d'autres au rang d'instrument ____2____ en France, c'est travailler à la fin de la langue ____3____ . Veiller à préserver les langues régionales – l'alsacien, le basque, le breton – où elles sont employées d'habitude; voilà qui n'est que justice et bon ____4____ ; mais encourager des parlers d'outre-mer, c'est donner un coup de pouce____5____ à l'anglais.

ITEM

J

1	**A** enlever	2	**A** français	3	**A** régionale	4	**A** sens	5	**A** nécessaire
	B abandonner		**B** officiel		**B** supérieure		**B** goût		**B** de moins
	C abaisser		**C** militaire		**C** nationale		**C** chic		**C** soudain
	D élever		**D** littéraire		**D** célèbre		**D** ton		**D** de plus

Here is another passage, in two parts. The first part is supplied with marginal clues; the second is not. It is a passage about the French schoolteacher of the recent past.

furniture: where is this found?

charged (with) (made responsible for).

the second war

from 'tenir' to hold ('held' or 'required')

C'était un type dont on se moquait bien facilement. Un des **meubles** de la ____6____ **écolière**; un humble fonctionnaire **chargé** de ____7____ les institutions de l'état. Je parle du professeur de lycée dans les années d'avant et d'après la **deuxième guerre** ____8____. Il était **nommé** par le ministre de l'Education ____9____, et **tenu** d'occuper une place ____10____ élevée dans la rigide hierarchie des **Proviseurs**, des Inspecteurs d'Académie, des Recteurs, et des Inspecteurs Généraux ....

adjective from 'école'

Number 7 will need to mean 'uphold'

nominated

headmasters

6	**A** prison	7	**A** critiquer	8	**A** mondiale	9	**A** gouvernementale
	B maison		**B** juger		**B** universelle		**B** départmentale
	C situation		**C** soutenir		**C** historique		**C** parlementaire
	D ville		**D** surprendre		**D** politique		**D** nationale

10	**A** bien
	B peu
	C très
	D moins

Il était ____11____ de suivre dans son enseignement des programmes déterminés dans le détail le plus ____12____ par le ministre; et les inspecteurs visitaient ses ____13____ assez souvent afin de s'assurer qu'il suivait les méthodes d'____14____ délimitées dans les ____15____ ministérielles.

11	**A** invité	12	**A** précis	13	**A** élèves	14	**A** enseignement
	B obligé		**B** nuancé		**B** collèges		**B** étudier
	C encouragé		**C** secret		**C** classes		**C** apprendre
	D privé		**D** sensible		**D** études		**D** enregistrement

15	**A** formules
	B protestations
	C émissions
	D circulaires

Part One
Medical Milestones

Medicine arose both from a natural curiosity about the structure of the body (anatomy) and its inner workings (physiology); and from an interest in the causes of disease (pathology in general, and bacteriology in particular), with a view to a cure (therapy) by one of a number of means. Here we will be looking at three of those means: pharmacology, psychiatry, and radiology.

Egyptian Sorcery
Greek Science
Roman Sanitation

HIPPOCRATES
(c. 460–370 BC)

GALEN
(AD 130–200)

Jewish Hygiene
Indian Herbalism
Chinese Acupuncture

ANATOMY
Versalius (1514–64) published first illustrated textbook of anatomy; made it a scientific study.
Fabricius (1537–1619) showed valves in blood vessels; founded modern embryology.
Malpighi (1628–94) provided anatomic basis for histology and study of physiological exchanges.

DIAGNOSTICS
René Laënnec (1781–1826) invented basic stethoscope.
Auenbrugger (1722–1809) devised chest percussion as diagnostic tool.
Hermann Helmholz (1821–94) invented ophthalmoscope (1851) for examination of retinal blood vessels.

PHYSIOLOGY
William Harvey (1578–1657) described blood circulation and the function of heart as a pump.
Thos. Sydenham (1624–89) studied epidemics; emphasized observation in clinical medicine.
Joh. Muller (1801–58) established structure and function of nerves and glands.

SURGERY
Alex. Munro (1697–1767) had new ideas for surgical dressings and instruments.
Wm. Hunter (1718–93) rescued obstetrics from midwives and made it a branch of medicine.
Joseph Lister (1827–1912) used carbolic acid as antiseptic for wounds, saving lives of amputees.

BACTERIOLOGY
Van Leeuwenhoek (1632–1723) first to observe bacteria and protozoa (or 'animalcules').
Louis Pasteur (1822–95) showed that fermentation and souring is the work of micro-organisms.
Robert Koch (1843–1910) discovered tubercle and cholera bacilli
Paul Ehrlich (1854–1915) found antibiotic against syphilis.

PATHOLOGY
E. Jenner (1749–1823) used cowpox vaccine to inoculate against smallpox.
Rudolf Virchow (1821–1902) used developing cell theory to explain effects of disease on organs, tissue.
Alph. Laveran (1845–1922) discovered parasite responsible for malaria (**Ross** [1857–1932] located it in anopheles mosquito).

ANAESTHETICS
C. Long (1815–78) used sulphuric ether in removal of cyst (1842).
H. Wells (1845) used nitrous oxide in dental operation.
Wm. Morton (1819–68) used ether in excision of tumour.
Jas. Sims (1813–83) used chloroform in gynaecological operations; first US specialist in gynaecology.

THERAPY

PHARMACOLOGY
Paracelsus (1493–1541) recognized effects of minerals in water; applied chemistry to medicine.
Gerh. Domagk (1895–1964) first sulfonamide drug: Prontosil.
Alexander Fleming (1881–1955) discovered Penicillin.
E. Chain (1906–79) and **M. Florey** (1898–1968) isolated and purified Penicillin.

PSYCHIATRY
Sigmund Freud (1856–1939) founded psychoanalysis based on free association of ideas and analysis of dreams.
Carl Jung (1875–1961) concepts of introversion and extraversion.
Carl Rogers (1902–87) client-centred psychotherapy and non-directive counselling.

RADIOLOGY
Wilm. Röntgen (1845–1923) discovered X-Rays.
Henri Becquerel (1852–1908) discovered uranium salts emitted radiation.
Marie Curie (1867–1934) and **Pierre Curie** (1859–1906) discovered radium and developed radiology as a branch of medicine.

Which is which?
1 Science of the incidence of disease affecting populations.
2 Scientific study and practice of childbirth and delivery.
3 Branch of medicine treating women's diseases.
4 Study of the minute structure of tissues of organisms.
5 Science of the formation and development of the foetus.
6 Branch of medicine concerning symptoms of illness.

A DIAGNOSTICS
B EMBRYOLOGY
C EPIDEMIOLOGY
D GYNAECOLOGY
E HISTOLOGY
F OBSTETRICS

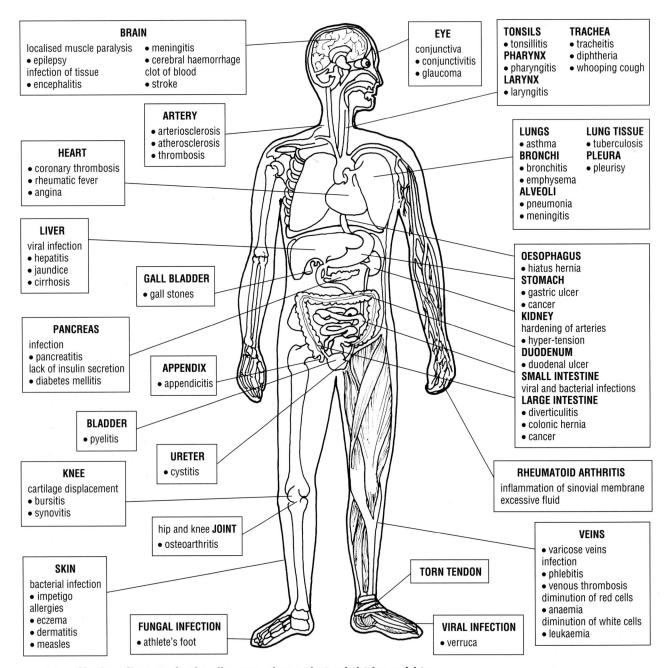

Part Two
Anatomy of Ailments

The ills that man is heir to are many; and ambient germs double the hazard. Organs typically respond to attack by becoming inflamed: the associated ailment is denoted by the suffix –*itis*. The suffix –*osis* denotes a condition, or a process.

BRAIN
localised muscle paralysis
• epilepsy
infection of tissue
• encephalitis
• meningitis
• cerebral haemorrhage
clot of blood
• stroke

EYE
conjunctiva
• conjunctivitis
• glaucoma

TONSILS
• tonsillitis
PHARYNX
• pharyngitis
LARYNX
• laryngitis
TRACHEA
• tracheitis
• diphtheria
• whooping cough

ARTERY
• arteriosclerosis
• atherosclerosis
• thrombosis

LUNGS
• asthma
BRONCHI
• bronchitis
• emphysema
ALVEOLI
• pneumonia
• meningitis
LUNG TISSUE
• tuberculosis
PLEURA
• pleurisy

HEART
• coronary thrombosis
• rheumatic fever
• angina

LIVER
viral infection
• hepatitis
• jaundice
• cirrhosis

GALL BLADDER
• gall stones

OESOPHAGUS
• hiatus hernia
STOMACH
• gastric ulcer
• cancer
KIDNEY
hardening of arteries
• hyper-tension
DUODENUM
• duodenal ulcer
SMALL INTESTINE
viral and bacterial infections
LARGE INTESTINE
• diverticulitis
• colonic hernia
• cancer

PANCREAS
infection
• pancreatitis
lack of insulin secretion
• diabetes mellitus

APPENDIX
• appendicitis

BLADDER
• pyelitis

URETER
• cystitis

RHEUMATOID ARTHRITIS
inflammation of sinovial membrane
excessive fluid

KNEE
cartilage displacement
• bursitis
• synovitis

hip and knee **JOINT**
• osteoarthritis

VEINS
• varicose veins
infection
• phlebitis
• venous thrombosis
diminution of red cells
• anaemia
diminution of white cells
• leukaemia

SKIN
bacterial infection
• impetigo
allergies
• eczema
• dermatitis
• measles

FUNGAL INFECTION
• athlete's foot

TORN TENDON

VIRAL INFECTION
• verruca

A Identify the ailments in the diagram above that might be said to be (at least in part) brought on by the careless or wilful behaviour of 'man' himself?

B Which ailment is which?

1 Bile finds its way into the circulation resulting in yellowing of the skin.
2 A respiratory infection indicated by a chronic, persistent cough.
3 The formation of a blood clot in an artery or vein.
4 Inflammation of the stomach, with nausea and vomiting.
5 Internal or external breach of one of the surfaces of the body.
6 Iron deficiency as one cause of failure of blood to transport enough oxygen.
7 Harmful reaction by a part of the body to some external substance.
8 Painful disability in the joints or the tissues associated with them.

A ALLERGY
B ANAEMIA
C BRONCHITIS
D GASTRITIS
E JAUNDICE
F RHEUMATISM
G THROMBOSIS
H ULCER

Part Three
The Hippocratic Oath

Hippocrates (c.460–c.370 BC) has been called the Father of Medicine. He practised in Greece, in the time of Socrates. He had no time for the common view that disease was a punishment from the gods. Of epilepsy, for example, he wrote: 'it has a natural cause, and its supposed divine origin is due to man's inexperience. Every disease has its own nature, and arises from external causes.' The so-called Oath is taken from a large collection of writings attributed to him.

I will look upon him who shall have taught me this Art even as one of my parents. I will share my substance with him, and I will supply his necessities, if he be in need. I will regard his offspring even as my own brethren, and I will teach them this Art, if they would learn it, without fee or covenant. I will impart this Art by precept, by lecture, and by every mode of teaching, not only to my own sons but to the sons of him who has taught me, and to disciples bound by covenant and oath, according to the Law of Medicine.

The regimen I adopt shall be for the benefit of my patients according to my ability and judgement, and not for their hurt or for any wrong. I will give no deadly drug to any, though it be asked of me, nor will I counsel such, and especially I will not aid a woman to procure abortion. Whatsoever house I enter, there will I go for the benefit of the sick, refraining from all wrongdoing or corruption, and especially from any act of seduction, of male or female, of bond or free. Whatsoever things I see or hear concerning the life of men in my attendance on the sick or even apart therefrom, which ought not to be noised abroad, I will keep silence thereon, counting such things to be as sacred secrets.

1 Find words in the passage that mean the same as the following:
   (a) advise;
   (b) contract;
   (c) command;
   (d) procedure.
2 What is the 'Art' to which Hippocrates refers, and why does he give it a capital 'A'?
3 What do the references to 'parents', 'offspring', and 'brethren' give us to understand about the writer's attitude to medicine?
4 What does Hippocrates rule out that modern medicine is increasingly prepared to rule in?
5 What misdeeds might Hippocrates be referring to as 'corruption'?
6 Rewrite the final sentence in your own words. Which of the following words sums up its meaning:
   (a) consultancy;
   (b) confidentiality;
   (c) diplomacy;
   (d) hypocrisy?

Part Four
Alternatives

Acupuncture, Homeopathy, Herbalism, Osteopathy, Chiropractic, Reflexology: they used to be called 'alternative', now they are seen as 'complementary' to orthodox medicine. When we think of modern medicine, we think of 'magic-bullet' drugs and micro-surgery. **Do complementary therapies have something to add to modern medicine, in your view?**

1

One of the most important reasons why doctors, as a group, have tended to ignore the natural healing powers of the human body and mind is because their attitude towards the body and towards illness was largely formulated by ... Descartes who believed that the human body is little more than a piece of machinery.

(Vernon Coleman, *Mind Power*, 1986)

2

When people are being hypnotized, or doing self-hypnosis, it is the influence of the words, converted to thoughts or feelings, which have such a marked effect. The mind, like a computer, accepts the words in a way that is special for that person. Based on experience, memory and a thousand other factors, the mind will produce a result in the form of a thought, picture or feeling. ... The question of how hypnosis works has been discussed for centuries and no real agreement has been reached.

(Brian Root, *Hypnosis: A Gateway to Better Health*, 1986)

3

The holistic health philosophy of medicine stands in stark contrast to mechanistic health because it acknowledges the importance of the spiritual element of health; the mental and emotional factors in well-being and disease are recognized and treated.

(Brent Hafen and Kathryn Frandsen, *An A-Z of Alternative Medicine*, 1984)

4

The use of fasting and other forms of dietary control, the inclusion of fibre, the avoidance of refined carbohydrates, the teaching of relaxation and meditation techniques are all part of traditional naturopathic practice which has recently attracted greater interest among the medical profession. ... Naturopathic practice is based on the recognition that the body possesses an inherent ability to heal itself.

(Roger Newman Turner, *Naturopathic Medicine*, 1990)

5

A friend of mine in Strasbourg developed acute appendicitis, for which of course the orthodox treatment would have been an immediate operation. This she refused to consider. Instead, she asked for her own special doctor, who cured her by the simple but surprising method of sticking a needle into the skin below her knee. Within fifteen minutes the nausea, the pain and muscular rigidity of the abdomen completely disappeared, nor was there any recurrence of these symptoms.

(Felix Mann, *Acupuncture: Cure of Many Diseases*, 1992)

6

How do you know if you have healing ability? Well, your first test is quite simple. Hold your hands apart in front of you: just a few inches will do. Feel the flow of energy between your hands. Have you got it? If not, vary the distance a little, and seek to feel the flow going from one hand to the other. ... Not everyone, not even some quite successful healers, feel this power strongly in their hands, but most do. Some feel heat, others cold, a few just feel the energy flow. You will know when that power is there; that's all that matters.

(Patrick Butler, *The Healing Handbook*, 1990)

7

I became convinced that emotional disturbance was a major contributory cause of cancer in many cases when both my father and uncle died from cancer within a year or so of having marital difficulties. Among my patients at least half who had cancer were subjected to extreme emotional pressure.

(Patrick Butler, *The Healing Handbook*, 1990)

8

The body can be thought of as a universe in its own right – a system of order and harmony which, when faced with problems or disturbances will always try to re-establish its balance. There is constant communication within the body, through circulation of the blood, circulation of energy currents throughout the nervous system, and circulation of vital energy. ... Although it has not been possible yet to work out scientifically exactly what sort of energy we are talking about here, its existence is indisputable.

(Anya Gore, *Alternative Health: Reflexology*, 1990)

Part Five
Euthanasia

In the last thirty or forty years, we have changed the law in respect of suicide, abortion, divorce, homosexuality, and fertility control. **Would reform of the law on euthanasia, in your view, be taking one liberty too many?**

1   We used to believe in the sanctity of life. We've compromised on abortion, and we withdraw feeding from patients on life-support machines, like the Hillsborough victim, Tony Bland. How much further are we prepared to go down the slippery slope? If we deny the specialness of human life, we remove our surest safeguard against abuse.

2   The irony is that suicide is perfectly legal. The senile, the incapacitated, the bedridden are often simply unable to take their lives, though this may be their dearest wish. We condemn them to live; we prevent them from doing what is legal, yet we prosecute the doctor, or friend, or relative who assists them in this legal act.

3   It's one thing to accept that we should honour the wishes of the old and sick for a good death, but what about those who can't express their wishes – who are beyond rationality? Can we assume that they'd rather die than live, just because we wouldn't want to live like that? When people can't claim the right to life themselves, we must defend it on their behalf.

4   The law as it stands is hypocritical: a doctor is within the law if she increases a dose of painkiller, in spite of the fact that death may well take time and be intermittently painful; but if she administers an effective toxin, like potassium chloride, she's charged with attempted murder, like Nigel Cox was in 1992.

5   Doctors themselves want the law changed, so that it's more in line with Dutch law. In Holland, a doctor can't be prosecuted for complying with a patient's wish to die, if that wish is expressed repeatedly, and is witnessed. Surveys show that six out of ten doctors have been asked for euthanasia by their patients. As it stands, the law puts them in an impossible position.

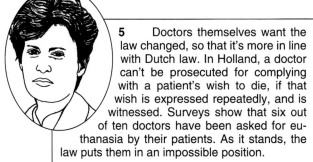

6   When you ask doctors to take life – however diminished that life is – you are asking them to renege on the most fundamental ethic enshrined in the Hippocratic Oath: to do all in their power to preserve life. You're asking them to preserve, and to go on preserving, and then suddenly – to destroy, in one final act of bad faith. Ultimately, it's the doctor–patient relationship that suffers.

7   Suicide may be legal, but we do all we can not to allow it. We don't stand and watch. We try to talk suicidal people out of their intention and, later, they're generally glad we did. The decision to take your life is seldom a rational one. So why is euthanasia any different? There is always something to live for; it can never be rational to choose nothing.

8   We must distinguish between active and passive euthanasia. When pain is unbearable and illness is terminal, we owe it to the dying not to be over-zealous about 'saving' their life. But active termination – when a doctor takes active steps to end a patient's life – that smacks too much of Nazi genetic selection.

Literary Terms and Examples

The crossword on page 57 is answered with twenty-six literary terms. The clues are definitions of those terms. The same twenty-six terms are listed again below left and, opposite them, are twenty-six quotations from literature, some well known and others more obscure. Each quotation is an example of a literary device defined by one of the terms. Match each quotation with its appropriate term.

A   Alliteration
B   Analogy
C   Bathos
D   Burlesque
E   Epic
F   Eulogy
G   Euphemism
H   Idiom
I   Irony
J   Malapropism
K   Metaphor
L   Metre
M   Ode
N   Onomatopoeia
O   Paradox
P   Paronym
Q   Pun
R   Sarcasm
S   Satire
T   Simile
U   Slang
V   Spoonerism
W   Synonym
X   Syntax
Y   Tautology
Z   Type

1 'Parting is such sweet sorrow.' – *Shakespeare*
2 'Season of mists and mellow fruitfulness,
   Close bosom-friend of the maturing sun.' – *Keats*
3 'Here lies the body of Amy Tew who fell asleep on 4th April, 1893.' – *Anon*
4 'Then out spake brave Horatius,
   The Captain of the Gate:
   "To every man upon this earth
   Death cometh soon or late."' – *Macaulay*
5 'The poor blighter went for a burton over the drink.' – *Anon*
6 'Satire is a sort of glass, wherein beholders do generally discover everybody's face but their own.' – *Swift*
7 'Just are / the ways / of God
   And justi/fiable / to men.' – *Milton*
8 'Love is like the measles; we all have to go through it.' – *Jerome K. Jerome*
9 'Ding, dong, bell
   Pussy's in the well!' – *Trad.*
10 'For Brutus is an honourable man; So are they all, all honourable men.' – *Shakespeare*
11 'We listened to Schubert lieder by Lake Como, read Keats odes, and ate fish and chips.' – *Anon*
12 '... as in Adam all die, even so in Christ shall all be made alive.' – *St. Paul*
13 'There is not in the universe a more ridiculous, nor a more contemptible animal, than a proud clergyman.' – *Fielding*
14 'I can get no remedy against this consumption of the purse.' – *Shakespeare*
15 'She's as headstrong as an allegory on the banks of the Nile.' – *Sheridan*
16 'His speech was a soliloquy, which he made all on his own.' – *Anon*
17 'Speech is the small change of silence.' – *Meredith*
18 I (first person pronoun subject) saw (verb) Esau (proper noun object).
19 'You have deliberately tasted two worms, and you can leave Oxford by the town drain.'
20 'He's parked outside the station. Stationary, he is.' – *Anon*
21 'The author of *Amelia*, the most singular genius which their island ever produced.' – *Borrow*
22 'Be merciful! Look with clement eyes on my state.' – *Anon*
23 'Nay, you had both felt his desperate deadly, daunting dagger: there are your d's for you!' – *Wycherley*
24 'The Book of Life begins with a man and a woman in a garden. It ends with Revelations.' – *Wilde*
25 'Reading is to the mind what exercise is to the body.' – *Steele*
26 'Napoleon's armies always used to march on their stomachs.' – *Sellars and Yeatman*

The All-Purpose Project Plan

A project (or 'coursework assignment') is not merely an essay writ large. An essay is a tight unit; a project is the sum of a number of parts. However, the triangular plan for an essay, recommended at the beginning of this book, can be adapted to meet the demands of the longer project.

The NEAB Syllabus Scheme II allows for the substitution of 'one major project' for essays on the Scheme I examination papers. This project should be 'multidisciplinary': the title is to be chosen by the candidate, but it is intended that the project should cover at least two out of the three subject areas: The Arts, Science and Technology, and the Social Sciences.

A coursework project is an option, similarly, in the Cambridge (UCLES) syllabus. The requirement here is that it be 'cross-disciplinary', and that the subject be unrelated to work done on any of the candidate's other A-level courses. The candidate is free to choose the title of the project, subject to approval by the Syndicate.

Coursework is a compulsory part of the AEB syllabus. Titles are prescribed annually (four of them, each appropriate to one of the four Paper I themes), and they are published in the syllabus.

Unlike an essay, a project does need an Introduction. Otherwise, the shape is much as before.

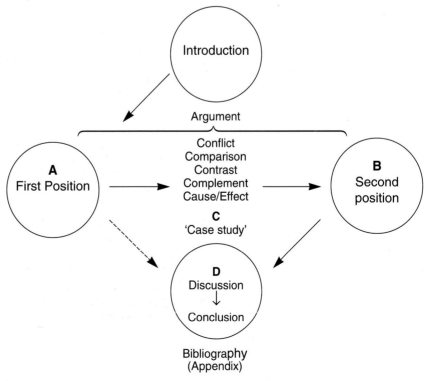

Title

If you have the choice of title, how do you go about making that choice? The subject should be one that: interests you; is researchable (i.e. information is available); is quite sharply focused; can be done in the time at your disposal.

It is helpful to frame the title as a question. This helps to sharpen the focus; it ensures that your project is a genuine **enquiry**; and it brings your conclusion to a neat end in the form of an **answer**.

Thus, instead of finding out all that there is to know about Queen Elizabeth I (about whom large volumes have been written), ask:

Elizabeth I: Why do we call her 'Good Queen Bess?'

and instead of writing the umpteenth project entitled: 'Anorexia Nervosa' (or 'Bulimia', or 'Alcohol Abuse', or 'Smoking', or 'Drugs'), ask:

Anorexia: Could it happen to you?

If there is no one subject that suggests itself (a long-standing passion; a university degree subject that it would be useful to know something more about) you could do worse than look at what your predecessors have done (or indeed, at specimen titles supplied by an examining board).

Let us look at a specimen title:

The M25: The Ultimate Motorway Madness?

(This is a provocative title: but to those who live close to it, and to those who use it, the M25 provokes some strong feelings).

How might you set about answering this question? You might map it out as follows:

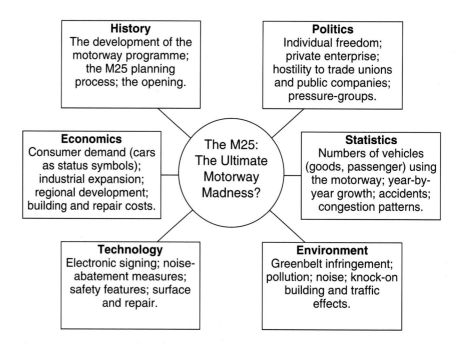

The headings for such a mapping, or brain-storming, exercise might be taken from the subheadings under the AEB Theme headings, or from the subjects of the academic curriculum. You may not want to pursue all these leads, but a map like this does make it obvious what it is you will need to find out about to answer your question.

Introduction

Because the project is likely to be three, four or five times as long as an essay, it is important that it is divided into sections, or chapters. Similarly, it is important that there is a contents page at the beginning to give the reader an overview of these sections, or chapters.

The introduction is the place to: define your terms; state your intentions (i.e. outline your argument); put the subject into its historical context.

To understand anything at all in the present, you have to know something of its past. That is why Part One of most of the Units is broadly historical. Every tree has its roots, and every villain his antecedents.

The contents page of this (the M25) project might look something like this:

Contents

There are no problematic terms to define in the title; but you would need to explain in your introduction why 'madness' might be an appropriate word to use in discussing a motorway which was planned and built with an eye to supposed benefits. Then it would be useful to refer to its place in the motorway-building programme, and to the optimism expressed (by ministers) at its opening.

Argument

It is evident that your argument (your A and B positions) will present the conflict between the advantages claimed for building the motorway – by politicians, industrialists, hauliers and others, – and the disadvantages complained of by environmentalists, local residents, and frustrated road-users. You will not be expected to have all the necessary information available, but you will (on the contrary) be expected to make reference to relevant, reasonably up-to-date material, and to make your use of this material explicit both in the text and in the bibliography at the end.

Your argument might look (at the planning stage) something like this:

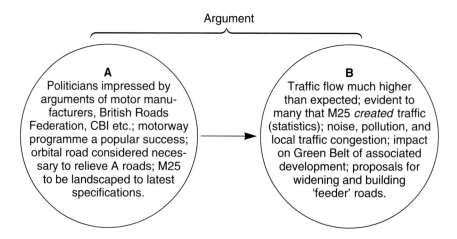

There is useful material in *Ways to Move* (Roger Robinson, 1976), and in *London 2001* (Peter Hall, 1989). If you were to make use of texts of this sort, you might do so like this:

> According to Robinson (1976) arguments for a motorway are often national and commercial, whilst arguments against it are local and environmental. It has been proposed that large new park-and-ride complexes be laid out at strategic points around the M25 (Hall, 1989): would these be perceived to confer local, or national benefits?

The work is referred to by the author's (or editor's) name, followed (in brackets) by the date of publication. When you refer to information from a particular source – even though you may not quote from it – it is good practice to cite the author and date in brackets after the reference to indicate that your information is 'authoritative'. Quotations should not be long, nor should you use too many, but, used carefully, they can help you to make your point more tellingly than if you were to paraphrase the argument. The following passage is appropriate to the B position:

> It was proposed that the 12-mile section between Junctions 8 and 10 be widened to four lanes. The Department of Transport made much of the steps that would be taken to reduce the impact of this widening on the environment: yet it could not be denied that the motorway runs through Green Belt land here, that it is a designated area of Outstanding Natural Beauty, even that 'there are several Ancient Monuments, Listed Buildings and Archaeological Sites adjacent to the motorway' (Department of Transport, 1994). The ruinous effects of an 8-lane motorway on amenities like these must be considerable.

(See below under 'Bibliography' for the manner in which the above, and other titles would be listed.)

Just as quotations can illustrate your text, so, of course, can photographs, diagrams, tables, drawings and – vital in this context – simple line maps. Such illustrative material is not merely useful, it is expected.

Your case-study section might well take the form of a brief questionnaire administered to:

• householders living close by the motorway;

• retailers on the A25;

• casual or habitual users of the motorway.

It might instead, or in addition, include a census of traffic using the motorway on, say, a busy weekday, a Sunday morning and a holiday weekend, in something like the following categories:

1   large lorries and vans;

2   light commercial vehicles;

3   cars and 4-wheel drive vehicles;

4   cars and towing caravans;

5   motorbikes.

(You would probably need to be on a bridge, noting the traffic flowing in one direction only). One or two representative, completed questionnaire forms, or census tally sheets, could be submitted in an appendix.

Conclusion

It may be that your opinion of the motorway was formed before embarking on the project. There is no need to claim scrupulous neutrality at any point; but the arguments under the A position should be given a fair hearing; and in your conclusion, you should make it clear which aspect(s) of your presented evidence you find more compelling. Mere assertion is not enough; you must provide evidence to support your arguments.

Your D position (in the planning) might look something like this:

D
Traffic on the M25 has been above forecast (census); early relief for other roads, but plenty of evidence that M25 traffic is **new** traffic; present congestion; D of T tried to assuage public concern at exhibitions etc., but proved wrong on noise-levels, and nothing can prevent 50 m width of tarmac through Green Belt from being intrusive; traffic forecasts into 21st Century, and 'feed-er' roads; where will it stop?

Bibliography

Sources should be listed in alphabetical order by author, or editor surname (or by publisher if no author is named). The name is followed by the date of publication (in brackets), then the title (underlined, or in italics); the place of publication, and the publisher's name. The idea is that the reader can turn to the bibliography for further details about the source (its recency, its respectability) referred to by the first two items of information in your text.

Here is a sample of relevant texts from the Geography shelves of a fairly typical College library. (Note the recommended layout when a chapter or a quotation is taken from an edited collection of readings where the author is not identical with the editor, as in Munton 1986, and Squire, 1991.)

Department of the Environment (1992) *The UK Environment*, Brown, A. (ed.), London: HMSO.
Department of Transport (1994) *Motorway Widening Scheme: Environmental Impact*, London: DoT.

Hall, P. (1989) *London 2001*, London: Unwin Hyman.

HMSO (1984) *Royal Commission on Environmental Pollution* (Tenth Report: Tackling Pollution – Experience and Prospects. Cmnd 9149), London: HMSO.

Mercer, D. & Puttnam, D. (1988) *Rural England: Our Countryside at the Crossroads*, London: Queen Anne Press.

Munton, R. (1986) 'The Metropolitan Green Belt', in Clout, H. & Wood, P. (eds) *London: Problems of Change*, Harlow: Longman.

Squire, G. (1991) 'The Impact of Industrial Change in the M4 Corridor', in Slator, F. (ed.) *Societies, Choices and Environments*, London: Collins Educational.

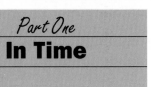

Part One
In Time

The music of ancient Egypt and of Greece is hidden from us within paintings of musicians with lyres. We cannot know what music was being played in such scenes, as no written scores have survived. This is because a notation was not devised until well into the Christian era. Our own word 'lyric' is testimony to the importance of the lyre.

Period	*Genres/ features*	*Instruments*	*Composers*	*Compositions*
MIDDLE AGES	Plainsong chant in unison (monophonic) Minstrel songs: rondeau, ballade	(voices only) lute	Leonin, Perotin (Fr.)	
1100s–1200s 1300s–1400s	Beginnings of polyphony (Fr.) Polyphonic madrigals (It.)			
RENAISSANCE c. 1400–c. 1600	Sacred music: masses Secular 3-, 4- and 5-part songs, madrigals		Palestrina (It.) Byrd, Morley, Gibbons, Dowland (E.)	
BAROQUE c. 1600–c. 1750	More complex harmonies All 12 tones of octave (chromaticism) used Major and minor keys Opera, oratorio, cantata Dances: courante, bourée, sarabänd, gigue, minuet Prelude, fugue, toccata Concerto grosso Overture (It. 'sinfonia')	recorder virginal viol organ violin violoncello harpiscord trumpet horn	Monteverdi, Scarletti, Corelli (It.) Blow, Purcell (E.) Lully, Rameau, Couperin (Fr.) Schütz, J.S. Bach (G.) Handel (G./E.) Vivaldi (It.) Telemann (G.)	*Dido and Aeneas –* Purcell *The Well-Tempered Klavier, Mass in B Minor –* Bach *Messiah, Water Music –* Handel *The Four Seasons –* Vivaldi
CLASSICAL c. 1750–c. 1805	Heavy sonorities give way to simpler forms 3-movement sonata, divertimento, serenade Symphonies, concertos	standardisation of orchestra string quartet (2 violins, viola and 'cello) piano	Haydn, Mozart (Aus.) Beethoven (G.)	*Creation –* Haydn *Eine Kleine Nachtmusik, Requiem, Magic Flute –* Mozart *Choral Symphony, Moonlight Sonata, Emperor Concerto –* Beethoven
ROMANTIC c. 1805–c. 1900	Programme music, rhapsodies, tone poems Nationalistic music	expanded symphony orchestra	Schumann, Mendelssohn (G); Schubert (Aus); Rossinni (It.); Liszt (Hung.); Chopin (Pol.); Glinka (R.); Wagner, Brahms (G.); Berlioz (Fr.); Borodin, Mussorgsky (R.); Albeniz, Granados (Sp.); Smetana, Dvorak (Cz.); Verdi (It.); Grieg (N.); Tchaikovsky (R.)	*Trout Quintet –* Schubert *Ring of the Nibelungs –* Wagner *German Requiem –* Brahms *The Trojans –* Berlioz *Boris Godunov –* Mussorgsky *New World Symphony –* Dvorak *Aïda –* Verdi *Swan Lake –* Tchaikovsky
MODERN c. 1900–	Impressionist pieces Jazz, Polytonality, atonality	saxophone wind quintet electronic music	Debussy, Ravel (Fr.) Elgar, Vaughan-Williams, Britten (Br.); Schoenberg (Aus.); Gershwin, Copland (US); Prokoviev, Shostakovitch, Stravinsky (R.)	*Rite of Spring –* Stravinsky *Appalachian Spring –* Copland *Peter Grimes –* Britten

A Bring the chart up to date by listing instruments, composers, genres and compositions in music (of all sorts) since the 1950s.

B Who wrote the following pieces?

1	The Planets	**A**	BACH
2	1812 Overture	**B**	BEETHOVEN
3	Peter and the Wolf	**C**	ELGAR
4	Pastoral Symphony	**D**	GERSHWIN
5	Pomp and Circumstance marches	**E**	HOLST
6	Brandenburg Concertos	**F**	MOZART
7	Rhapsody in Blue	**G**	PROKOVIEV
8	The Marriage of Figaro	**H**	TCHAIKOVSKY

Part Two
The Orchestra

The arrangement of the orchestra is a matter of convention rather than of rule. The conductor may place the player where he or she wishes, and as the interpretation of the music requires. The arrangement illustrated here, however, would not be unusual. The number of instruments in each category would answer the demands of the composer and of the piece.

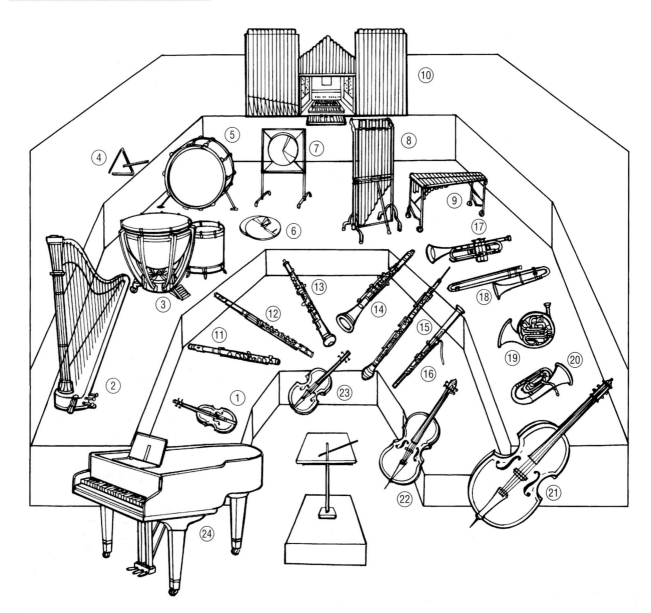

Which instrument is which?

1

A	BASS DRUM	**G**	DOUBLE BASS	**M**	OBOE	**S**	TRUMPET
B	BASSOON	**H**	FLUTE	**N**	ORGAN	**T**	TUBA
C	CELLO	**I**	FRENCH HORN	**O**	PIANO	**U**	TUBULAR BELLS
D	CLARINET	**J**	GONG	**P**	PICCOLO	**V**	VIOLA
E	COR ANGLAIS	**K**	HARP	**Q**	TRIANGLE	**W**	VIOLIN
F	CYMBALS	**L**	KETTLE DRUM	**R**	TROMBONE	**X**	XYLOPHONE

2
A Jointed wind-instrument with seven finger holes and a thumbhole.
B Similar to virginals, keyboard instrument of the 18th Century.
C Brass-wind, similar to a trumpet, used in military bands.
D A stringed, plucked instrument in 'Dixieland' music.
E Small wooden hoop, vellum-covered, hung with metal discs.
F A plucked string instrument played on the table or lap.
G Metal-stringed, plucked instrument like a lute.
H Hybrid, single-reeded, metal, jazz-band instrument.

1 BANJO
2 CORNET
3 MANDOLIN
4 RECORDER
5 SAXOPHONE
6 SPINET
7 TAMBOURINE
8 ZITHER

Part Three
Popular Music

Since the advent of the gramophone, and more particularly the wireless, music of a sort is everywhere and at every time; in the heavens, the lower parts of the earth, the mountains, the forest and every tree therein. It is a Psalmist's nightmare. At one time a cautious glance round the room assured one, through the absence of a piano, that there would be at least no music after dinner. But today the chances are that one's host is a gramophone bore, intent on exhibiting his fifty-seven varieties of soundbox, or a wireless fiend intent on obtaining the obscurest stations irrespective of programme. It is to be noticed that the more people use the wireless the less they listen to it. Some business men actually leave the wireless on all day so that the noise will be heard as they come up the garden path, and they will be spared the ghastly hiatus of silence that elapses between the slam of the front door and the first atmospheric.

What people do in their own homes is fortunately still their own concern, but what takes place in public streets and public-houses concerns us all.

The principal objections to music provided by the now almost universal loud speaker are its monotony and unsuitability. Whereas you can escape from a mechanical piano by going to the next café, you can rarely escape from a BBC gramophone hour by going to the next public-house because they are almost bound to be presenting the same entertainment to their clients. The whole of London, whatever it is doing, and whatever its moods, is made to listen to the choice of a privileged few, or even a privileged one.

We live in an age of tonal debauch where the blunting of the finer edge of pleasure leads only to a more hysterical and frenetic attempt to recapture it. It is obvious that second-rate mechanical music is the most suitable fare for those to whom musical experience is no more than a mere aural tickling, just as the prostitute provides the most suitable outlet for those to whom sexual experience is no more than the periodic removal of a recurring itch.

(Constant Lambert, *Music Ho!* 1934)

1 What do you suppose Lambert means by:
   (a) 'a Psalmist's nightmare'? (line 4)
   (b) 'the ghastly hiatus'? (line 14)
   (c) 'tonal debauch'? (line 28)
   (d) 'a mere aural tickling'? (line 32)
2 By what means does he signal his disapproval of the 'business men' whom he refers to in line 12?
3 The passage is taken from a section entitled 'The Appalling Popularity of Music'. What is it, in summary, that so appals Lambert?
4 Lambert was writing in the 1930s. How far would you agree or disagree that we suffer from a surfeit of recorded music in our own day?

Part Four

Music and Communication

It is said that music is an international language, but can it be seen as having something to say, or is it more a vehicle of communication? Use any of the quotations below as a starting point from which to answer the question: **How far can music be compared with the written word as a medium of communication?**

1

A composer who cannot in advance calculate to some extent the effect of his piece on the listening public is in for some rude awakenings. Whether or not he ought to take this effect upon an audience into account at the time of composing is another matter. ... Composers vary widely in their attitude. But whatever they tell you, I think it is safe to assume that although a conscious desire for communication may not be in the forefront of their minds, every move toward logic and coherence in composing is in fact a move toward communication.

(Aaron Copland, *Music and Imagination*, 1959)

2

The meaning of music, we need hardly remind ourselves, cannot be put into words; for that matter, the 'meaning' of a poem can not be conveyed except in the words and rhythms chosen by the poet for a special purpose .... Music is no more 'abstract' than poetry; it is a language in and through which composers have expressed themselves, their conceptions and visions of the world, precisely as Shakespeare, Goethe, Dante, Cervantes and Lewis Carroll have expressed theirs.

(Neville Cardus, *Talking of Music*, 1957)

3

It may be that Schoenberg's final loosening of tonal ties bore some relation to events in his personal life. In the summer of 1908, at the very time of his first atonal compositions, his wife left him for a while to live with their friend, the painter Richard Gerstl. The experience of disillusionment, dejection, and regret is certainly reflected in the Second String Quartet ... the exposure of the deepest springs of personality required musical means of an utterly personal kind, not those learned from tradition. Atonality was the only possible medium for musical Expressionism.

(Paul Griffiths, *Modern Music*, 1978)

4

On her earliest recordings with Teddy Wilson, we hear Billie Holiday obeying the custom of the day, lining up with the instrumental soloists .... But with Holiday, jazz made the happy discovery that words could be of paramount importance. Such were Holiday's powers of evocation, her capacity to illuminate conflicting emotions with the slightest turn of phrase, that in her wake we expect the finest women jazz singers to be great dramatic actresses as well, and judge them harshly when they come up short.

(Francis Davis, *Outcats*, 1990)

5

To a musician the important thing is that a record should be made, pressed and delivered to the public, like a message sent out. The things that are important to a fan – who played on it, when, what tunes, how many takes – are much less important to a player .... It may seem odd that such a personal, warm, unpredictable music as jazz should be charted in such cold, analytical volumes as discographies ....

(Miles Kington, *The Jazz Anthology*, 1992)

6

Along with every other form of communication, music has expanded its vocabulary .... To draw on an obvious analogy, musical styles are like languages. All too many people speak only one language – in both a literal and figurative sense. ... The classical music listener who thinks music died with Brahms, the Jazz buff who thinks music started with King Oliver, the rock fan who can't listen to anything without a beat – they're all unwilling to hear anything but their own musical language.

(John Schaeffer, *New Sounds: The Virgin Guide to New Music*, 1990)

Make use of any of the opinions expressed below to write an answer to the following question: **Does music have a function beyond that of affording pleasure?**

1 Music has all sorts of functions, but then so does writing. Not all writing is literature, but then you wouldn't want it to be. You don't buy a newspaper for its heightened language, but you don't despise good journalism.

2 My favourite sort of music is soft and romantic – soothing music, to relax to. When you've been at work all day, you want to listen to music with your shoes off.

3 You can't really talk about music having a *function* at all. It's part of the definition of any art-form that it *isn't* functional. Music that has a *use* probably isn't art at all: it's just a sound-track filling in silence.

4 I suppose the most important 'function' music has had down the ages has been to worship God. Look at all the music written for church services: oratorios, masses, anthems. God had all the best tunes when the Church commissioned the music.

5 I like music I can dance to; music with a good beat to it, to liven things up. My sort of music has got to get me up on my feet and make me want to stay there.

6 Music has been used to stir up people's emotions, of course, in war-time for instance: marches and patriotic music. Wasn't it Cromwell who marched his troops into battle singing psalms? Lots of music has been quite nationalistic, like 'God save the Queen' and 'I vow to thee, my country'.

7 Isn't all art, ultimately designed to give pleasure. Even religious music is supposed to please God. Different people get their pleasure from different sorts of music. The fact that A gets his pleasure from Beethoven, and B gets his from the Beatles doesn't make one sort of music better than the other.

8 Music is a sort of drug: it keeps you going. It picks you up when you're down. It is, if you like, an anaesthetic.

ITEM

L

Proverbs

A proverb is a short, memorable saying which, in one succint line, summarises a whole fable, or embodies a simple, closely-observed truth. Generally, they are of the same pre-industrial kind as in the Similes in Item E (see page 35). Proverbs are the compressed folk-wisdom of a culture; potted popular philosophy.

Below are the beginnings of 50 proverbs: unite each with its appropriate ending.

1	Actions speak …	A	make good neighbours
2	All that glistens …	B	on the other side of the fence
3	All work and no play …	C	louder than words
4	A bird in the hand …	D	try, try and try again
5	Blood is thicker …	E	make light work
6	The Devil makes work …	F	are soon parted
7	Early to bed, early to rise …	G	that blows nobody any good
8	Empty vessels …	H	than water
9	Every cloud …	I	better than no bread
10	A fool and his money …	J	while the sun shines
11	A friend in need …	K	is not gold
12	Good walls …	L	has a silver lining
13	The grass is always greener …	M	is a friend indeed
14	Half a loaf is …	N	but it pours
15	He who laughs last …	O	wear it
16	He who lives by the sword …	P	is worth two in the bush
17	If at first you don't succeed …	Q	make the most noise
18	If the cap fits …	R	that catches the worm
19	It's an ill wind …	S	you leap
20	It's the early bird …	T	dies by the sword
21	It never rains …	U	for idle hands
22	Lightning never strikes …	V	makes Jack a dull boy
23	Look before …	W	in the same place twice
24	Make hay …	X	laughs longest
25	Many hands …	Y	makes a man healthy, wealthy and wise
26	A miss is as good …	Z	twice shy
27	A nod is as good …	AA	run deep
28	Nothing ventured …	BB	is another man's poison
29	Once bitten …	CC	the iron is hot
30	One man's meat …	DD	and spoil the child
31	One swallow does not …	EE	nothing gained
32	The pen is mightier …	FF	are better than one
33	A penny saved …	GG	want not
34	People who live in glasshouses …	HH	make a summer
35	Pride comes …	II	as a mile
36	The proof of the pudding …	JJ	spoil the broth
37	The road to Hell …	KK	saves nine
38	A rolling stone …	LL	than the sword
39	Spare the rod …	MM	never boils
40	Still waters …	NN	without fire
41	A stitch in time …	OO	but you cannot make it drink
42	Strike while …	PP	the mice will play
43	There's no smoke …	QQ	before a fall
44	Too many cooks …	RR	do as the Romans do
45	Two heads …	SS	gathers no moss
46	Waste not …	TT	is paved with good intentions
47	A watched pot …	UU	shouldn't throw stones
48	When in Rome …	VV	is a penny gained
49	When the cat's away …	WW	as a wink to a blind man
50	You can take a horse to water …	XX	is in the eating

Many of the proverbs claim to tell more or less 'scientific' truths in a rather dogmatic way. How might you test the truth-value of these three proverbs?
(a) The best fish swim near the bottom.
(b) Cast not a clout till May is out.
(c) Take care of the pence, and the pounds will take care of themselves.

Part One
Painters, Periods and Places

Taste in painting has alternated between the sweet wine of the Medieval, Baroque and Romantic periods, and the dry wine of the early Renaissance, and the Rococo – between ebullience and restraint. The most important painters in each period are listed below.

Prehistoric	• Cave paintings of game animals and the hunt				
Egyptian	• Wall paintings in the tombs of the Pharaohs				
Greek	• Wall and vase paintings of gods and heroes				
Roman	• Architectural frescoes at Pompeii and Herculaneum				
Early Medieval	• Illuminated manuscripts and religious frescoes				

	FLEMISH • DUTCH • GERMAN	BRITISH	ITALIAN	SPANISH	FRENCH

Late Medieval
c. 1200s–1300s

Religious subjects still predominated, but figures were increasingly realistic and three dimensional. Bosch specialised in the fantastic.

Early Renaissance
c. 1400s

(Fr. 'Rebirth')

Italian painters painted religious frescoes, but figures were more fully human and serene. Northern European painters pioneered portraiture and landscapes.

High Renaissance
c. 1500s

Baroque
c. 1600s

(Fr. 'Odd, curious')

The intellectual refinement of the Renaissance gave way to emotion, to huge scale and theatrical effect. Portraits and landscapes now abounded.

Classicism/Rococo
c. 1700s

(Fr. 'Rocaille' – shell-work)

Romanticism
c. 1789–1800s

Blake, Fuseli, Goya, David expressed wartime angst; busy heroic canvases followed in France, troubled landscapes in England. Pre-Raphaelites and Courbet were 'socialists' in the Chardin tradition.

Pre-Raphaelite Brotherhood
1848–1860

FLEMISH • DUTCH • GERMAN
Jan van Eyck 1385–1441
Roger van der Weyden 1398–1464
Hieronymus Bosch 1450–1516
Albrecht Durer 1471–1528
Hans Holbein 1497–1543
Pieter Breughel 1530–69
Peter Paul Rubens 1577–1640
A. van Dyck 1599–1641
Franz Hals 1580–1666
Jan Vermeer 1632–75
Rembrandt 1606–69

BRITISH
Joshua Reynolds 1723–92
Thomas Gainsborough 1727–88
William Hogarth 1697–1764
William Blake 1757–1827
Henry Fuseli 1741–1825
John Constable 1776–1837
G.M.W. Turner 1775–1851
D.G. Rossetti 1828–82
John Millais 1829–96
Holman Hunt 1827–1910
Ford Madox Brown 1821–93

ITALIAN
Giotto 1266–1337
Masaccio 1401–28
Fra Angelico 1387–1455
Filippo Lippi 1406–69
Botticelli 1444–1510
Leonardo da Vinci 1452–1519
Della Francesca 1416–82
Andrea Mantegna 1431–1506
Michelangelo 1475–1564
Raphael 1483–1520
Titian 1480–1576
Caravaggio 1569–1609
Tiepolo 1696–1770
Antonio Canaletto 1697–1768
Francois Guardi 1712–93

SPANISH
El Greco 1541–1614
Velasquez 1599–1660
Murillo 1618–82
Francisco Goya 1746–1828

FRENCH
Nicolas Poussin 1594–1665
Claude Lorrain 1600–82
Antoine Watteau 1684–1721
Francois Boucher 1703–70
Honoré Fragonard 1732–1806
J-B. Chardin 1699–1779
Jacques-Louis David 1748–1825
J.A.D. Ingres 1781–1867
Eugène Delacroix 1798–1863
Louis A.T. Géricault 1791–1824
Gustave Courbet 1819–77

A Name the most celebrated paintings of each of the most celebrated artists listed above.

B Who painted which of the following paintings?

1	Arnolfini and his Wife	**A**	BOTTICELLI
2	Birth of Venus	**B**	CONSTABLE
3	The Blue Boy	**C**	DA VINCI
4	Creation of Man	**D**	DAVID
5	The Death of Marat	**E**	GAINSBOROUGH
6	Execution of 3rd May, 1808	**F**	GOYA
7	The Hay Wain	**G**	HALS
8	The Last Supper	**H**	VELASQUEZ
9	The Laughing Cavalier	**I**	MICHELANGELO
10	The Rokeby Venus	**J**	VAN EYCK

Part Two
Impressionism and After

Movements that took centuries and decades to flower before the 1800s blossomed and died in a matter of years in the 1900s. Earlier schools were named by later generations. Modern '–isms' have been given names by their self-consciously innovative practitioners. Painters who lived long lives belonged to more than one 'school'.

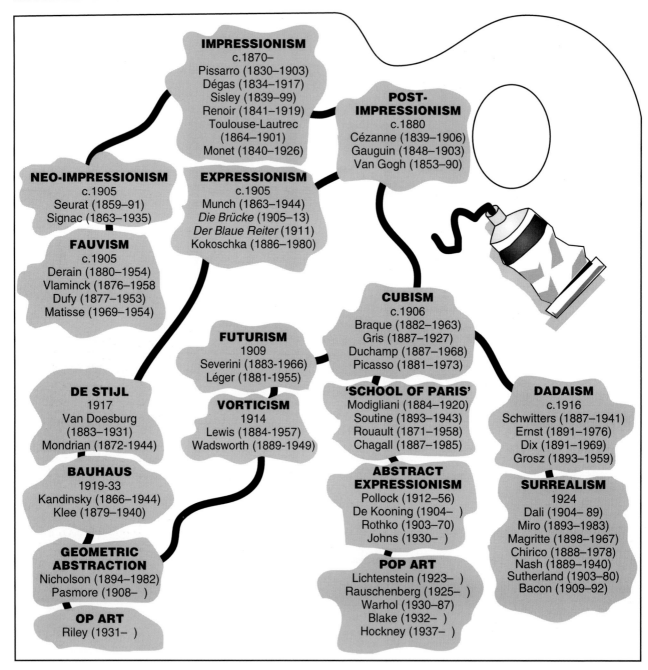

IMPRESSIONISM
c.1870–
Pissarro (1830–1903)
Dégas (1834–1917)
Sisley (1839–99)
Renoir (1841–1919)
Toulouse-Lautrec
(1864–1901)
Monet (1840–1926)

POST-IMPRESSIONISM
c.1880
Cézanne (1839–1906)
Gauguin (1848–1903)
Van Gogh (1853–90)

NEO-IMPRESSIONISM
c.1905
Seurat (1859–91)
Signac (1863–1935)

EXPRESSIONISM
c.1905
Munch (1863–1944)
Die Brücke (1905–13)
Der Blaue Reiter (1911)
Kokoschka (1886–1980)

FAUVISM
c.1905
Derain (1880–1954)
Vlaminck (1876–1958
Dufy (1877–1953)
Matisse (1969–1954)

CUBISM
c.1906
Braque (1882–1963)
Gris (1887–1927)
Duchamp (1887–1968)
Picasso (1881–1973)

FUTURISM
1909
Severini (1883-1966)
Léger (1881-1955)

DE STIJL
1917
Van Doesburg
(1883–1931)
Mondrian (1872-1944)

VORTICISM
1914
Lewis (1884-1957)
Wadsworth (1889-1949)

'SCHOOL OF PARIS'
Modigliani (1884–1920)
Soutine (1893–1943)
Rouault (1871–1958)
Chagall (1887–1985)

DADAISM
c.1916
Schwitters (1887–1941)
Ernst (1891–1976)
Dix (1891–1969)
Grosz (1893–1959)

BAUHAUS
1919-33
Kandinsky (1866–1944)
Klee (1879–1940)

ABSTRACT EXPRESSIONISM
Pollock (1912–56)
De Kooning (1904–)
Rothko (1903–70)
Johns (1930–)

SURREALISM
1924
Dali (1904– 89)
Miro (1893–1983)
Magritte (1898–1967)
Chirico (1888–1978)
Nash (1889–1940)
Sutherland (1903–80)
Bacon (1909–92)

GEOMETRIC ABSTRACTION
Nicholson (1894–1982)
Pasmore (1908–)

POP ART
Lichtenstein (1923–)
Rauschenberg (1925–)
Warhol (1930–87)
Blake (1932–)
Hockney (1937–)

OP ART
Riley (1931–)

Which is which?

1 Bold lines and strident colours earned this group the label 'wild beast'.
2 An attempt to capture fleeting effects of light in tiny dabs of colour.
3 A free use of paint applied spontaneously, in 'unconscious' action.
4 An interpretation of the twentieth century in terms of machinery, speed and movement.
5 Resolution of nature in geometric form viewed from different aspects.
6 An expression of the times (in Britain) in harsh, angular or swirling shapes.
7 Use of the imagery of advertisements and popular cultural icons.
8 Communication of the feelings of the artist, often angst-ridden.
9 A protest against war in a deliberate ridicule of traditional culture.
10 Free play of the unconscious mind and of the language of dreams.

A ABSTRACT EXPRESSIONISM
B CUBISM
C DADAISM
D EXPRESSIONISM
E FAUVISM
F FUTURISM
G IMPRESSIONISM
H POP ART
I SURREALISM
J VORTICISM

Part Three
We the Patrons

It is just as thoughtless to be 'for modern art' as it is to be 'against it'. The situation in which it grew is just as much our own doing as that of the artists. There are certainly painters and sculptors alive today who would have done honour to any age. If we do not ask them to do anything in particular, what right have we to blame them if their work appears to be obscure and aimless?

The general public has settled down to the notion that an artist is a fellow who should produce Art much in the way a bootmaker produces boots. By this they mean that he should produce the kind of paintings or sculptures they have seen labelled as Art before. One can understand this vague demand, but alas, it is the one job the artist cannot do. What has been done presents no problem any more. There is no task in it that could put the artist on his mettle. But critics and 'highbrows' too, are sometimes guilty of a similar misunderstanding. They, too, tell the artist to produce Art, they, too, are inclined to think of pictures and statues as specimens for future museums. The only task they set the artist is that of creating 'something new' – if they had their way, each work would represent a new style, a new 'ism'. In the absence of any more concrete jobs even the most gifted modern artists sometimes fall in with their demands. Their solutions of the problem of how to be original are sometimes of a wit and brilliance not to be despised, but in the long run this is hardly a task worth pursuing. That, I believe, is the ultimate reason why modern artists so often turn to various theories, new and old, about the nature of art. It is probably no more true to say that 'art is expression' or that 'art is construction' than it was to say that 'art is the imitation of nature'. But any such theory, even the most obscure one, may contain that proverbial grain of truth which might do for the pearl ....

Artists, we trust, will always be born. But whether there will also be art depends to no small extent on ourselves, their public. By our indifference or our interest, by our prejudice or our understanding we may yet decide the issue.

(E.H. Gombrich, *The Story of Art*, 1972)

1 **(a)** What does it mean to put an 'artist on his mettle'? (lines 14–15)
  (b) Whom do you suppose Gombrich means by 'highbrows'? (line 15)
  (c) What more 'concrete jobs' might artists be given? (line 21)
  (d) What is meant by 'that proverbial grain of truth which might do for the pearl'? (lines 30–31)
2 How does Gombrich justify the claim that 'modern art is just as much our own doing as that of the artists'?
3 Why, in his view, can an artist not produce Art, as a boot-maker produces boots?
4 What should the critic be looking for in Art, according to Gombrich, if not originality?
5 What does his attitude appear to be towards 'theories' of art?

Part Four
Critical Canons

What are the criteria by which art-critics make judgements about paintings, when these are so various as to include religious frescoes and collages of hessian and press-cuttings? Base an answer to this question on any or all of the following critical opinions: **What do you look for in the sort of painting that you would be prepared to hang over your bed?**

1

An extraordinary succession of technical develop-ments has replaced artistic intuition by mechanical marvels. With its unchallenged perfection the photo-graphic lens has assumed the task of portraying the whole objective world. Also, the film camera has in-fused the breath of life into static pictures, enabling them, after a sleep of a thousand years, to step out of their frames and act. Is this the end of painting? It is not painting but only the old conception of painting which must be extended.

(Peter Thoene, *Modern German Painting*, 1938)

2

If the reader wishes to understand the art of the pre-sent day he must not judge everything by ready-made standards. Every period has to solve its problems in its own way. ... Today, as always, art re-mains the unmistakable finger-print of the age. That many people do not understand its language is due, on the one hand, to their artistic education, in which the emphasis is always on historical elements or the con-tents of the museums, and on the other hand to the complicated and indecipherable aspect of the modern world. Not art alone, but also physics or chemistry is far more difficult to understand than it used to be, and yet no-one reproaches the natural sciences on this account, as art is constantly reproached.

(Hermann Leicht, *History of the World's Art*, 1963)

3

By what standard are we to appraise [abstract ex-pressionist works]? Evidently any relation with external reality must be left out of account by the na-ture of the artist's aim. The main question involved is whether these paintings convey to you the emotional experience of the artist. It may be found in the person-ality the cryptic shapes take on, the feeling of animation they give, the surge and insistence of colour, the pres-ence of non-material force. They are a kind of rhapsody.

(William Gaunt, *The Observer's Book of Modern Art*, 1964)

4

The psychological truth in Rembrandt's paintings goes beyond that of any other artist who has ever lived. Of course they are masterpieces of sheer picture-making. In the *Bathsheba* he makes use of studies from nature and from antique reliefs to achieve a perfectly balanced design. We may think we admire it as pure painting, but in the end we come back to the head. Bathsheba's thoughts and feelings as she ponders on David's letter are rendered with a subtlety and a human sympathy which a great novelist could scarcely achieve in many pages.

(Kenneth Clark, *Civilization*, 1969)

5

It is the chief characteristic of great art to evoke fresh and often totally divergent reactions from the viewer, but what is important is that before these comes the ini-tial response. This may vary from sheer amazement at the precision with which the artist has been able to de-pict an object, to an acknowledgement of his prowess in transforming existing shapes or forms into objects that are entirely new.

(Christopher Lloyd, *A Picture History of Art*, 1979)

6

In a society of consumers, many artists have turned into purveyors of fast art. In the United States, food and its packaging became an obsessive subject – the soup tins of Warhol, the beer cans cast by Jasper Johns, the 'EAT' neon signs of Robert Indiana .... [Joseph] Beuys sold whatever he signed, but he claimed that every human being was an artist. Nurses and doctors, teachers and students were artists. Doing anything was art. 'All other definitions of this term "art" end up say-ing that there are artists and there are non-artists – people who can do something, and people who can't do anything.' But Beuys himself seemed a non-artist to many people who would not accept his definition of the artist in the broadest possible terms.

(Andrew Sinclair, *The Need to Give: The Patrons and the Arts*, 1990)

Part Five

But Is It Art?

If we do not know much about modern art, at least we know what we like. Few now expect a modern painting to be representational – photographic in its faithfulness to its subject. **But what *do* we expect of a modern painting?** Answer this question with reference to one or more of the following examples.

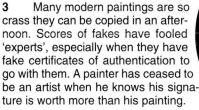

1 I expect to see something that I couldn't do myself, and I don't expect to see a ridiculous price-tag on it. Critics say the paintings of Robert Ryman (mostly plain white) 'draw attention to the importance of light in painting'. Ryman says his paintings have no meaning – and he laughs all the way to the bank.

2 I don't expect a painting to *be* of anything, but I do expect it to have been inspired by something. Picasso's *Guernica*, for example, isn't *of* the bombed city, but he was moved *by* the bombing to paint stark, screaming images of broken animals and people. The event moved him, and the images move us.

3 Many modern paintings are so crass they can be copied in an afternoon. Scores of fakes have fooled 'experts', especially when they have fake certificates of authentication to go with them. A painter has ceased to be an artist when he knows his signature is worth more than his painting.

4 People look at Pop Art and say: 'I could do that!' The point is, as Joe Tilson said, 'We did it. We did it first.' Tilson painted an A–Z of Family and Friends in 1963. It was new; it broke new ground. Paintings like his only looked easy when they'd been done.

5 You see a piece of modern art and you say: 'a 4-year-old could do that.' Carly Johnson was 4 when she painted *Rhythm of the Trees*, and it was accepted by Manchester City Art Gallery for its annual show. The fact is it was a fresh, lovely and lively painting. Real art is ageless.

6 A painting should be the working out of an idea – an idea in the painter's head before he begins to paint. You can't write a novel or a concerto without being 'aware' of what you're doing. Why should a painting be any different? Art is the product of a heightened awareness, not of unawareness.

7 For me, Salvador Dali did most to combine sheer skill (he called his paintings 'handmade photography') with imagination and inventiveness. His *Persistence of Memory* for example, (his 'limp watches') stops you in your tracks. Surrealists painted *ideas*; they painted metaphors.

8 I like a colourful, busy canvas, where there's lots going on and plenty of detail for the eye to linger over: a Max Ernst, or Henri Rousseau. I've no time for patterns of the sort you see on primary school classroom walls. A painting has got to bustle with life: a Dufy, or L.S. Lowry.

Maths 4: Coping with Algebra

Q1: Which of the following algebraic statements is not equivalent to the other three?

(a) $a + b = ab$

(b) $\dfrac{ab}{a + b} = 1$

(c) $1 = \dfrac{1}{a} + \dfrac{1}{b}$

(d) $b = \dfrac{a}{1 - a}$

In theory, a student trying to answer this question is supposed to have the necessary grasp of algebra learnt at GCSE to be able to see that (d) is the one that is different. In practice, even many students of A-Level Mathematics would make some silly mistakes with this question. The trick is to try some arbitrary numbers. Decide which looks the easiest example. In this case it is (c). Putting both a and b equal to 2 gives us $1 = \frac{1}{2} + \frac{1}{2}$, which is correct. Does this work for the others? Option (a) gives $2 + 2 = 2 \times 2$ which is right. Option (b) gives $\frac{2 \times 2}{2 + 2} = 1$ which is also correct. That leaves (d) which gives $2 \neq \frac{2}{1-2}$. Thus we arrive at the correct answer simply by substituting some numbers.

Let us now look at a question that many students would think looked horrendous:

Q2: A sequence of numbers a_1 a_2 a_3 ... is calculated using the rule

$$a_{n+1} = \sqrt{1 + a_n}$$

and beginning with $a_1 = 1.5$. After the first few terms all the numbers are approximately:

(a) 2.618
(b) 1.618
(c) 1.000
(d) 0.618

Although this question looks quite forbidding, it is in fact fairly straightforward. It is a case of simple substitution, as in the previous question, only this time we are given the number to substitute.

What are we given? We have a rule about a sequence of numbers. They do not look like numbers but we should be used to the idea that letters can represent numbers. The first one is a_1. The subscript 1 indicates that it is the first term. We are told that it is equal to 1.5. The next stage is to accept that the second number is a_2, the third a_3 and so on.

The rule, $a_{n+1} = \sqrt{1 + a_n}$ is a device for working out the next term. If you know a_n it is possible to work out the subsequent term a_{n+1}. It is done, using a calculator, like this:

$$a_2 = \sqrt{1 + a_1}$$
$$= \sqrt{1 + 1.5}$$
$$= \sqrt{2.5}$$
$$= 1.581113\ldots$$

Now, keeping all the figures on your calculator, use this number to calculate a_3:

$$a_3 = \sqrt{1 + a_2}$$
$$= \sqrt{1 + 581113\ldots}$$
$$= \sqrt{2.581113\ldots}$$
$$= 1.606559\ldots$$

Repeating the process, which is fairly quick on a calculator, gives us:

$$a_4 = \sqrt{1 + a_3}$$
$$= \sqrt{1 + 1.606\ldots}$$
$$= \sqrt{2.606\ldots}$$
$$= 1.614494\ldots$$

There is no need to calculate further. It is clear that the correct answer is (b).

There is a major lesson to be learnt from this, quite apart from how to do this kind of question. It is that you

ITEM

should not allow yourself to be discouraged by the unpleasant appearance of a question. Try. If the question is full of unpleasant algebra, substitute some numbers instead.

Q3: The numbers 1, 4, 9 and 16 are the squares of the positive integers. What number in the sequence follows the square of *n*?

(a) $n^2 + 1$
(b) $n^2 + 2n + 1$
(c) $n^2 + 9$
(d) $(n - 1)^2$

The number after *n* is *n* + 1. Squaring this gives $(n + 1)^2$. This does not look like any of the possible answers, but at least we can eliminate (d). We are supposed to be able to multiply out $(n + 1)^2$ but for some students this may be a dangerous move. Even some A-Level mathematicians may make the mistake of choosing (a) as the answer so, to be sure, we can substitute some numbers.

Let us choose *n* = 4. The square of 4 is 16. The square of the next number is 25. Put *n* = 4 into the four possible answers and we get:

(a) $4^2 + 1 = 16 + 1 = 17$
(b) $4^2 + (2 \times 4) + 1 = 25$
(c) $4^2 + 9 = 25$
(d) $(4 - 1)^2 = 3^2 = 9$

This is a nuisance. The answer is now (b) or (c). Most people would opt for (b) but just to make sure we try *n* = 5 and hope that we get the answer 36 which is the square of 6.

(b) $5^2 + (2 \times 5) + 1 = 36$
(c) $5^2 + 9 = 34$

We now have the answer.

This trick will work for any question of this type. Remember that the word 'number' does not necessarily have to mean a whole positive number. Negative numbers and fractions are numbers too, as are irrationals. Irrational numbers are those that cannot be equal to a fraction, proper or improper. This means that they cannot

be expressed as the *ratio* of two whole numbers, hence the name. They include π, the ratio of the circumference of a circle to its diameter. Many people are brought up to write π as $\frac{22}{7}$, but this is just an approximation. Other irrationals include the square roots of any prime number such as $\sqrt{2}$ or $\sqrt{5}$ or any combination of them with rationals such as $3 + \sqrt{2}$. Irrational numbers have decimal parts that go on forever without repeating. In fact, the answer to the second question we attempted in this section, 1.618, is

$$\frac{1 + \sqrt{5}}{2}$$

which is irrational.

Part One
Schools of Thought

The business of philosophy is to ask questions. At different times, philosophers have been moved to ask different *sorts* of questions. The eight groups of philosophers listed below must be understood to be loose groupings only; and the style given to their questions is merely indicative likewise.

6ᵗʰ CENTURY BC

A THALES · ANAXIMANDER · ANAXIMENES · PYTHAGORAS · HERACLITUS · PARMENIDES — asked **cosmological** questions e.g.:
What is the underlying nature of reality?
What is the archetypal form of matter?
What is the vital force that sustains all living things?

4ᵗʰ CENTURY BC

B SOCRATES · ARISTOTLE · PLATO · PLOTINUS (3rd Century AD) — asked **metaphysical** questions e.g.:
How is one to live virtuously?
What propositions are necessarily true?
What is the relationship between soul and body?

5ᵗʰ–14ᵗʰ CENTURY

C AUGUSTINE · AQUINAS · ANSELM · WILLIAM OF OCKHAM · DUNS SCOTUS — asked **theological** questions e.g.:
How did evil irrupt into God's world?
How does God's existing differ from ours?
Did God create his creatures of necessity?

16ᵗʰ–19ᵗʰ CENTURY

D MACHIAVELLI · HOBBES · LOCKE · ROUSSEAU · MARX — asked **political** questions e.g.:
Is a ruler bound by ordinary moral values?
What is man like in a state of nature?
When might one resist lawful authority?

17ᵗʰ–19ᵗʰ CENTURY

E DESCARTES · SPINOZA · LOCKE · LEIBNIZ · BERKELEY · HUME — asked **epistemological** questions e.g.:
Of what knowledge can we be certain?
Is mathematical truth the type of all truth?
Does reason contradict or reinforce our sense-experience?

18ᵗʰ–20ᵗʰ CENTURY

F KANT · BENTHAM · MILL · MOORE — asked **moral** questions e.g.:
Can we define the good objectively?
How is one to bring about the greatest good?
When are we justified in curbing another's liberty?

19ᵗʰ–20ᵗʰ CENTURY

G KIERKEGAARD · NIETZSCHE · HEIDEGGER · SARTRE — asked **existential** questions e.g.:
What is the truth by which I can live?
What is the nature of being?
What does a man do when he chooses himself?

20ᵗʰ CENTURY

H SCHLICK · WITTGENSTEIN · CARNAP · RUSSELL · AYER — asked **analytical** questions e.g.:
How are propositions representations of reality?
By what means do we test propositions?
What is the criterion of meaningfulness?

What group of philosophers is most likely to have asked these questions?

1 Are reason and faith complementary or are they in confict with each other?
2 Is man free, and therefore responsible for his deeds?
3 Is the world timeless and unchanging, or is it in constant flux?
4 What is it like to be a human being?
5 What is the nature of the contract between ruler and ruled?
6 Are ethical questions really questions about language and meaning?
7 How do we arrive at the conception of cause and effect?
8 What is the relationship between what is visible and what is intelligible?

Part Two
A History of –isms

Below is a diagrammatic representation of twenty-four philosophies (or positions), their place in history, and their founders, or principal proponents. No –ism is entirely self-contained: ideas occur and then recur in new forms.

c. 400BC	**Cynicism** Antisthenes	The pursuit of virtue through the simple life.
c. 350BC	**Epicureanism** Epicurus	The primacy of sense-experience and indulgence in the good life.
c. 300BC	**Stoicism** Zeno	Harmony with nature and equanimity in face of hardship.
	Asceticism	Self-denial and bodily discomfort in imitation of Christ.
	Mysticism	Unity of the self with the divine being.
	Scholasticism Aquinas	Syllogistic logic and disputation based on the work of Aristotle.
1509	**Humanism** More and Erasmus	Man should seek to know himself and improve his condition.
1637	**Rationalism** Descartes	Reliance on reason and deductive argument to establish the truth.
1663	**Determinism** Spinoza	The impossibility of things being other than as they are.
1675	**Quietism** De Molinos	Absolute surrender to God and forswearing of worldly ambition.
1690	**Empiricism** Locke	Knowledge is derived from experience and is not available *a priori*.
1710	**Idealism** Berkeley	Reality is essentially a mental or spiritual construct.
1740	**Scepticism** Hume	Knowledge is ultimately doubtful because phenomena are contingent.
1789	**Utilitarianism** Bentham	Actions are moral insofar as they maximize happiness.
1841	**Positivism** Comte	Exaltation of science and its contribution to human progress.
1841	**Atheism** Feuerbach	Denial of the existence of God.
1843	**Existentialism** Kierkegaard	The primacy of the individual, and importance of moral choice.
1848	**Dialectical materialism** Marx	What is real in history and in life is the nature and ownership of the means of subsistence.
1860	**Agnosticism** Huxley	The impossibility of knowing whether God exists or not.
1873	**Aestheticism** Pater	Art exists for its own sake.
1878	**Pragmatism** Pierce	The truth of a statement depends on its practical use-value.
1913	**Behaviourism** Watson	Mental states are explicable only in terms of observable behaviour.
1922	**Verificationism** Schlick and Carnap	The meaning of statements is the method by which their truth is known.
	Relativism	In a plural world, no one philosophy can claim a monopoly on truth.

Match the following statements and –isms.
1 All knowledge is deducible from a few self-evident principles.
2 The truth of a proposition is determined by whether or not it works.
3 An action is wrong if it tends more to mischief than to pleasure.
4 A statement is true if it is attested to by sense-experience.
5 Man creates his own essence uncontrolled from outside.
6 Physical hardship is good for a man's soul.
7 What we know rests on observations of things as they are.
8 Experience and inductive logic make for ever-increasing knowledge.
9 Man must understand his own condition in order to advance.
10 An object has being only when it is perceived by a subject.

A ASCETICISM
B EMPIRICISM
C EXISTENTIALISM
D HUMANISM
E IDEALISM
F POSITIVISM
G PRAGMATISM
H RATIONALISM
I UTILITARIANISM
J VERIFICATIONISM

Part Three
No Man's Land

Philosophy, as I shall understand the word, is something intermediate between theology and science. Like theology, it consists of speculations on matters as to which definite knowledge has, so far, been unascertainable; but, like science, it appeals to human reason rather than to authority, whether that of tradition or that of revelation. All definite knowledge – so I shall contend – belongs to science; all dogma as to what surpasses definite knowledge belongs to theology. But between theology and science there is a No Man's Land, exposed to attack from both sides; this No Man's Land is philosophy. Almost all the questions of most interest to speculative minds are such as science cannot answer, and the confident answers of theologians no longer seem so convincing as they did in former centuries. Is the world divided into mind and matter, and if so, what is mind and what is matter? Is mind subject to matter, or is it possessed of independent powers? Has the universe any unity or purpose? Is it evolving towards some goal? Are there really laws of nature, or do we believe in them only because of our innate love of order? Is man what he seems to the astronomer, a tiny lump of impure carbon and water impotently crawling on a small and unimportant planet? Or is he what he appears to Hamlet? Is he perhaps both at once? Is there a way of living that is noble and another that is base, or are all ways of living merely futile? If there is a way of living that is noble, in what does it consist, and how shall we achieve it? Must the good be eternal in order to deserve to be valued, or is it worth seeking even if the universe is inexorably moving towards death? Is there such a thing as wisdom, or is what seems such merely the ultimate refinement of folly? To such questions no answer can be found in the laboratory. Theologies have professed to give answers all too definite; but their very definiteness causes modern minds to view them with suspicion. The studying of these questions, if not the answering of them, is the business of philosophy.

5

10

15

20

25

30

(Bertrand Russell, *History of Western Philosophy*, 1946)

1 (a) What does one do when one *speculates*? (line 3)
   (b) What does it mean to appeal to 'revelation'? (lines 5–6)
   (c) What is a love that is 'innate'? (line 18)
   (d) Find a substitute word or phrase for 'inexorably'. (line 26)
2 What does Russell appear to think of the knowledge that theology purports to give us? Quote the basis for your answer.
3 Why do you suppose Russell chooses the astronomer rather than, say, the chemist, as the scientist to whom man seems to be mere carbon and water?
4 Do you know how man appears to Hamlet? If not, can you work out from the text how he sees man?
5 Why should definiteness be an object of suspicion to the modern mind? (lines 31–2)

Part Four
Philosophizing

At one time, the whole of human knowledge was the province of philosophy. What do philosophers do now? What is philosophy for? Can we, by philosophizing, gain knowledge that we cannot gain by pursuing science? Here are some ingredients for a possible answer to these questions.

1

It was when almost all the necessities of life and the things that make for comfort and recreation were present, that (philosophical) knowledge began to be sought. Evidently then we do not seek it for the sake of any other advantage; but as the man is free, we say, who exists for himself and not for another, so we pursue [philosophy] as the only free science, for it alone exists for itself.

(Aristotle, in W.D. Ross, ed., *Metaphysics*, 1927)

2

We must try to seize it in its original freshness if we wish to understand the associations the word 'philosophy' came to have for the Greeks. To state it briefly, it is the view that man is something intermediate between God and 'the other animals'. ... For a being subject to error and death, wisdom (Sophia) in the full sense is impossible; that is for God alone. On the other hand, man cannot be content, like 'the other animals' to remain in ignorance. If he cannot be wise, he can at least be a lover of wisdom.

(R.W. Livingstone, ed., *The legacy of Greece*, 1922)

3

One has to 'leave philosophy aside', one has to leap out of it and devote oneself like an ordinary man to the study of actuality. ... Philosophy and the study of the actual world have the same relation to one another as masturbation and sexual love ... The philosophers have only *interpreted* the world, in various ways; the point is to *change* it.

(Marx and Engels, in C.J. Arthur, ed., *The German Ideology*, 1970)

4

Philosophy, like all other studies, aims primarily at knowledge. The knowledge it aims at is the kind of knowledge which gives unity and system to the body of the sciences .... It cannot be maintained that philosophy has had any very great measure of success in its attempts to provide definite answers to its questions. ... This is partly accounted for by the fact that, as soon as definite knowledge concerning any subject becomes possible, this subject ceases to be called philosophy, and becomes a separate science.

(Bertrand Russell, *The Problems of Philosophy*, 1912)

5

If the philosopher is to uphold his claim to make a special contribution to the stock of our knowledge, he must not attempt to formulate speculative truths, or to look for first principles, or to make *a priori* judgements about the validity of our empirical beliefs. He must confine himself to works of clarification and analysis.

(A.J. Ayer, *Language, Truth and Logic*, 1936)

6

Philosophy is not to be valued only for its indirect practical effects but for itself; and the best way of securing these good practical effects is to pursue philosophy for its own sake. In order to find truth we must aim at it disinterestedly. . . . Beliefs are useful because they are true, not true because they are useful.

(A.C. Ewing, *The Fundamental Questions of Philosophy*, 1951)

7

Philosophical problems are, of course, not empirical problems; they are solved, rather by looking into the workings of our language, and that in such a way as to make us recognise those workings. The problems are solved not by giving new information, but by arranging what we have always known. Philosophy is a battle against the bewitchment of our intelligence by means of language.

(Ludwig Wittgenstein, *Philosophical Investigations*, 2nd edn, 1958)

8

Philosophers, Wittgenstein came to think, had made the mistake of trying to model their activities on those of scientists – as, indeed, the very phrase 'logical atomism' suggests .... Exact definitions would make philosophy look like a species of science; philosophy, as Wittgenstein envisages it, explains nothing, analyses nothing – it simply describes.

(John Passmore, *A Hundred Years of Philosophy*, 1957)

Part Five

Morals and Motives

Each of the eight opinions expressed below represents a well-established philosophy of morals (Utilitarianism, Intuitionism, Emotivism, Situationism, Existentialism, Kantianism, Natural Law and Divine Command Theory). Which is which? Use any or all of them to answer this question: **On what grounds do we make moral decisions?**

1   We know that stealing, killing, causing injury, and so on are immoral because these acts have always been forbidden in religious writings. They run counter to God's will. Morals are summed up in the command to love your neighbour as yourself.

2   A moral judgement has no objective truth-value. When we say: 'Adultery is wrong', or 'killing animals is unethical', all we're doing is expressing a personal feeling. That murder is illegal is a matter of fact: to say it's 'wrong' is an expression of disgust, or emotion.

3   The human condition is the same everywhere. Our moral nature, our awareness of the moral order, springs from our shared human nature. Our sense of natural justice, of natural rights, are reflections of that immutable order.

4   There are no objective morals. The only thing that makes an act right or wrong is the presence or absence of love. Love is the one thing in the world that is intrinsically good, that *defines* good and evil.

5   We all seek pleasure and shun pain. This fundamental individual preference is the basis for saying that morality is all about securing the maximum happiness for the maximum number of people. Behaviour is moral when it has a balance of good consequences over bad ones.

6   There are no rules where moral decisions are concerned. We all have intuitions about what's right and wrong – it often comes down to common sense. Motives are what are really important. If you *mean* well, you can't, by definition, do *moral* ill.

7   We know what it is our duty to do. Kant called it the Categorical Imperative. It is *a priori* knowledge of what is good and bad – an independent standard by which we know what is good for its own sake, irrespective of consequences.

8   There is nothing given; no set of moral principles as it were, 'out there'. We have to invent our own. Individuals choose a course of action – course A rather than course B – and in doing so, in acting upon their choice, they choose their morals.

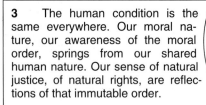

ITEM
N

Greek and Roman Gods and Heroes

Below is a family tree of the classical gods. Their Greek names are given in capitals, and their Roman equivalents in lower-case letters underneath. Zeus was the king and father of gods and men, with power over all the deities except the Fates.

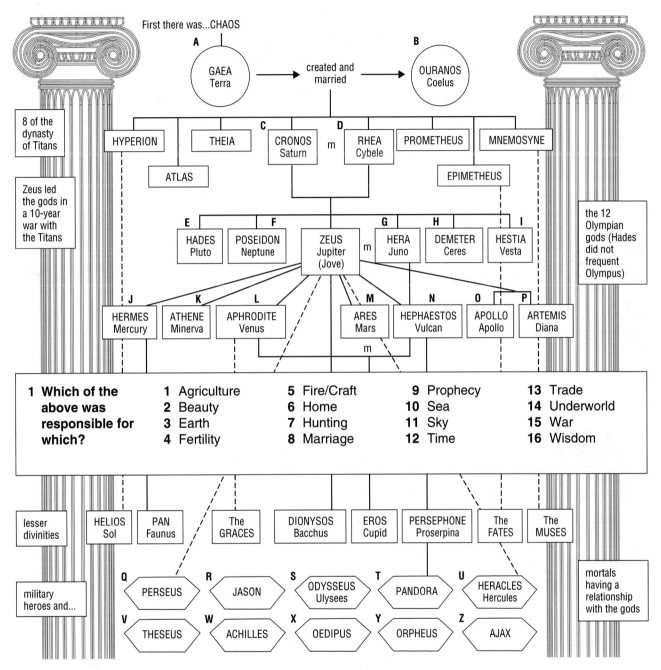

First there was...CHAOS

A GAEA Terra → created and married → **B** OURANOS Coelus

8 of the dynasty of Titans

Zeus led the gods in a 10-year war with the Titans

C CRONOS Saturn m **D** RHEA Cybele

HYPERION　THEIA　PROMETHEUS　MNEMOSYNE

ATLAS　EPIMETHEUS

the 12 Olympian gods (Hades did not frequent Olympus)

E HADES Pluto　**F** POSEIDON Neptune　ZEUS Jupiter (Jove) m **G** HERA Juno　**H** DEMETER Ceres　**I** HESTIA Vesta

J HERMES Mercury　**K** ATHENE Minerva　**L** APHRODITE Venus　**M** ARES Mars　HEPHAESTOS Vulcan　**N** APOLLO Apollo　**O** ARTEMIS Diana　**P**

m

1 Which of the above was responsible for which?

1 Agriculture	5 Fire/Craft	9 Prophecy	13 Trade
2 Beauty	6 Home	10 Sea	14 Underworld
3 Earth	7 Hunting	11 Sky	15 War
4 Fertility	8 Marriage	12 Time	16 Wisdom

lesser divinities

HELIOS Sol　PAN Faunus　The GRACES　DIONYSOS Bacchus　EROS Cupid　PERSEPHONE Proserpina　The FATES　The MUSES

military heroes and...

mortals having a relationship with the gods

Q PERSEUS　**R** JASON　**S** ODYSSEUS Ulysees　**T** PANDORA　**U** HERACLES Hercules

V THESEUS　**W** ACHILLES　**X** OEDIPUS　**Y** ORPHEUS　**Z** AJAX

2 Which of the Heroes and Mortals did which of the following deeds?

1. Wandered for ten years after the Trojan War before returning to his wife.
2. Performed twelve prodigious feats of strength (or 'labours').
3. Cut off the head of the Gorgon, Medusa.
4. Died of a poisoned arrow in his heel, loosed at him by Paris.
5. Unwittingly killed his father, and married his mother.
6. Charmed Pluto with his playing on the lyre, but lost Eurydice.
7. Captain of the Argonauts who sought the Golden Fleece.
8. A courageous warrior, he led the troops of Salamis against Troy.
9. Let loose from her box all the evils that afflict mankind.
10. Killed many villains, including Procrustes and the Cretan Minotaur.

Part One
Learning

Learning takes place on a continuum between unconscious conditioning and conscious thinking (or cognition). All learning is ultimately the result of the ASSOCIATION of one item in the environment with another.

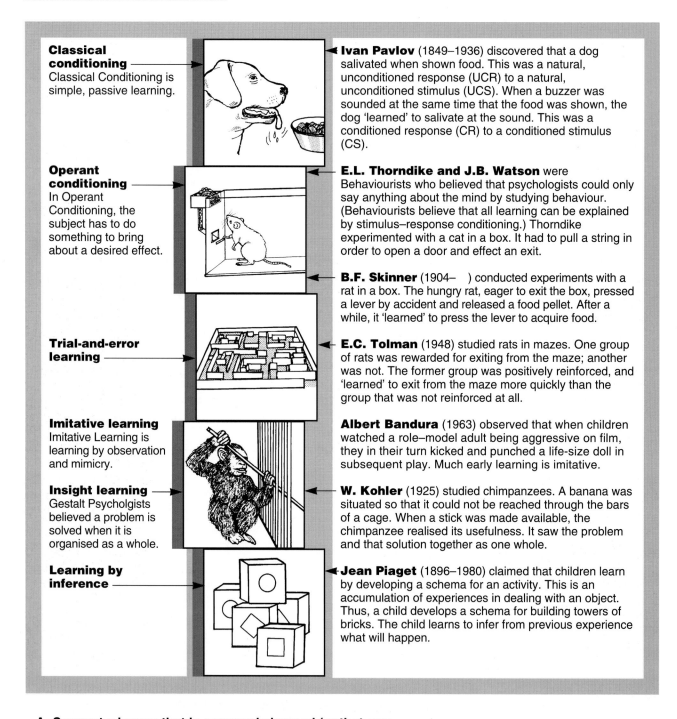

Classical conditioning
Classical Conditioning is simple, passive learning.

Ivan Pavlov (1849–1936) discovered that a dog salivated when shown food. This was a natural, unconditioned response (UCR) to a natural, unconditioned stimulus (UCS). When a buzzer was sounded at the same time that the food was shown, the dog 'learned' to salivate at the sound. This was a conditioned response (CR) to a conditioned stimulus (CS).

Operant conditioning
In Operant Conditioning, the subject has to do something to bring about a desired effect.

E.L. Thorndike and J.B. Watson were Behaviourists who believed that psychologists could only say anything about the mind by studying behaviour. (Behaviourists believe that all learning can be explained by stimulus–response conditioning.) Thorndike experimented with a cat in a box. It had to pull a string in order to open a door and effect an exit.

B.F. Skinner (1904–) conducted experiments with a rat in a box. The hungry rat, eager to exit the box, pressed a lever by accident and released a food pellet. After a while, it 'learned' to press the lever to acquire food.

Trial-and-error learning

E.C. Tolman (1948) studied rats in mazes. One group of rats was rewarded for exiting from the maze; another was not. The former group was positively reinforced, and 'learned' to exit from the maze more quickly than the group that was not reinforced at all.

Imitative learning
Imitative Learning is learning by observation and mimicry.

Albert Bandura (1963) observed that when children watched a role–model adult being aggressive on film, they in their turn kicked and punched a life-size doll in subsequent play. Much early learning is imitative.

Insight learning
Gestalt Psycholgists believed a problem is solved when it is organised as a whole.

W. Kohler (1925) studied chimpanzees. A banana was situated so that it could not be reached through the bars of a cage. When a stick was made available, the chimpanzee realised its usefulness. It saw the problem and that solution together as one whole.

Learning by inference

Jean Piaget (1896–1980) claimed that children learn by developing a schema for an activity. This is an accumulation of experiences in dealing with an object. Thus, a child develops a schema for building towers of bricks. The child learns to infer from previous experience what will happen.

A Suggest a lesson that is commonly learned (or that *you* learned) by each of the six methods referred to above.

B Fit the appropriate words in the spaces.

1 Children receive _____ when they are rewarded.
2 Simple _____ is responsible for most early learning.
3 Truly reflective, inferential learning is known as _____.
4 The _____ association is a powerful mechanism for learning.
5 The belief that we are confined to studying what people do is _____.
6 We learn by _____ from repeated experience.

A Behaviourism
B Cognition
C Conditioning
D Inference
E Reinforcement
F Stimulus-response

Part Two
Development of Language

The diagram below illustrates the development of language in a child from birth to 3 years of age. Naturally, the stages are approximations only. On the left are three theories of the way in which language is acquired; and on the right, three theories of the relationship between language and thinking.

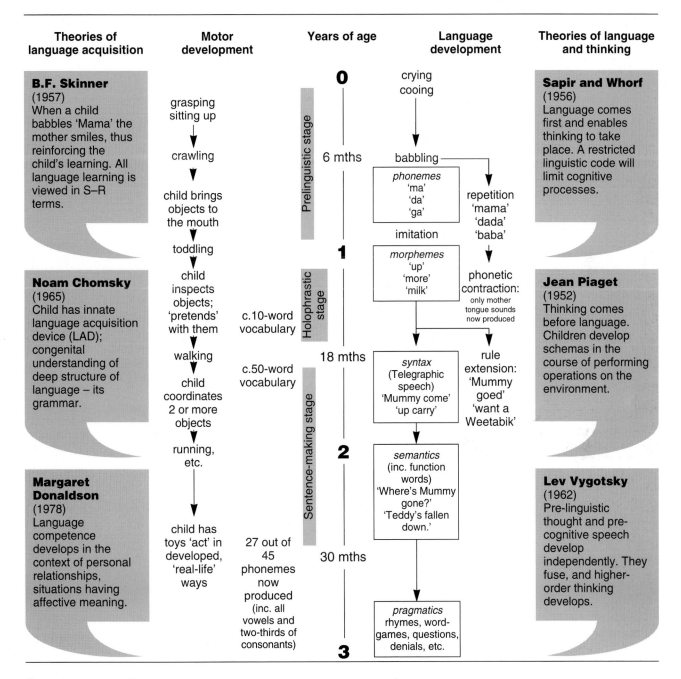

Theories of language acquisition	Motor development	Years of age	Language development	Theories of language and thinking
B.F. Skinner (1957) When a child babbles 'Mama' the mother smiles, thus reinforcing the child's learning. All language learning is viewed in S–R terms.	grasping sitting up ↓ crawling ↓ child brings objects to the mouth ↓ toddling ↓ child inspects objects; 'pretends' with them ↓ walking ↓ child coordinates 2 or more objects ↓ running, etc. ↓ child has toys 'act' in developed, 'real-life' ways	**0** — 6 mths — **1** — c.10-word vocabulary — 18 mths — c.50-word vocabulary — **2** — 30 mths — 27 out of 45 phonemes now produced (inc. all vowels and two-thirds of consonants) — **3**	**Prelinguistic stage** crying cooing → babbling — *phonemes* 'ma' 'da' 'ga' — imitation → repetition 'mama' 'dada' 'baba'	**Sapir and Whorf** (1956) Language comes first and enables thinking to take place. A restricted linguistic code will limit cognitive processes.

Some open questions

1. Skinner's view was that all language learning is the result of positive reinforcement. Chomsky disagreed, saying that children do not say 'mummy goed' because an adult has 'rewarded' them for doing so. They are over-extending an innately-known grammatical rule. Do you find either view convincing?
2. Debate has raged over whether children 'think' before they can speak, or whether speech comes before thought. Do you believe that one can think without language?
3. At the holophrastic stage, a child speaks often in sentences of one word (e.g. 'Up!'). What can we say in general about the words and phrases that young children utter?

Part Three
Infant Conditioning

The brave new world is characterized by scientific socialism. The Director shows a group of students round the Central London Hatchery and Conditioning Centre. He takes them to the nurseries to witness an exercise in 'Neo-Pavlovian Conditioning'.

The Director opened a door. They were in a large bare room, very bright and sunny; for the whole of the southern wall was a single window. Half a dozen nurses, trousered and jacketed in the regulation white viscose-linen uniform, were engaged in setting out bowls of roses in a long row across the floor. Big bowls packed tight with blossom. 5

The nurses stiffened to attention and the DHC came in.

'Set out the books,' he said curtly.

In silence the nurses obeyed his command. Between the rose bowls the books were duly set out – a row of nursery quartos opened invitingly at some gaily-coloured image of beast or fish or bird. 10

'Now bring in the children.'

They hurried out of the room and returned in a minute or two, each pushing a kind of tall dumb-waiter laden, on its four wire-netted shelves with eight-month-old babies, all exactly alike, and all dressed in khaki. 15

'Put them down on the floor.'

The infants were unloaded.

'Now turn them so that they can see the flowers and books.'

Turned, the babies at once fell silent, then began to crawl towards those clusters of sleek colours, those shapes so gay and brilliant on the white pages. As they approached, the sun came out of a momentary 20 eclipse behind a cloud. From the ranks of the crawling babies came little squeals of excitement, gurgles and twitterings of pleasure.

The swiftest crawlers were already at their goal. Small hands reached out uncertainly, touched, grasped, unpetalling the transfigured roses, crumpling the illuminated pages of the books. The Director waited until 25 all were happily busy. Then, 'Watch carefully,' he said. And, lifting his hand, he gave the signal. The Head Nurse, who was standing by a switchboard at the other end of the room, pressed down a little lever.

There was a violent explosion. Shriller and even shriller, a siren 30 shrieked. Alarm bells maddeningly sounded.

The children started, screamed; their faces were distorted with terror.

'And now,' the Director shouted (for the noise was deafening), 'now we proceed to rub in the lesson with a mild electric shock. ...'

'They'll grow up with what the psychologists used to call an "instinc- 35 tive" hatred of books and flowers. Reflexes unalterably conditioned. They'll be safe from books and botany all their lives.'

(Abridged from Aldous Huxley, *Brave New World*, 1932)

1 (a) What is a 'curt' speech? (line 7)
  (b) What is it that has 'transfigured' the roses? (line 24)
  (c) What alternative word, or words, might have been used for 'started'? (line 31)
  (d) What is meant by 'conditioned' here? (line 35)

2 What would a commentator mean who referred to Huxley's style of writing in this passage as 'objective', or 'dispassionate'?

3 What is Huxley's purpose in adopting such a style, do you suppose?

4 What (rather less coercive) measures are commonly adopted in today's schools to 'condition' pupils – to 'reinforce' learning?

Part Four
Artificial Intelligence

Artificial Intelligence is about programming computers to do the sorts of things that human minds can do (in part) so that we may better understand how the human mind works. Make use of any combinations of the following views to construct an answer to this question: **Will computers (or 'thinking machines') make the human brain redundant?**

1

Not until a machine can write a sonnet or compose a concerto because of thoughts and emotions felt, and not by a chance fall of symbols, could we agree that machine equals brain – that is, not only write it but know that it had written it.

(G. Jefferson, 'The Mind of Mechanical Man', in *British Medical Journal*, 1949)

2

I believe that at the end of the century the use of words and general educated opinion will have altered so much that one will be able to speak of machines thinking without expecting to be contradicted. I believe further that no useful purpose is served by concealing these beliefs.

(Alan Turing, 'Computing Machinery and Intelligence', in *Mind*, 1950)

3

Computers give information as if they had thoughts, but they are just complicated pieces of machinery that human beings have constructed to provide information; they only do what we program them to do. They do not go through thought-processes and they do not possess knowledge.

(John Hospers, *An Introduction to Philosophical Analysis*, 1953)

4

Minds exist in brains and may come to exist in programmed machines. If and when such machines come about, their causal powers will derive not from the substances they are made of, but from their design and the programs that run in them. And the way we will know they have those causal processes is by talking to them and listening carefully to what they have to say.

(Douglas R. Hofstadter and Daniel C. Dennell, *The Mind's I*, 1981)

5

A human may know just what kind of emotional impact touching another person's hand will have both on the other person and on himself. The acquisition of knowledge is certainly not a function of the brain alone; ... There are some things humans know by virtue of having a human body. No organism that does not have a human body can know these things in the same way humans know them.

(Joseph Weizenbaum, *Computer Power and Human Reason*, 1976)

6

No-one supposes that computer simulations of a five-alarm fire will burn the neighbourhood down or that a computer simulation of a rain storm will leave us all drenched. Why on earth would anyone suppose that a computer simulation of understanding actually understood anything?

(John Searle, 'Minds, Brains and Programs', in *The Behavioural and Brain Sciences*, 1980)

7

I assume that there is nothing magical about neurones; they are part of the natural world. That is, they can in principle be described by physics and chemistry, just as bone and steel – and silicon chips – can too. I assume that there is no special physical property that is essential to intelligence, which is possessed only by brain-proteins.

(Margaret A. Boden, *Artificial Intelligence in Psychology*, 1989)

8

The aspects of brain function that we most critically need to understand in order to build a more mind-like computer are the manner in which cell-to-cell connections code information differently in the various modules, and the manner in which this information becomes so widely distributed, and redundant in various brain regions. If we do manage to develop such a model, much of what appears mysterious in brain function would rapidly be disclosed to scientific understanding.

(Robert L. Nadeau, *Mind, Machines & Human Consciousness*, 1991)

Part Five

Science and the Psychic

We know rather little about the mind. Ignorance leaves room for fascination with, and speculation about, extra-sensory perception, or the paranormal. Science has put psychic phenomena to the test, however, and there is at least one chair in parapsychology at a British University. Base an answer to the following question on any or all of the opinions below. **Is the study of the paranormal a legitimate scientific pursuit?**

1   It's an extraordinary sort of arrogance to suppose that we know all there is to know about nature, and what is normal, so that we can confidently deny the existence of super-nature or the paranormal. Scientists of a modest kind admit that there is far more that we *don't* know than that we *do*.

2   There are simply too many well-attested sightings of ghosts and other manifestations (doors banging, objects moving and so on) to write them off as the product of fevered imaginations. Many of the witnesses are people who would have a lot to lose if they were thought to be cranks, or worse, tricksters.

3   Belief in the paranormal passes in and out of fashion. It comes in, someone does something unusual (there have always been illusionists and conjurors), they're discredited, and it's forgotten again. There's something in us that wants to believe in the paranormal. It's a substitute for religion, if you like.

4   So-called paranormal phenomena can be ascribed to manifestations of the collective unconscious mind of people who participate in a séance. They've a sort of wish-fulfilment that can be explained in straightforwardly psychological terms.

5   We know enough about perception to make it more likely that a person who claims to have seen a ghost is deluded, than that all we've learnt about the structure of matter is false, merely in order to accommodate a few visions.

6   The mind is the last great frontier. We still know very little about it, and what it can do. Hindu yogis, Uri Geller, Matthew Manning and others offer lots of evidence of the power of mind over matter. The power of the mind to heal the body is well known to psychiatrists and healers of all sorts.

7   There is a good deal of evidence for telepathy being genuine. Time and again identical twins testify to the transfer of thought between them when they were distant from each other. And J.B. Rhine demonstrated thought-transfer that couldn't be ascribed to chance.

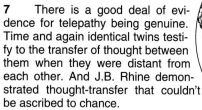

8   Scientists acquire knowledge only after rigorous testing of hypotheses, in controlled conditions. Parapsychologists claim to be able to acquire knowledge by a psychic short cut. Parapsychology isn't a science because its exponents don't operate scientifically.

French: Text and multiple-choice questions in English

The main objective of an exercise in French (and something like 80 per cent of candidates for the NEAB General Studies examination tackle the French section on the paper) is to test 'reading comprehension'. This is done by means of multiple-choice questions (MCQs) in English. (There may also be a text and MCQs in French: see Item R). Here is part of a text about astronomy, together with five MCQs in English. The correct answers are indicated, and the three distractors are explained.

Saint-Michel-l'Observatoire se trouve à quelques kilomètres de For-calquier dans les Alpes-de-Haute-Provence. Ses dômes métalliques blancs, imposants, dominent une forêt de chênes-lièges. Le Centre National de Recherche Scientifique a ouvert l'Observatoire au public pour le circonstance de l'observation rapprochée de la Comète Halley, en 1985. 5
Les sondes Vega et Giotto lancées à la fin 1984 et au début juillet 1985 ont permis de savoir plus sur la comète; et le visiteur a pu s'en profiter.

Il a été plongé dans l'actualité astronomique avec une maquette représentant un mobile conduit par micro-ordinateur simulant la trajectoire de la comète par rapport au Soleil et à la terre. Cette comète 10
n'est qu'une boule de neige sale, mais elle cache la mémoire de notre système solaire. La maquette a entraîné le visiteur dans le temps: la comète parcourt une révolution complète autour du soleil. La trajectoire elliptique de la comète dure soixante-seize ans, donc la privilège d'une observation tellement rapprochée ne reviendra qu'en 2061. 15

Le CRNS a embauché des étudiants en astrophysique pour satisfaire la curiosité des visiteurs de Saint-Michel. Ceux-ci ont dû laisser tomber leur timidité s'ils ont voulu comprendre ce qu'on leur a montré. Le directeur leur a demandé de ne pas hésiter à poser des questions aux étudiants ... 20

---

1 Saint-Michel presents itself in the form of:
A an imposing forest of oak and cork trees. ◄— the observatory dominates this forest
B a number of imposing, white, metallic domes. ✓ see lines 2–3
C an army of white-painted radio-telescopes. ◄— no reference to telescopes so far
D buildings dominated by the glistening Alps ◄— it's the observatory that's doing the 'dominating'.

2 The observatory was opened to the public:
A at a time suitable for observing Halley's Comet. ✓ see line 5
B to celebrate the launch of the Vega satellite. ◄— this was launched to observe the comet
C by the astronomer Edmund Halley. ◄— Halley is very dead
D for the purpose of scientific research. ◄— this is the purpose of the 'centre'

3 A micro-ordinateur (line 9) is a:
A public address-system. ◄— no connection with microphones
B space command-module. ◄— this is not NASA
C micro-computer. ✓ you know it, or you infer it
D model of the universe. ◄— the 'maquette' is the model

4 The importance of Halley's Comet is that it:
A can only be seen once every 76 years. ◄— true, but unimportant
B travels on a path between Sun and Earth. ◄— it doesn't; it orbits the sun (line 13)
C can tell us the history of the Solar System. ✓ see lines 11–12
D is a privilege to observe it. ◄— because it's important for other reasons

5 Visitors to Saint-Michel:
A had not to be shy about asking questions. ✓ see lines 17–18
B could enrol as students of astrophysics. ◄— this is hardly likely
C must not ask questions of the students. ◄— on the contrary
D hesitated to ask questions. ◄— they were asked **not** to hesitate

ITEM

Here is another section of the same passage, together with five more questions. This time, you need to work out the answers yourself.

Le Directeur, titulaire d'un DEA d'astronomie, a appris aux visiteurs que le soleil est une étoile très ordinaire, perdue au milieu de quatre cents milliards d'autres qui constituent notre galaxie, la Voie Lactée. Les galaxies sont des nuées d'étoiles faites de gaz et de poussière liées par la force gravitationelle. Tournant sur elles-mêmes, elles s'eloignent les unes des autres, par suite de l'expansion de l'univers.

On a été invité à pénétrer dans l'une des coupoles de l'observatoire qui abrite un téléscope de 120 cm de diamètre. Toutes les nuits, les astronomes en mission observent le ciel depuis des onze coupoles du site à Saint Michel. Les téléscopes permettent de collecter la lumière venue d'une étoile pour l'analyser. Bien entendu, il n'y avait rien à voir pendant les heures de visite; et, en outre, les coupoles sont fermées dans la journée, pour limiter les variations de température et éviter les turbulences qui brouillent l'image.

6 The Director said of the sun that:
   A it is the only star of its kind in the galaxy.
   B of all the stars in the galaxy it is the only sun.
   C it is otherwise called the Milky Way.
   D it is a very ordinary star among billions of others.

7 One factor in the expansion of the universe is that:
   A the force of gravity is weakening over time.
   B the dust and gas are being dissipated.
   C the galaxies are receding from each other.
   D the galaxies turn in upon themselves.

8 Visitors were permitted to enter a dome:
   A where there was a 120cm telescope.
   B to observe the night sky.
   C from which they could see the other eleven domes.
   D that was only 120 cms in diameter.

9 The visitors could not make observations themselves:
   A in spite of the Director's best intentions.
   B because their visit was made during the day.
   C there being nothing to see in the sky at the time.
   D because starlight was being collected and analysed.

10 The domes are shut during daylight hours:
   A because the astronomers are busy receiving the public.
   B so as to keep the domes at night-time temperature.
   C to avoid the effects on the telescopes of too much heat and light.
   D so that the astronomers can collect light for analysis.

Part One
World Religions

The diagram below represents the spread of the major world religions in both time (on the vertical axis) and in place (on the horizontal axis). The 'Western' religions (Judaism, Christianity and Islam) have been thought of as monotheistic (worshipping one God) and the 'Eastern' religions as polytheistic (worshipping many gods). The more learned among Hindus, however, would say that Vishnu, Krishna and others are not themselves gods, but are revelations ('avatars') of the one spirit, Brahman.

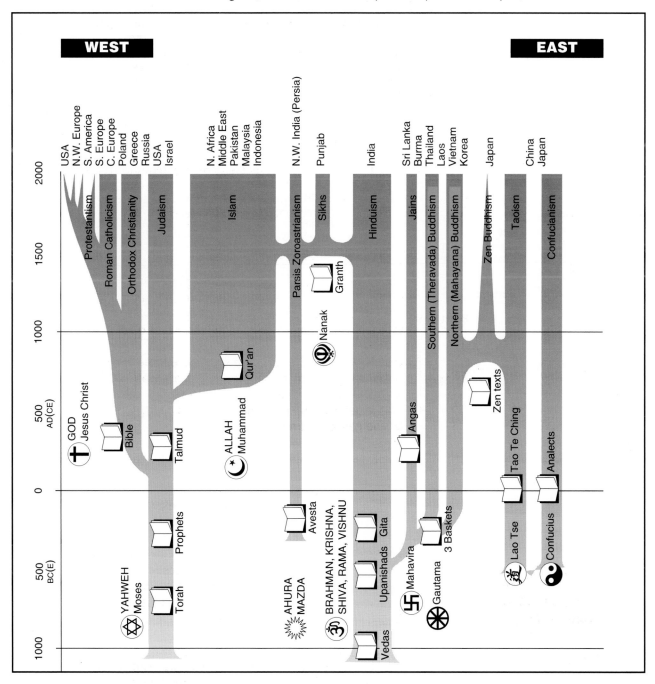

A Summarize what you take to be the principal differences between Eastern and Western religions.

B To which of the major religions (Buddhism, Christianity, Hinduism, Islam and Judaism) does each of the following belong?

1 BAR MITZVAH	ceremony of initiation;	**6** PASSOVER	8-day celebration of deliverance;
2 EUCHARIST	re-enactment of Last Supper;	**7** RAMADAN	month of fasting;
3 JIHAD	holy war against unbelievers;	**8** SACRAMENT	outward sign of inward grace;
4 KARMA	sum of acts influencing future reincarnation;	**9** SAMSARA	endless wheel of life;
5 NIRVANA	release from cycle of rebirth;	**10** YOGA	discipline whose object is union with the divine.

Part Two
Protestantism

The Christian Church was united (more or less) until the Great Schism of AD 1034. The Western, Latin-speaking, 'Catholic' (or universal) Church had been growing apart from the Eastern, Greek-speaking, 'Orthodox' Church for some time. In that year, they broke apart for good.

Ever since the Reformation of the 1500s (when reformers protested against abuses in the Roman Catholic Church) one group after another has disagreed on a point of doctrine or practice, and gone its separate way. The diagram below represents an extension of the left-hand end of the map of world religions in Part One on the previous page.

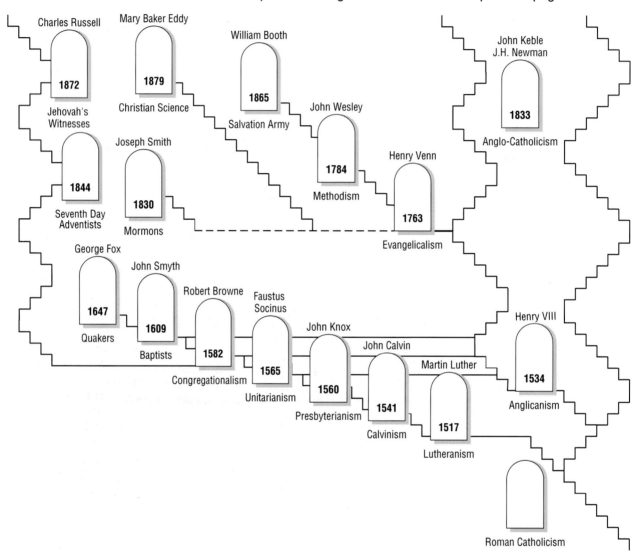

A Which of the above sects and denominations are shrinking, and which are growing?

B What new sects have emerged in the twentieth century?

C Which is which?

1 Practise believers' (adult) baptism by total immersion.
2 So named because of their systematic study of the Bible.
3 Otherwise called the Church of Jesus Christ of Latter-Day Saints.
4 Pacifists who believe that there is something of God in everyone.
5 Do not believe in the Trinity, but in the divinity of God the father only.
6 Hold to Episcopal organization and communion with the see of Canterbury.
7 Believe Christ will return in person and observe the Sabbath on Saturday.
8 Regard prayer as the sufficient means of solving moral and physical problems.
9 Stress the sovereignty of God and the predestination of souls.
10 Place faith in the imminent kingdom and in their own election to it.

A QUAKERS
B CALVINISM
C ANGLICANISM
D MORMONS
E METHODISM
F BAPTISTS
G UNITARIANISM
H JEHOVAH'S WITNESSES
I CHRISTIAN SCIENCE
J SEVENTH DAY ADVENTISTS

Part Three
Varieties of Religion

Ought it to be assumed that in all men the mixture of religion with other elements should be identical? Ought it, indeed, to be assumed that the lives of all men should show identical religious elements? In other words, is the existence of so many religious types and sects and creeds 5 regrettable?

To these questions I answer 'No' emphatically. And my reason is that I do not see how it is possible that creatures in such different positions and with such different powers as human individuals are, should have exactly the same func- 10 tions and the same duties. No two of us have identical difficulties, nor should we be expected to work out identical solutions. Each, from his peculiar angle of observation, takes in a certain sphere of fact and trouble, which each must deal with in a unique manner. One of us must soften himself, an- 15 other must harden himself; one must yield a point, another must stand firm – in order the better to defend the position assigned him. The divine can mean no single quality, it must mean a group of qualities, by being champions of which in alternation, different men may all find worthy missions. 20 Each attitude being a syllable in human nature's total message, it takes the whole of us to spell the meaning out completely. So a 'god of battles' must be allowed to be the god for one kind of person, a god of peace and heaven and home, the god for another. We must frankly recognize the 25 fact that we live in partial systems and that parts are not interchangeable in the spiritual life. If we are peevish and jealous, destruction of the self must be an element of our religion; why need it be one if we are good and sympathetic from the outset? If we are sick souls we require a religion of 30 deliverance; but why think so much of deliverance if we are healthy-minded?

(William James, *The Varieties of Religious Experience*, 1902)

1 (a) What does 'peculiar' mean in this sense? (line 13)
  (b) What does one do when one 'yields a point'? (line 16)
  (c) By whom or by what might one be 'assigned' a position? (line 18)
  (d) What is it to be 'peevish'? (line 27)
2 What is meant by 'elements' in line 2, and subsequently?
3 What does James appear to say about religion when he refers to it as a 'solution'? (line 13)
4 What is meant literally by the metaphor used in lines 21–3?
5 Do you understand James to mean that there is one god, that there are many gods, or that there are no gods at all?

Part Four
The Image of God

Below are a number of propositions having to do with apprehensions of the nature of God. Base an answer to the following question on any or all of them: **To what extent would you agree that believers have a problem where the image of God is concerned?**

1

What further can be known about God must be sought in the region of particular experiences, and therefore rests on an empirical basis. In respect to the interpretation of these experiences, mankind has differed profoundly. He has been named respectively, Jehovah, Allah, Brahman, Father in Heaven, Order of Heaven, First Cause, Supreme Being, Chance. Each name corresponds to a system of thought derived from the experiences of those who have used it.

(A.N. Whitehead, *Science and the Modern World*, 1925)

2

You will not find one among the profounder sort of scientific minds without a religious feeling of his own. But it is different from the religiosity of the naive man. For the latter God is a being from whose care one hopes to benefit and whose punishment one fears; a sublimation of a feeling similar to that of a child for its father, a being to whom one stands, so to speak, in a personal relation, however deeply it may be tinged with awe. But the scientist is possessed by the sense of universal causation .... His religious feeling takes the form of a rapturous amazement at the harmony of natural law, which reveals an intelligence of such superiority that, compared with it, all the systematic thinking and acting of human beings is an utterly insignificant reflection.

(Albert Einstein, *The Religious Spirit of Science*, 1934)

3

The name of this infinite and inexhaustible depth and ground of all being is *God*. That depth is what the word God means. And if that word has not much meaning for you, translate it, and speak of the depths of your life, of the source of your being, of your ultimate concern, of what you take seriously without any reservation. Perhaps, in order to do so, you must forget everything traditional that you have learned about God, perhaps even that word itself.

(Paul Tillich, *The Shaking of the Foundations*, 1949)

4

I prefer the term 'The Unconscious' knowing that I might equally well speak of 'God', or 'daimon' if I wished to express myself in mythic language. When I do use such mythic language I am aware that 'mana', 'daimon', and 'God' are synonyms for the Unconscious – that is to say, we know just as much or just as little about them as about the latter. ... The great advantage of the concepts 'daimon' and 'God' lies in making possible a much better objectification of the *vis à vis*, namely a *personification* of it.

(C.G. Jung, *Memories, Dreams, Reflections*, 1963)

5

A statement is 'theological' not because it relates to a particular Being called 'God', but because it asks ultimate questions about the meaning of existence .... To assert that 'God is love' is to believe that in love one comes into touch with the most fundamental reality in the universe, that Being itself ultimately has this character.

(John A.T. Robinson, *Honest to God*, 1963)

6

God (and this is a definition) is the sum of our values, representing to us their ideal unity, their claims upon us and their creative power. Mythologically, he has been portrayed as an objective being, because ancient thought tended to personify values in the belief that important words must stand for things. ... Just as you should not think of justice and truth as independent beings, so you should not think of God as an objectively existing superperson.

(Don Cupitt, *The Sea of Faith*, 1984)

Part Five

Who needs it?

Religion would appear to be in decline in North-Western Europe, except among immigrant groups from Islamic countries. Observance would seem to be holding up in North America, where new cults claim committed adherents, and martyrs. Is a belief in God, a god, or gods essential to the human condition? Do we need religion?

1 Freud believed science would replace religion, as monotheism had replaced animism. He thought it was impossible to go on believing in a transcendent god in an Einsteinian universe. But even he valued religion for its contribution to the spiritual health of a society, and its image of itself.

2 Even someone who doesn't believe in a good, eternal, omnipotent, omniscient, omnipresent god has to admit that there has never been a finer statement of moral ideals than the one represented in the Sermon on the Mount – and that, from what we know of him, Jesus would seem to have been a moral prodigy.

3 'Do as you would be done by' is the ethic that underlies all religions and moral codes. Religious observance is simply the way a society or culture gives expression to that ethic. It doesn't change anybody. One is not the sort of person one is because one is religious; one is religious because of the sort of person one is.

4 We simply cannot deny that man has always looked for meanings for life and death outside himself – outside his own petty experiences of these things. Our spiritual yearnings are as much a part of us as our physical appetites. Look how religion has returned to Eastern Europe to fill the vacuum left by communism.

5 Science and religion can coexist, of course. But what sort of God does a modern astrophysicist believe in? Not the God of the Old Testament, or the New. If you've dispensed with a 'Father' to whom you can pray, whose 'Son' died, and 'rose again', what's left? Religion is a sort of nostalgia for lost innocence, and scientists are as human as the rest of us.

6 The religious impulse goes pretty deep. In Hinduism, Islam and Buddhism, for example, religion is a part of a culture, the philosophy, the world view of the people of what we call the 'East'. In communist China, the people made a god of Mao, in North Korea, of Kim Il Sung. We are not without our gods in the west.

7 We have made a great mistake when we have supposed that morality is somehow dependent upon religion. Belief in God never was a motive for moral conduct. It isn't moral to be 'good' in hope of heaven, or in fear of hell; truly moral behaviour is freely chosen, and other-centred. Sticks and carrots are for donkeys.

8 We really must look for other purposes for our lives – other meanings – than those taught by religion. 'God made us, and it is our duty to please Him' is a pretty feeble excuse for existence. The sooner we realize that there is no 'ultimate' meaning of life, the sooner we'll settle for what we can do to make it more bearable.

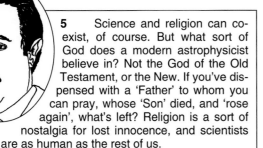

Maths 5: Star problems

Q1: Given that $a*b = ab + a + b$, what is $4*(3*a)$? What is the solution of $x*7 = (x*2) + (x*3)$? If $a*y = 0$, what is y?

Questions like this seem to be designed to dissuade students from answering. Even students of A-Level Mathematics will find them unfamiliar. They are based on some of the simpler ideas of Abstract Algebra Theory and are really very easy. The thing to do is to profit from the lesson of the previous section and substitute some numbers.

The star represents an operator. There are all sorts of operators in mathematics. The four most common are addition $(+)$, subtraction $(-)$, multiplication $(\times)$ and division $(\div)$. They are always written between two numbers to get a result. For example: $2 + 3 = 5$, $7 - 3 = 4$, $3 \times 5 = 15$, $6 \div \frac{1}{2} = 12$. Simple isn't it?

Now we can try something a little more complicated! Let $a*b = a^2 + b$. To attempt to understand this, put $a = 2$ and $b = 3$ (the actual values are irrelevant). $2*3$ is then the same as $2^2 + 3 = 4 + 3 = 7$. It only continues to mean this until we are told that it means something else. The meaning of the star operator is not constant in the way that $+$ is always addition and $\times$ is always multiplication. But for now,

$$3*4 = 3^2 + 4 = 9 + 4 = 13$$

$$2*1 = 2^2 + 1 = 4 + 1 = 5$$

$$1*2 = 1^2 + 2 = 1 + 2 = 3$$

Notice that reversing the numbers does not give the same result. Mathematicians will say that the operation is not 'commutative'. Addition and multiplication are commutative; subtraction and division are not.

We can make up any definition we like for $*$. Here is another: $a*b = 2a + 3b$. Here are some calculations:

$$2*3 = 2 \times 2 + 3 \times 3 = 4 + 9 = 13$$

Remember to do the multiplications before the additions.

$$3*2 = 2 \times 3 + 3 \times 2 = 6 + 6 = 12$$

Again this operation is not commutative. Here are a few more to help you see how it works:

$$5*4 = 2 \times 5 + 3 \times 4 = 10 + 12 = 22$$

$$3*7 = 2 \times 3 + 3 \times 7 = 6 + 21 = 27$$

Exercise 5.1

Try these using the same definition $(a*b = 2a + 3b)$.

1 4*3
2 6*1
3 −2*4
4 5*−2
5 −5*6

Your answers should be

1 17
2 15
3 8
4 4
5 8

Let us now return to the question at the beginning of this section: Given that $a*b = ab + a + b$, what is $4*(3*a)$? Let a be a simple number, say 5. Then $3*5$ is $3 \times 5 + 3 + 5 = 15 + 3 + 5 = 23$. (Remember the rule in algebra always to carry out multiplications and divisions before additions and subtractions.)

Now try $3*a$. This is $3 \times a + 3 + a = 3a + a = 4a + 3$. $4*(3*a)$ is therefore $4*(4a + 3)$. This is $4 \times (4a + 3) + 4 + (4a + 3) = (16a + 12) + 4 + (4a + 3) = 20a + 19$.

Now let us tackle the second part. What is the solution of $x*7 = (x*2) + (x*3)$? Break down the question into smaller bits:

$$x*7 = 7x + x + 7 = 8x + 7$$
$$x*2 = 2x + x + 2 = 3x + 2$$
$$x*3 + 3x + x + 3 = 4x + 3$$

So if $x*7 = (x*2) + (x*3)$, then $8x + 7 = 3x + 2 + 4x + 3$. This gives $8x + 7 = 7x = 5$ or $x = -2$.

Now for the last part. If $a*y = 0$, what is y? Let us try $a = 2$.

$2*y = 2y + 2 + y = 3y + 2$

Now try $a = 3$, to see what happens:

$3*y = 3y + 3 + y = 4y + 3$

Interesting. Then $a = 4$ gives:

$4*y = 4y + 4 + y = 5y + 4$

So, $a*y = ay + a + y = (a + 1)y + a$. Put this equal to 0 and we get:

$(a + 1)y + a = 0$

$(a + 1)y = -a$

$y = \dfrac{-a}{(a + 1)}$

Now this is not very pleasant for anyone who is unsure of algebra, but questions of this type are usually multiple choice, and substituting simple numbers in the possible answers should give sufficient clues to picking the right one.

Sometimes, the examiners make the questions still more complicated. A similar question to this appeared recently:

Q2: Pairs of integers are combined to form another pair according to the following rule:

$(a, b)*(c, d) = (a + c, b - d)$

Rule number one is don't panic!. Rule number two is try some numbers. Let us split it into two bits. What happens in the two halves? This says:

$a*c = a + c$

$b*d = b - d$

So, the first numbers in each pair are added up and the second numbers in each pair are subtracted. For example,

$(2, 3)*(4, 5) = (2 + 4, 3 - 5) = (6, -2)$

$(-1, 3)*(2, -1) = (-1 + 2, 3 - (-1))$
$= (1,4)$

Exercise 5.2

What are:

1   $(2, 4)*(1, 3)$
2   $(7, 8)*(-2, 5)$
3   $(4, 5)*(2, 3)$
4   $(2, -1)*(-1, 3)$
5   $(6, 3)*(4, 1)$
6   $(4, 1)*(6, 3)$
7   $(0, 0)*(3, 4)$
8   $(3, 4)*(0, 0)$

Part One
Scientific Method

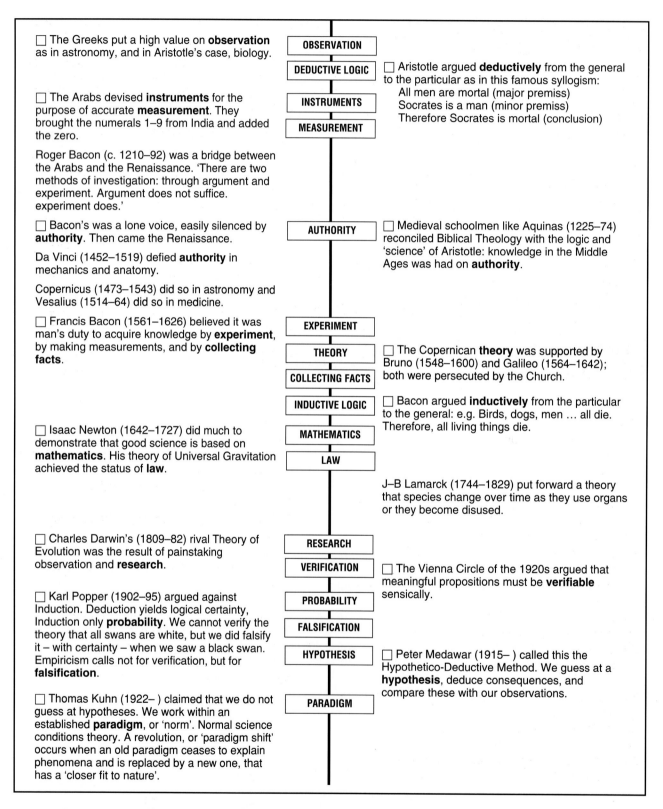

☐ The Greeks put a high value on **observation** as in astronomy, and in Aristotle's case, biology.

OBSERVATION

DEDUCTIVE LOGIC

☐ Aristotle argued **deductively** from the general to the particular as in this famous syllogism:
  All men are mortal (major premiss)
  Socrates is a man (minor premiss)
  Therefore Socrates is mortal (conclusion)

☐ The Arabs devised **instruments** for the purpose of accurate **measurement**. They brought the numerals 1–9 from India and added the zero.

INSTRUMENTS

MEASUREMENT

Roger Bacon (c. 1210–92) was a bridge between the Arabs and the Renaissance. 'There are two methods of investigation: through argument and experiment. Argument does not suffice. experiment does.'

☐ Bacon's was a lone voice, easily silenced by **authority**. Then came the Renaissance.

AUTHORITY

☐ Medieval schoolmen like Aquinas (1225–74) reconciled Biblical Theology with the logic and 'science' of Aristotle: knowledge in the Middle Ages was had on **authority**.

Da Vinci (1452–1519) defied **authority** in mechanics and anatomy.

Copernicus (1473–1543) did so in astronomy and Vesalius (1514–64) did so in medicine.

☐ Francis Bacon (1561–1626) believed it was man's duty to acquire knowledge by **experiment**, by making measurements, and by **collecting facts**.

EXPERIMENT

THEORY

COLLECTING FACTS

☐ The Copernican **theory** was supported by Bruno (1548–1600) and Galileo (1564–1642); both were persecuted by the Church.

INDUCTIVE LOGIC

☐ Bacon argued **inductively** from the particular to the general: e.g. Birds, dogs, men … all die. Therefore, all living things die.

☐ Isaac Newton (1642–1727) did much to demonstrate that good science is based on **mathematics**. His theory of Universal Gravitation achieved the status of **law**.

MATHEMATICS

LAW

J–B Lamarck (1744–1829) put forward a theory that species change over time as they use organs or they become disused.

☐ Charles Darwin's (1809–82) rival Theory of Evolution was the result of painstaking observation and **research**.

RESEARCH

VERIFICATION

☐ The Vienna Circle of the 1920s argued that meaningful propositions must be **verifiable** sensically.

☐ Karl Popper (1902–95) argued against Induction. Deduction yields logical certainty, Induction only **probability**. We cannot verify the theory that all swans are white, but we did falsify it – with certainty – when we saw a black swan. Empiricism calls not for verification, but for **falsification**.

PROBABILITY

FALSIFICATION

HYPOTHESIS

☐ Peter Medawar (1915–) called this the Hypothetico-Deductive Method. We guess at a **hypothesis**, deduce consequences, and compare these with our observations.

☐ Thomas Kuhn (1922–) claimed that we do not guess at hypotheses. We work within an established **paradigm**, or 'norm'. Normal science conditions theory. A revolution, or 'paradigm shift' occurs when an old paradigm ceases to explain phenomena and is replaced by a new one, that has a 'closer fit to nature'.

PARADIGM

1 Devise a syllogism of your own whose conclusion is certain.

2 Identify one or more 'paradigm shifts' in the above account.

3 Use the terms in capitals above to make a flow-diagram of the 'logic' of a scientific discovery.

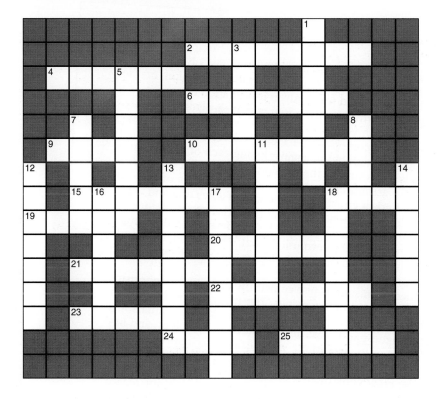

Part Two
Scientific Terms

The crossword below has spaces for twenty-six words. Choose the appropriate terms from the list of fifty-two words alongside the crossword, by reference to the clues below.

1 ACID	27 MEMBRANE
2 ALKALI	28 METAL
3 AMINO	29 MITOSIS
4 ATOM	30 MOLECULE
5 BACTERIA	31 NEON
6 CARBON	32 NEUTRON
7 CATALYST	33 NODE
8 CELL	34 NUCLEUS
9 COMPOUND	35 OZONE
10 CRYSTAL	36 PLASMA
11 ELECTRON	37 POLYMER
12 ELEMENT	38 POSITRON
13 ENERGY	39 PROTON
14 ENTROPY	40 QUANTA
15 ESTER	41 RADON
16 FISSION	42 SODIUM
17 GENE	43 SOLID
18 GERM	44 SULPHUR
19 HALOGEN	45 TITRATE
20 HORMONE	46 URANIUM
21 HYDROGEN	47 VALENCY
22 ISOTOPE	48 VALVE
23 KINETIC	49 VIRUS
24 LATENT	50 VITAMIN
25 LIPID	51 VOLT
26 MASS	52 WAVE

Clues Across

2 Substance made up of a number of resolvable parts, or elements.
4 Naturally fixed minimum amounts of energy emitted.
6 Measure of energy unavailable for purpose of doing work.
9 Unit of electromotive force.
10 Smallest particle of substance retaining properties of the substance.
15 One of a set of chemically identical species of atom.
18 Unit-mass of organic matter.
19 Radioactive yet unreactive, noble yet inert gas.
20 Capacity of a material body to perform work.
21 Energy possessed by a body in virtue of its motion.
22 Measurement of strength of a solution by adding one of known strength.
23 Pertaining to a derivative of ammonia.
24 A gas used in lighting.
25 Natural or mechanical regulator of flow or passage.

Clues Down

1 Yellow, non-metallic element.
3 Opaque elementary substance having readiness to form positive ions.
5 An uncharged fundamental particle.
7 Neither liquid nor gas.
8 Unit of DNA responsible for the transmission of specific characteristics.
11 Substance irreducible to a simpler substance.
12 Secretion bringing about some physiological action.
13 Electron having a positive charge.
14 Basic compound highly soluble in water.
16 Silver-white metallic element.
17 Indivisible unit of negative electricity.
18 Solid having certain molecular structure and faceted surface.

Part Three
Humane Science

The scientist who considers himself absolutely 'objective' and believes that he can free himself from the compulsion of the 'merely' subjective should try – only in imagination of course – to kill in succession a lettuce, a fly, a frog, a guinea-pig, a cat, a dog, and finally a chimpanzee. He will then be aware how increasingly difficult murder becomes as the victim's level of organization rises. The degree of inhibition against killing each of these beings is a very precise measure for the considerably different values that we cannot help attributing to lower and higher forms of life. To any man who finds it equally easy to chop up a live dog and a live lettuce I would recommend suicide at his earliest convenience!

The principle that science should be indifferent to values must not lead to the belief that evolution, that most wonderful of all chains of naturally explicable processes, is not capable of creating new values ....

A sentimental misanthropist coined the often-cited aphorism: 'The more I see of human beings, the more I like animals.' I maintain the contrary: only the person who knows animals, including the highest and most nearly related to ourselves, and has gained insight into evolution, will be able to apprehend the unique position of man. We are the highest achievement reached so far by the great constructors of evolution. We are their 'latest' but certainly not their last word. The scientist must not regard anything as absolute, not even the laws of pure reason. He must remain aware of the great fact, discovered by Heraclitus, that nothing whatever really remains the same even for one moment, but that everything is perpetually changing. To regard man, the most ephemeral and rapidly evolving of all species, as the final and unsurpassable achievement of creation, especially at his present particularly dangerous and disagreeable stage of development, is certainly the most arrogant and dangerous of all untenable doctrines. If I thought of man as the final image of God, I should not know what to think of God. But when I consider that our ancestors, at a time fairly recent in relation to the earth's history, were perfectly ordinary apes, closely related to chimpanzees, I see a glimmer of hope.

5

10

15

20

25

30

35

(Konrad Lorenz, *On Aggression*, 1966)

1 Find words in the text that have similar meanings to the following:
   (a) transient;
   (b) ultimate;
   (c) impartial;
   (d) specious.
2 What do you understand Lorenz to mean by an organism's 'level of organization'?
3 Is it a valid test of objectivity that Lorenz proposes in the first paragraph? On what grounds do you agree, or disagree that it is?
4 What do you think Lorenz means when he calls the author of the aphorism 'sentimental', and a 'misanthropist'? (line 16)
5 Is Lorenz justified, in your view, in suggesting that *nothing* is absolute?

Part Four

Science and Serendipity

Serendipity means discovery by happy chance. Do scientists make their discoveries only after years of patient trial and error; are they the result of sudden illumination; or do they happen upon them by chance? Use any or all of the following quotations as a basis for a response to this instruction: **Assess the contributions of sheer hard work, and of inspiration, to the advancement of science**.

1
Often when one works at a hard question, nothing good is accomplished at the first attack. Then one takes a rest, longer or shorter, and sits down anew to the work. During the first half-hour, as before, nothing is found, and then all of a sudden the decisive idea presents itself to the mind .... This unconscious work is possible, and of a certainty it is only fruitful, if it is on the one hand preceded and on the other followed by a period of conscious work. These sudden inspirations never happen except after some days of voluntary effort which has appeared absolutely fruitless.

(Henri Poincaré, *Mathematical Creation*, 1913)

2
At the time when Pavlov was chiefly engaged in the study of digestion he would take an active part in the experiments himself. Most of the vivisection experiments were performed personally by him. In experiments on aseptically-operated animals which were subjected to long periods of observation, Pavlov would have his co-workers watch the animals. Pavlov simply could not bring himself to watch or carry on any procedure lasting a long time without any apparent results.

(G.V. Anrep, the Obituary of Ivan Pavlov, 1936)

3
Curiosity is not a product of innocence, but is a state which our minds constantly seek to achieve. We are at all times sorting and re-sorting our sense-impressions, other data, and our ideas about them and testing them all against each other. Perversely we hope not only for unexpected felicities, the fitting together of mental jig-saws, but also for unexpected discords. Either may lead us forward.

(D.R. Newth, 'On Scientific Method', 1964)

4
At first there were so very few who believed in the existence of bodies smaller than atoms. I was even told long afterward by a distinguished physicist who had been present at my lecture at the Royal Institution that he thought I had been 'pulling their legs'. I was not surprised at this, as I had myself come to this explanation of my experiments with great reluctance, and it was only after I was convinced that the experiment left no escape from it that I published my belief in the existence of bodies smaller than atoms.

(J.J. Thomson, *Recollections and Reflections*, 1936)

5
Dalton was a man of regular habits. For 57 years he walked out of Manchester every day; he measured the rainfall, the temperature – a singularly monotonous enterprise in this climate. Of all that mass of data, nothing whatever came. But of the one searching, almost childlike question about the weights that enter the construction of these simple molecules – out of that came modern atomic theory. That is the essence of science: ask an impertinent question, and you are on your way to the pertinent answer.

(Jacob Bronowski, *The Ascent of Man*, 1973)

6
In analysing the part that chance plays in science, one can distinguish three different types of discovery in which it is the vital factor: an intuition from random juxtaposition of ideas, a eureka intuition, and serendipity. The origin of the first is entirely mental, the second arises from interaction of mental activity with the external world, the third is found externally without an active mental contribution.

(W.I.B. Beveridge, *Seeds of Discovery*, 1980)

Part Five
The Drift from Science

Politicians worry that we produce too few scientists and engineers. Make use of any combination of the following views to write an essay in answer to this question: **Why does it prove so difficult to attract young people to careers in science and engineering?**

1   Scientists and engineers don't have a very wonderful image among young people. Say 'chemist' to them, and they think of a rather unkempt, other-worldly, bespectacled boffin in an ancient Austin. And engineers are people who wear soiled overalls and have oil on their hands.

2   Science and technology are bound to be harder than Arts subjects. There's a lot of information to be learnt, and a certain level of mathematical understanding to be reached, before you get to the really exciting bits.

3   Specialization at 16+ or even earlier, has a lot to do with it. If all 16–19 year olds had to take science and maths to gain a university place, more would go on to study science or engineering at degree level.

4   Women have been put off entering science and engineering. They're perceived to be 'masculine' subjects, to do with machines. Girls are by nature more interested in people than in things.

5   It begins in the maths classes. The language of maths is one few children really learn with confidence. They learn what works – what gets the right answers – but not how or why. And there's no reinforcement in society. Famous people say: 'Oh! I couldn't do maths.' They don't say: 'I never learned to read and write.'

6   Science teachers themselves are to blame. The young women who train as primary teachers are very likely refugees from science themselves. They simply haven't the confidence to teach it. On the other hand, good scientists who do teach don't necessarily make very good teachers – they aren't on their pupils' wavelength.

7   It's our culture; we tend to glorify achievements in the arts more than in the sciences. Look at the arts festivals, and all the space given to the media *in* the media. When did you last see a fuss made about a congress of scientists – or even about a Nobel prize-winner? Look at all the publicity given to the Booker Prize, BAFTA awards and Oscars. Science just isn't sexy.

8   There simply aren't the jobs in science and engineering; and those that there are don't carry huge salaries. The high flyers can see where the money is: it's in the City and the board-rooms – not in science labs or workshops. The Government won't fund basic research. And we wonder why there's a brain-drain to countries that do.

ITEM

Classical Allusions

There are many phrases in English that allude to the gods and heroes of classical mythology, and to historical figures.
Complete the following sentences by filling in the appropriate phrase or letter from the alphabetic list of phrases below.

1
A ACHILLES HEEL
B AUGEAN STABLES
C AUGUSTAN AGE
D BACCHANALIAN ORGY
E DAMOCLEAN SWORD
F GOLDEN FLEECE
G GORDIAN KNOT
H HERCULEAN TASK
I HERMETIC BOOKS
J HIPPOCRATIC OATH
K HOMERIC LAUGHTER
L MARTIAL LAW
M MIDAS TOUCH
N OEDIPUS COMPLEX
O OLYMPIAN DISDAIN
P PANDORA'S BOX
Q PARTHIAN SHOT
R PLATONIC LOVE
S PROCRUSTEAN BED
T PROTEAN SHAPE
U PYRRHIC VICTORY
V SPARTAN DIET
W STYGIAN GLOOM
X TITANIC STRUGGLE
Y TROJAN HORSE
Z VENEREAL DISEASE

1 Lucky man, he had the _____ in business affairs.
2 Had I known it was such a _____ I wouldn't have volunteered.
3 It opened up a _____ of misfortunes.
4 All entertainment ceased when _____ was imposed.
5 Greed was my _____. It brought an end to my career.
6 Theirs was a _____, soul to soul.
7 They dismissed them all; made a clean sweep of the _____.
8 His _____ was what alienated his father.
9 The celebration degenerated into a veritable _____.
10 He died from _____; syphilis I think.
11 The threat hung over him like a _____.
12 His _____ was a devastating piece of sarcasm.
13 The contents of the _____ remained shrouded in mystery.
14 I am bound by the _____ to do all I can to save her.
15 The _____ was magnificent in its cultural self-confidence.
16 Imagine the _____ between two such heavy-weight boxers.
17 It was a holy grail, a _____ that had to be procured.
18 They rowed in the _____ of a night mist.
19 It was a _____ of a gift: apparently a promise, in fact a threat.
20 When drunk, he gave way to _____, loud and unstoppable.
21 I've been on a _____ since Christmas, to keep in trim.
22 They viewed their lowly fellow countrymen with _____.
23 He seemed to be able to adopt one _____ after another.
24 It was a _____, costly in men and munitions.
25 The test was a _____ for all, irrespective of their abilities.
26 At last I have solved it. I have cut the _____.

Again, complete the sentences with the appropriate word or letter. This time, the adjectives are single words which derive from classical sources.

2
A CEREAL
B DELPHIC
C EROTIC
D JOVIAL
E LUNATIC
F MERCURIAL
G ORPHIC
H PANIC
I SATURNINE
J VESTAL

1 Faced with such opposition, the Government took _____ measures.
2 He is given to _____ behaviour in almost monthly cycles.
3 At Christmas, he is at his most _____ and generous.
4 It is a region known for the quality of its _____ produce.
5 The music was _____ in its mystery and enchantment.
6 Later representations of Aphrodite are _____ and voluptous.
7 She was a _____ virgin to the end of her chaste days.
8 He fixed his audience with a glowering _____ expression.
9 He had an energy that was positively _____.
10 His utterances were _____ in their obscure profundity.

Part One
Stratification

What characteristics determine the 'stratum' or social class to which people have been, or continue to be, assigned? Government officials, market researchers, and social scientists (male or female) have given many different answers to this question.

Karl Marx (1818–83) divided society into two groups:
1 **the bourgeoisie** – owners of land or machinery;
2 **the proletariat** – owners only of their own labour.

Max Weber (1864–1920) believed this was too simple: he divided society into four classes:
1 **upper class**
2 **petit bourgeoisie**
3 **middle class**
4 **working class**

Weber recognized the importance of the large and growing, 'propertyless', white-collar middle class. Since Weber's time there have been further attempts to refine the structure of the social classes, and five of these are illustrated below.

Social class in the UK has been associated, since 1921, with occupation – that of the 'head of the household'. This includes neither the 'idle' rich, nor the unemployed 'poor'. Market researchers, therefore, added

a Class E. John Goldthorpe's scale is widely used by academics, but is not without its critics. Feminist sociologists at Surrey University, for instance, argued that the 'head of the household' criterion is outdated in a world of single-parent and dual-career households, and of widespread female employment. Hence the SOCS.

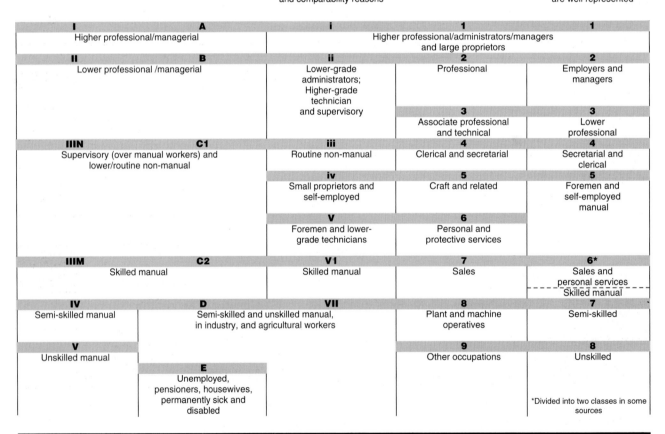

REGISTRAR GENERAL'S SCALE (RGS) – 1921 (with revisions)		SOCIAL GRADING SCALE (SGS) – used in market research	HOPE-GOLDTHORPE SCALE (HGS) – developed for the Oxford Social Mobility Enquiry (1972); excluded women for historical and comparability reasons	STANDARD OCCUPATIONAL CLASSIFICATION (SOC) – replacing the RGS for official purposes	SURREY OCCUPATIONAL CLASS SCALE (SOCS) – (1986) including women and discriminating more finely in occupations where women are well represented
I Higher professional/managerial		**A**	**i** Higher professional/administrators/managers and large proprietors	**1**	**1**
II Lower professional /managerial		**B**	**ii** Lower-grade administrators; Higher-grade technician and supervisory	**2** Professional	**2** Employers and managers
				3 Associate professional and technical	**3** Lower professional
IIIN Supervisory (over manual workers) and lower/routine non-manual		**C1**	**iii** Routine non-manual	**4** Clerical and secretarial	**4** Secretarial and clerical
			iv Small proprietors and self-employed	**5** Craft and related	**5** Foremen and self-employed manual
			v Foremen and lower-grade technicians	**6** Personal and protective services	
IIIM Skilled manual		**C2**	**VI** Skilled manual	**7** Sales	**6*** Sales and personal services / Skilled manual
IV Semi-skilled manual	**D** Semi-skilled and unskilled manual, in industry, and agricultural workers		**VII**	**8** Plant and machine operatives	**7** Semi-skilled
V Unskilled manual				**9** Other occupations	**8** Unskilled
	E Unemployed, pensioners, housewives, permanently sick and disabled				*Divided into two classes in some sources

To which numbered, or lettered, class would you assign the following occupations on the accompanying scales?

1 Typing/word-processing worker   **(a)** RGS   **(b)** SOCS
2 Unemployed hospital porter   **(a)** SGS   **(b)** SOC
3 Librarian in a public library   **(a)** HGS   **(b)** SOC
4 Architect in private practice   **(a)** RGS   **(b)** SOCS
5 Assembly-line worker   **(a)** HGS   **(b)** SOC
6 Self-employed technician   **(a)** SGS   **(b)** SOCS

Part Two
Schooling and Sifting

Do schools create a certain sort of society, or does society create schools in its own image? What is the relationship between schooling and occupational status?

Marxist sociologists tend to look for equalizing changes in society as a *precondition* for bringing about equality of opportunity in schools, and *equality of outcome*.

Liberals are more optimistic that equality of social and economic opportunity can be promoted by *reform*

of the school system. They do not look for equality of outcome.

Functionalists tend to accept that the system does what it sets out to do: it sorts people according to their abilities, actual and potential.

Interactionists focus on relationships

at the level of the classroom, and on the influence of the 'hidden curriculum'.

There have been three social, political and economic 'ideologies' dominant at different times since the Second World War, and each has had its effects on the workings of the school system.

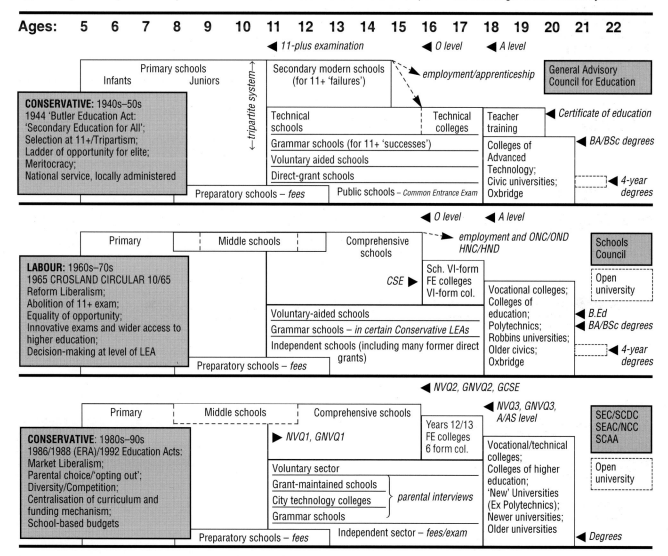

Ages: 5 6 7 8 9 10 11 12 13 14 15 16 17 18 19 20 21 22

A   **Summarize the principal differences between the education policies of the 'left wing' and 'right wing' in British politics.**

B   **Which institution was intended ...?**

1   In the post-war period, for boys 'good with their hands'.
2   To give power to parents at the expense of local education authorities.
3   As 'beacons', examples of 'academic excellence' for all schools to follow.
4   To supply a 'practical', locally-accountable higher education.
5   As schools for all 11–16 year olds, irrespective of their ability.
6   To sift children into 'academic' and 'vocational' education.

A   City technical colleges
B   Comprehensives
C   Eleven plus
D   Opting out
E   Polytechnics
F   Technical schools

Part Three
Homelessness

This is the most basic of housing problems. When restricted to few people it has raised scarcely a whisper of public concern. At other times it has been masked, at least temporarily, by living with in-laws, sharing, or greater multi-occupation. When many people are affected, however, and have demonstrated, then the seismograph of political representation has registered the subterranean rumblings. In 1945 and 1946, for example, the housing shortage was sharply brought to the Government's attention by the large-scale squatting in empty properties. Thereafter, throughout the late 1940s and 1950s such protest was rare. It surfaced again in the late 1960s when the continuing problem of finding decent affordable accommodation in central London was partially overcome by some households who squatted in empty properties. This protest was incorporated by most London boroughs, who handed empty property over to squatters' groups; it presented a solution to long housing waiting lists and the embarrassment of holding empty derelict property. From the 1970s the protest of the squatters worked hand in hand, in London at least, with the local authorities. The most successful housing protest did not involve demonstrations in the street; it was a television drama. In 1966 the BBC showed a powerful drama called *Cathy Come Home* written by Jeremy Sandford about the problems of one family who had been made homeless and their tribulations in seeking temporary accommodation. The impact was enormous. Arthur Greenwood, the housing minister of the time, ordered a private showing for all his officials. More important, the housing ginger-group Shelter was established. The atmosphere of public discussion concerning *Cathy Come Home* gave Shelter a tremendous boost. And what could have turned out to be just another ephemeral association was transformed into an important pressure group which has been an important voice in subsequent debate.

The problem of homelessness has been bedevilled by the lack of muscle of the victims. Homeless households represent a failure but not a threat. The homelessness issue has also been bedevilled by the stigmatization of the victims. At worst they are portrayed as scroungers, queue-jumpers, outsiders or, at middling, as inadequates unable to organize their lives properly. From this perspective, their problem is seen in terms of personal inadequacy rather than a malfunctioning of the housing market; like the poor (and the rich) the homeless will therefore always be with us.

(John R. Short, *Housing in Britain: The Post-War Experience*, 1982)

1 Explain, in words or phrases of your own, what is meant, in the context of this passage, by:
   (a) 'incorporated'; (line 12-13)
   (b) 'derelict'; (line 15)
   (c) 'ephemeral'; (line 26)
   (d) 'stigmatization'. (line 31-2)
2 What is the combined effect of Short's reference to a 'seismograph', and to 'subterranean rumblings'? (lines 5 and 6)
3 What would you say the difference is between a 'ginger-group' and a 'pressure group'? (lines 24 and 27)
4 In what ways does the writer make it clear that he sees the homelessness problem as a struggle for power between the homeless and the authorities?
5 Is the author sincere in his view that the homeless will 'always be with us'? (lines 36–7)
6 To what extent is squatting a solution to the problem of homelessness, in your opinion?

Part Four
Equal Opportunities

Both Margaret Thatcher and John Major had modest origins: the latter rashly looked forward to a 'classless society'. The quotations below may suggest approaches to the following question: **A meritocratic society is one in which it is ability that makes for success – where the higher reaches are open to anyone with talent. Is Britain a meritocracy, in your view?**

1
The economic expansion which has been a major factor in the growth of the service class has made it possible, through rising real incomes and living standards, for a widespread sense of social advancement to be experienced even where at the same time a basic immobility of class position is recognized.

(John H. Goldthorpe, *Social Mobility and Class Structure in Modern Britain*, 1980)

2
Racism doesn't exactly help you feel secure as a person. I've been followed by the police and I don't look your sort of heavy dread guy. I've had the police follow me in a car all the way up Roundhay Road at ten o'clock at night, just cruising by the side of me not saying a word. It was really eerie and I just carried on walking, because I knew that if I stopped or jumped over a wall or something they'd have got me and there'd have been no witnesses.

(Charles Husband, *Race in Britain*, 1982)

3
Even the Equal Pay Act (1970) and the Sex Discrimination Act (1975), which appear to be women-centred policies, assume that the struggle for equality is an individual one waged by women who are able to perceive discrimination and bring a formal charge; which, if they win, affects only them and not the category of women or female employees to which they belong. Policies are conceived, directed and implemented by men.

(Carol Buswell, *Women in Contemporary Society*, 1989)

4
Black girls were not only impeded by teachers' assessments of their abilities, but their decision making was fundamentally influenced by the poverty of advice and information they received about job opportunities. Primarily because they were not given the opportunity to explore possibilities, young black women often chose their careers from a limited range of occupations, depending on their own knowledge and existing experience of the labour market.

(Heidi Safia Mirza, *Young, Female and Black*, 1992)

5
There are frequent complaints about Parliament's social unrepresentativeness, particularly its male and upper- and middle-class character .... A study of political and economic leaders in eighteen various sectors found that half had been educated at public schools and Oxbridge. Similar selectivity is seen among senior army officers, judges, bishops in the Church of England, and directors of the Bank of England and the 'Big Four' clearing banks.

(Dennis Kavanagh, *British Politics: Continuities and Change*, 2nd edn, 1990)

6
Both men and women believe that work is less important for women than for men and that men should have higher wages and more secure employment because of their role of supporting the family. Men are seen as 'bread-winners' whereas women are seen as domestic carers. ... [However] it would be quite possible for men and women to be seen equally as responsible for the economic support of the household and for the necessary domestic labour and child care.

(Pamela Abbott and Claire Wallace, *An Introduction to Sociology: Feminist Perspectives*, 1990)

7
The law passed in 1944 which said that 3 per cent of jobs in larger organizations should go to disabled people has been a dismal failure: the average today ranges from 0.7 per cent in the South-East to 1.5 per cent in Yorkshire. Schools and colleges, public places, transport systems, even health and welfare services continue to exclude, segregate and diminish disabled people, often forcing them into poverty and dependence.

(Craig Donnellan, *Disabilities and Discrimination*, 1992)

8
The vast majority of people agree that women should have the same participation opportunities as men, but few are willing to make the changes needed to bring about equity. They say that equity is great as long as women don't want to wrestle or do other 'unladylike' sports, as long as women don't want to play on men's teams, as long as we won't need to make any changes in opportunities available for men ...

(Jay J. Coakley, *Sport in Society: Issues and Controversies*, 5th edn, 1994)

Part One
Depraved or Deprived?

Are criminals born or made? Are young criminals, in particular, more sinned against than sinning? Refer to any of the opinions below to write an essay with this title: **Comment on the view that young offenders are criminals by intent, and that the answer to persistent offending is a prison term.**

1   The criminal chooses to commit crime. Most people – even most young males on council estates – *don't* make this choice. Each of us has an individual will, and a responsibility to choose. It's something of an insult to the majority of responsible individuals to suggest that they are merely the product of their environment and upbringing.

2   It can hardly be a coincidence that the vast majority of young offenders are from disadvantaged backgrounds. They're neglected at home, and they fail at school. They only 'succeed' as bullies, as joy-riders, or as petty thieves. Their peers in similar circumstances affirm their behaviour and give them respect that they receive from no-one else.

3   It's absurd to suggest that unemployment is to blame for inner-city crime. The unemployment of the 1930s didn't give rise to the sort of crime we see on our streets today; and there wasn't the safety-net of housing benefit and re-training programmes and what have you, that soften – and shorten – the blow of unemployment today.

4   There is some doubt about whether juvenile crime has increased and whether there is a distinguishable class of 'persistent young offenders'. More cars mean more car-crime; new laws mean more criminals; more efficient policing methods mean more convictions – and more places in secure units will mean there will be more young males sentenced to occupy them.

5   We're all aware that there has been a breakdown of social cohesion with the decline of the family, and the erosion of authority. I don't regret the 'death of God', but the ebbing of respect for all authority figures – clergymen, teachers, politicians, the police – has led inevitably to a society where the peer-group is the only point of reference and object of loyalty.

6   Persistent young offenders, more often than not, are the products of violent, perhaps abusing homes, or they have spent their formative years in care. They may well have been mistreated in local authority institutions. You can't love other people unless, and until, you've been loved yourself. Criminal behaviour is attention-seeking – a cry from the heart.

7   Non-custodial sentences are fine when they work – but we owe it to the actual and potential victims of theft, burglary, and vandalism, to send the right messages, of disapproval and deterrence – but also to give them intensive job-training. There is simply no feasible alternative to prison.

8   Locking a lot of young tearaways up together is Dickensian. Prisons are finishing schools for criminals: they learn the tricks of the trade, they make contacts – and they're brutalized into the bargain. A majority re-offend, and qualify for adult prison sentences. At £2,000 per inmate per week, sending them to prison is an extremely expensive way of demonstrating our failure.

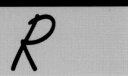

French: Text and multiple-choice questions in French

There is no doubt about it: this is the exercise in French that most candidates find difficult. However, the meanings of potential answers can quite easily be informed by reference to the text, and the language used is unlikely to be at a particularly difficult level. Here is part of a newspaper story about a mix-up at a Paris airport. Four alternative answers are offered and translations are provided.

> C'est une drôle d'affaire, ce que s'est passé dimanche soir à l'aéroport d'Orly-Ouest. Les passagers du vol Marseille-Bordeaux étaient déjà dans la salle d'embarquement. L'avion d'Air Inter était sur la piste, et les pilotes se disposaient à lancer les moteurs. L'heure du décollage a sonné mais rien n'a bougé. Un haut-parleur 5 a annoncé aux voyageurs que leur vol était annulé; qu'il leur fallait attendre le suivant. Puis, tout le monde a vu l'avion s'envoler, vide.
>
> Les pilotes d'Air Inter recoivent la consigne, comme tous les membres du Syndicat National des Pilotes de Ligne (SNPL); c'est à la police de fouiller les bagages à main et les passagers, et 10 les pilotes ont le droit de refuser de décoller en cas de défaut. C'est une question importante de sécurité. Bien sûr, dans la pratique, le refus de vol est extrêmement rare. Normalement, les pilotes ne sont pas 'militants'; de plus, ils sont tout à fait conscients que le moindre retard au décollage entraîne des perturbations sérieuses 15 dans la rotation des avions sur la ligne ....

1 Cette affaire s'est passé:
A au bureau d'Air Inter.
B à l'aeroport d'Orly-Ouest.
C de Marseille à Bordeaux.
D dans la salle d'embarquement.

This affair happened:
– at Air Inter's office.
– at Orly-West airport.
– en route from Marseille to Bordeaux.
– in the departure lounge.

2 Au moment de l'annonce, les passagers étaient:
A en Douane.
B a l'enregistrement.
C dans la salle d'embarquement.
D dans l'avion, sur la piste.

At the time of the announcement, the passengers were:
– passing through customs.
– at the baggage check-in.
– in the departure lounge.
– in the aeroplane, on the runway.

3 Les passagers ont entendu un annonce qui leur a dit que/qu':
A l'avion était au point de décoller.
B il n'y aurait plus de vols ce soir-là.
C l'avion allait décoller vide.
D il faudrait attendre le vol suivant.

The passengers heard an announcement telling them that:
– the plane was about to take off.
– there would be no more flights that evening.
– the aeroplane was going to take off empty.
– they would have to await the next flight.

4 'Fouiller' les bagages, c'est-à-dire:
A faire des recherches de valises.
B ouvrir les sacs à main.
C mettre les bagages à bord.
D fermer les bagages sûrement.

'Fouiller' the luggage means:
– search the cases.
– open hand-bags.
– take the luggage aboard.
– shut the bags securely.

5 Les pilotes peuvent refuser de décoller:
A en cas de non-fouille.
B quand ils ont le droit.
C quand il y a des perturbations sérieuses.
D si leurs collègues ne sont pas membres du SNPL.

Pilots can refuse to take off:
– when no search is conducted.
– when they have the right.
– when there are serious disturbances.
– when colleagues aren't members of the SNPL.

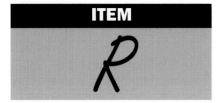

ITEM

Here is another section of the same passage, together with five more questions, this time without translation:

On se souvient de la crise de 'hijacking', pendant les années soixante-dix. Depuis ce terrorisme international, les contrôles de sécurité (portail magnétique, fouille personnelle en cabine) sont pratiqués sur tous les vols internationaux, et sur les lignes intérieures, elles aussi. Les salles d'embarquement sont équipées de ses installations dans tous les aéroports de Paris, et d'autre part. Mais en période de pointe (au début des grandes vacances, par exemple, et à Noël), la police a été incapable d'assurer tous les contrôles.

Dans cette circonstance, la police a eu recours à proposer aux compagnies un liste arbitraire des vols à contrôler – 40 pour cent, disons, des vols à courte distance. Les commandants de bord des avions non-fouillés sont partis (d'habitude satisfaits) avec un 'certificat de non-fouille', fourni par la police pour dégager leur responsabilité en cas de problème. Dimanche soir, on n'a pas pris cette mesure.

6 On est conscient de la sécurité depuis:
  A la fouille routinière des passagers.
  B le décollage des vols vides.
  C le terrorisme des années soixante-dix.
  D l'installation des portails métalliques.

7 Les portails métalliques se trouvent:
  A dans la cabine d'avion.
  B aux aéroports de Paris seulement.
  C à l'embarquement pour les vols internationaux.
  D dans tous les aéroports commerciaux.

8 Une 'période de pointe' est:
  A quand on est en vacances.
  B une fête annuelle chrétienne.
  C heures de presse et de voyage.
  D les premières heures tranquilles du matin.

9 Quand la police ne peut pas assurer tous les contrôles:
  A elle contrôle un pourcentage des vols.
  B les compagnies fouillent les passagers sans problème.
  C 40 pour cent des vols partent vides.
  D les commandants de bord sont bien satisfaits.

10 Le 'certificat de non-fouille':
  A est une admission de responsabilité du part de la police.
  B accorde la responsabilité aux compagnies.
  C provoque des problèmes pour les pilotes du Syndicat.
  D est une solution qui satisfait tout le monde.

Part One

Recreation in Retrospect

Sport in Britain has always been an affair of class: the upper class hunted on horseback, and the peasants baited on foot or played rough games without rules. It was only when the working class won weekends and brief holidays that sport was organized, urbanized and commercialized in the ways we know it.

	Upper Class	Lower Class
1000s	Jousting, Hawking	Stool-ball, Ninepins, Handball
	Deer-hunting, Archery, **Horse-riding**	Football Cock-fighting
		All played according to local rules or none at all
1100s	**Golf** (Scotland)	
1200s	Croquet (France), Billiards	
	Court **Tennis**, Bowling	Fist-fighting Badger-baiting
1300s		
1400s		
1500s	Henry VII played both Tennis and Bowling	
1552	**Golf** – St Andrews course laid out	
1600	Shooting, Fox-hunting	
	Puritans banned sports and games as tending to ungodliness	
1660s	Charles II patron of Newmarket – **Horse-racing**	
1700s	Cricket (Kent)	Prize-fighting Cock-fighting
	Gambling was the chief motive for engaging in sport in the 1700s. In theory, gambling was restricted among the upper class, and prohibited among the lower class – but all indulged	
1719	Duke of Cumberland patron of prize-fighter Jack Broughton at Figg's Amphitheatre London	
1728	**Cricket** (Kent vs. Surrey)	Hare-coursing
1743		Jack Broughton's rules for **Boxing** devised
		Dog-fighting
1744	**Golf** rules devised **Cricket** rules devised	
1750	**Horse-racing** rules (Jockey Club established)	
	Sports were regarded by churchmen as an idle pastime; yet public schools began to see the value of team-games to foster discipline, and 'muscular Christianity'	
1800s	The public schools began to play their own versions of **Football**	
1817	First track and field athletics meet at Necton, Norfolk	
1828	William Webb Ellis picks up soccer ball and runs with it	
		Birth of **Rugby Football**
		First law to protect animals
1835		Prize-fighting banned Cock-fighting banned
1844		First day-excursion train from London to Brighton
1847		Ten Hours Bill
1850		Half-day Saturday established by law in textile industry
		'La Semaine Anglaise' soon spread to other industries
1860	**Golf** Open Championship, Prestwick	
1863		**Football** Association established
1864	First Varsity Athletics Match	
1871		**Rugby** Union established
		Bank Holiday Act defines 'Saint Mondays' as holidays
1870s		Big railway companies give week's holiday with pay
1873	First County Championship **Cricket**	
1877		Lawn **Tennis** Association established
1878		Bicycle Tourists Club established
1885		**Football** League established
1886		Queensbury Rules introduced for boxing
1914		**Football** League now dominated by professional clubs
1920s	Eight-hour day achieved at work	
1938	Holidays with Pay Act (brought into effect after the Second World War)	

Some open questions

1 What are the main differences between 'upper-class' and 'lower-class' sports?

2 What changes did the coming of the railways make to sport and leisure?

3 What was the role of women and girls in any of the above pastimes?

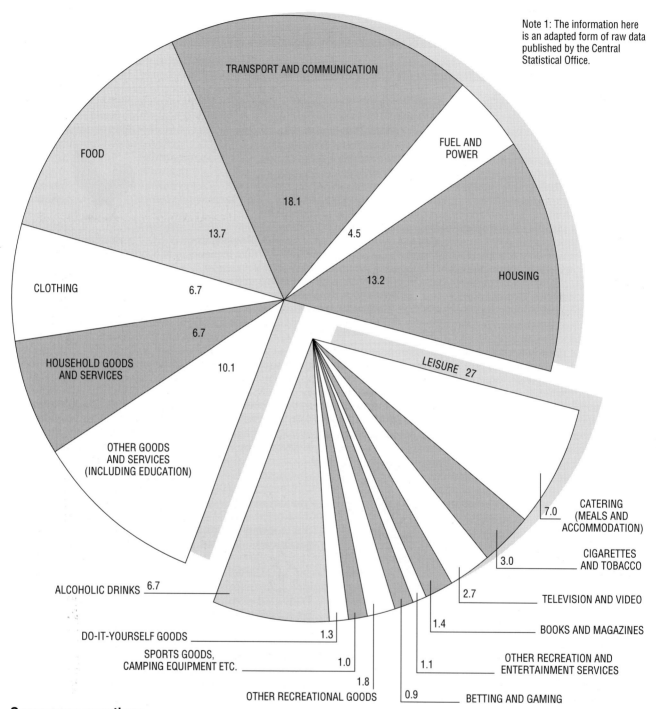

Part Two

Patterns of Leisure

The pie-chart below represents consumer expenditure. The mean averages of expenditures over ten years, under each of eight function heads, are expressed here as percentages of total expenditure at constant market prices. The 'Leisure' function is subdivided into ten more-or-less distinguishable items.

Note 1: The information here is an adapted form of raw data published by the Central Statistical Office.

TRANSPORT AND COMMUNICATION

FOOD

FUEL AND POWER

18.1

13.7

4.5

13.2

CLOTHING   6.7

HOUSING

6.7

HOUSEHOLD GOODS AND SERVICES

10.1

LEISURE 27

OTHER GOODS AND SERVICES (INCLUDING EDUCATION)

CATERING (MEALS AND ACCOMMODATION)   7.0

CIGARETTES AND TOBACCO   3.0

TELEVISION AND VIDEO   2.7

BOOKS AND MAGAZINES   1.4

ALCOHOLIC DRINKS   6.7

OTHER RECREATION AND ENTERTAINMENT SERVICES   1.1

DO-IT-YOURSELF GOODS   1.3

SPORTS GOODS, CAMPING EQUIPMENT ETC.   1.0

BETTING AND GAMING   0.9

OTHER RECREATIONAL GOODS   1.8

Some open questions

1 What expenditures included under non-leisure items in the diagram may, in fact, be expenditure on leisure items?
2 What items may feature under the heading 'other recreation and entertainment services', do you suppose?
3 Should all alcoholic drinks be regarded as 'leisure items' in your view?
4 Which do you imagine are the items under the 'leisure' heading that are likely to decrease in importance, in the future, and which are likely to grow?

Note 2: The above diagram is not to scale. Percentages are rounded to one place of decimals, and therefore do not add up to one hundred.

Part Three

Mass Entertainment

Sport (like religion) was a great social tranquillizer in the growing industrial towns. Churches and firms encouraged it, playing-fields were laid out, and games were scheduled on 'holy days'. The next phase in the sociology of sport took place in the 1920s and 1930s, between the World Wars.

Sport was a booming leisure activity, with two totally new evening sports being created in the inter-war period, greyhound racing – the first track opened in Belle Vue, Manchester in 1926 – and Speedway racing. Older sports achieved their definitive shape as forms of mass entertainment, including association football, cricket, boxing, motor racing, tennis, with their local and national celebrities. Football was still essentially a proletarian game, without the veneer of commercialism that was to develop after the Second World War. Though professionals, the players were still recognizably similar to the average working man, with wages which were pegged at a level near to those of skilled workmen. To many the advent of the football pools had added a distasteful aspect of gambling to the game. Similarly confined to a largely proletarian background was boxing. The inter-war period has been called the 'brutal hey-day of boxing'. More than football, it was a 'rags to riches' sport in an era which had no dearth of hungry fighters. The world of boxing was riddled with abuses until the Boxing Board of Control began to regulate the sport after 1934. Motor racing and tennis were largely middle-class sports, the former deriving great impetus from the ever-widening circles of car-ownership, whilst the latter offered one of the few areas in which female sporting stars could emerge. All of these sports saw a considerable rise in attendances. Cup finals, title fights, large race meetings and Wimbledon were becoming part of the leisure calendar for masses of the population, and at the same time big business. But the sport which left its greatest mark on the inter-war period was cricket, which was accorded a status today reserved for association football. Its personalities were national news; test matches were accorded the attention now devoted to the World Cup, and granted a much greater degree of respectability than almost any other sport. It retained a snobbish *cachet* which was evidenced in the distinction between 'gentlemen', the amateurs, and 'players', the professionals. Sport in general expanded massively in the twenties and thirties, in terms of both spectators and participants. It brought a wider range of sporting recreation to a seemingly insatiable public. As in so many other areas, the inter-war period saw in sport the birth of tendencies in leisure and recreation which were to be continued and amplified in the post-war period.

(John Stevenson, *Social Conditions in Britain between the Wars*, 1977)

1 What do the following words mean in the context of the passage?
(a) 'proletarian'; (line 7)
(b) 'dearth'; (line 15)
(c) 'impetus'; (line 18)
(d) 'insatiable'. (line 32)
2 Why is football specifically referred to as 'association football'? (line 25)
3 What does the word 'veneer' suggest about the professionalism that came later? (line 7)
4 Explain what is meant by the reference to boxing as a 'rags to riches' sport? (line 14)
5 How do we account for the emergence of the sports mentioned in the passage as 'mass entertainment' at this time? (lines 4-5)
6 Have the 'tendencies' that were born between the wars been sustained into our own time?

Part Four
Survival of the Fittest

'Mens sana in corpore sano'; a healthy mind in a healthy body. This maxim was taken to justify much school sport. Few would say that exercise is *bad* for you; if it is so good, if health makes for happiness, **is it our civic duty to keep fit?**

1

Like any machine, our bodies must be kept well-maintained. They are designed to be exercised frequently and pushed to the limits of physical endurance .... A routine programme of exercise has more than immediate pay-off because you are buying good health for possibly an additional decade at the end of your life. We do not have any proof that physical fitness automatically increases longevity, but we do know that unfit people are throwing away their chance to live a long and happy life.

(Miriam Stoppard, *Healthcare*, 1980)

2

Nearly every week some expert makes a new claim about the benefits of exercise, only to be shouted down the following week by another expert saying that it can be bad for you. In fact there is little hard scientific evidence that taking up exercise ensures any long term benefits because it is so difficult to measure or prove. Many factors such as where you work and what you eat affect your health and it is almost impossible to isolate the effects of these from the effects of exercise.

(Open University *et al.*, *The Good Health Guide*, 1980)

3

Claims about the 'protective' effects of exercise in heart disease have been simplified and exaggerated. They have led to large numbers of middle-aged adults jogging the streets. The jogging is good for them for many reasons provided they tackle it gradually but the motivation is a little suspect. Exercise should be a pleasant habit pursued for its own sake rather than as a dose of protective medicine.

(E.J. Bassey & P.H. Fentem, *Exercise: the Facts*, 1981)

4

If we swim or play badminton or visit a gym twice a week, and for some reason miss out on a session, we may (indeed we *should*) be aware of it. The more regular the exercise the more we will miss it. In the ballet world, dancers say that if they miss class for one day, they know it; if they miss for two days, their teacher knows it; if they miss for three days, the audience knows it! The body responds quickly to exercise, and equally rapidly to missing out on it.

(Derek and Julie Parker, *Do It Yourself Health*, 1982)

5

The earlier children start a balanced pattern of exercise the better. Children accustomed to regular physical training will gain greater self-confidence, and the physical and mental well-being that is induced will help them to make the most of their education and to develop into well-rounded human beings – not life-spectators hooked on hours of television each day.

(Miriam Polunin, ed., *The Health & Fitness Handbook*, 1982)

6

The best way to combat fatigue is not to conserve energy as Churchill recommended, but to get tired more often. You can encourage this healthy fatigue by swimming, riding, rowing, cycling, jogging or playing tennis and squash. But the most convenient conditioning activity of all is undoubtedly walking. This is the ideal, all-purpose exercise which requires no expensive sports equipment and can be done at any age and in virtually any place.

(Donald Norfolk, *Farewell to Fatigue*, 1985)

7

In teenagers and younger children, the greater the hours of TV watching the fatter the child. More specifically, the prevalence of adolescent obesity increases 2 per cent for each hour of television viewed daily. Also, the earlier in life TV watching begins the greater the obesity and the more profound the problem becomes in teenage years. In addition, the excess weight gain throughout life closely parallels reduced physical activity rather than increased calorie intake.

(Frank L. Katch and W.D. McArdle, *Nutrition, Weight Control, & Exercise*, 3rd edn, 1988)

8

Muscular fitness can help you cope with the demands of your job. It can improve your performance in an activity or sport. It can boost your ego .... When combined with aerobic fitness it may even improve your sex-life! 'Ridiculous!' you say. 'Fitness is not a panacea, a cure-all.' Of course it isn't. But in a society dedicated to the automobile, remote control devices, and robots ..., an age when we face the threat of a genuine energy crisis, who will be better able to adapt and survive? The fittest, that's who!

(Brian J. Sharkey, *Physiology of Fitness*, 3rd edn, 1990)

Part Five
The Use and Abuse of Drugs

There are medicinal drugs and there are what we have come to call 'recreational' drugs. Drugs used (illicitly) in sport fall somewhere in between. There are sound reasons for legalizing 'soft' drugs; and there are equally sound reasons for not doing so. If there were not, there would be no debate. **Where do you stand in the debate about the legalization of soft drugs?**

1 The medical and social services have problems enough as it is, coping with the victims of over-indulgence in tobacco and alcohol – and we know what the effects of these drugs are. Why add yet another category of problems when we don't even know what the long-term physiological and psychological effects of cannabis are?

2 It's a straightforward matter of civil liberties: Why should the state interfere in an individual's pleasure-seeking, when no harm to others is involved? Cannabis is a relaxant: it doesn't make you aggressive in the way alcohol often does. It could even have socially beneficent effects overall because of its pacifying quality.

3 Cannabis is known to ease the pain of multiple sclerosis, backache, even cancer. It can save the sight of glaucoma sufferers. Yet the 1971 Misuse of Drugs Act prevents doctors from prescribing it. It's an absurd prejudice when a fear of abuse inhibits responsible use. Some people abuse aspirin, but we don't prohibit it.

4 If anything, the trend is towards firmer controls, not relaxation. We've tightened up on drinking and driving, on alcohol sales at football matches, and on cigarette advertising. And as people have become more conscious of the dangers of passive smoking, so the habit has come to be seen as anti-social. To legalize pot would be to turn the clock back.

5 Do we really want a whole generation of young people turning on, tuning in, and dropping out? Adolescence is supposed to be a time for youthful energy, and idealism, not tranquillized passivity. Doesn't anyone read *Brave New World* any more? Better that religion should be the opium of the people than that opium should be the religion.

6 The law as it stands makes criminals of an entire generation. Tobacco and alcohol have always been the drugs of the older generation. Young people who prefer a less toxic drug are criminalized for horticulture! Why's growing grass any worse than brewing mead or guzzling meths?

7 It makes no sense to set the police on to kids for possession of soft drugs when they'd be better employed chasing the dealers and pushers of hard drugs. A law that's comprehensively breached is a bad law. It brings the law in general into disrepute. The police themselves are pressing now for the decriminalization of cannabis-use.

8 How would we prevent people under the influence of cannabis from driving? Or walking into cars if it comes to that? How would we prevent students hallucinating in lessons and lectures? Who'd be allowed to smoke it? Where? And when? We'd need a whole new set of laws, or tomorrow, it'll be hard drugs.

Maths 6: Statistics and Probability

We conclude these mathematics sections with a look at a branch of applied mathematics that is particularly useful to the social sciences. Statistics and probability have their origins in antiquity. Indeed, the word 'statistics' comes from the same root as 'state', betraying its origin as the tool of governments. Probability had a vague history until the French philosopher and mathematician Blaise Pascal received a letter from a professional gambler, the Chevalier de Méré, about the chances of getting certain combinations of cards. This led to the discovery of Pascal's Triangle (which had been known to the Chinese many centuries before) and to the development of a new branch of mathematics.

Q1: A parish priest writes to his bishop to report on the weekly plate collections. There were five Sundays in one month, and the plate was as follows:

Sunday	Collection
1	£212
2	£217
3	£411
4	£212
5	£219

What was the average collection?

The first thing we need to decide in this case is which type of average is needed. There are three different types of average.

The mean
Perhaps the most obvious way to tackle this is to find the total collection for the five Sundays and divide by five. This will give us the mean (or arithmetic mean to distinguish it from various other types of mean). In this case, the total is £1,271 which, divided by 5, gives us £244.20. The difficulty with this approach is that the bishop would get the idea that this parish collected about £240 every Sunday, whereas the collection is more like £215. The figure has been distorted by the sum for week 3, when there may have been a special service or a particularly generous visitor.

The mode
A more appropriate average for this example might be the mode (sometimes known as the norm). This is the figure which appears most often: in this case £212.

The median
The third type of average is the median. This is the figure which appears in the centre of the list of figures when they are arranged in numerical order. So here it would not be £411, which is in the centre of the table, but it is £217, which is the central number in the following list: £212, £212, £217, £219, £411. In normal circumstances this would be the one to use.

It is important to understand which is the most appropriate average that can be calculated in any given example to give the most typical result. For example: to find an average shoe size, you would calculate a mode, whereas to determine the average salary of a number of workers, you would calculate a median.

4 Witnesses to a robbery were asked to estimate the height of a thief. Their answers were 5′ 9″, 5′ 10″, 5′ 10″, 5′ 11″ and 6′ 0″.

Q2: The number of children per family on a housing estate were recorded as follows:

No. of children	No. of families
0	11
1	16
2	4
3	2
4	1

What is the average number of children per family?

The appropriate average in this case is the mean, but students can go wrong with this type of question because there is a tendency to add up the figures in the number of families row and then divide by five. Instead, the correct procedure is to find out the total number of children and divide by the number of families. The total number of children is worked out like this:

$(0 \times 11) + (1 \times 16) + (2 \times 4) + (3 \times 2) + 4 \times 1) = 0 + 16 + 8 + 6 + 4 = 34$

The total number of families is $11 + 16 + 4 + 2 + 1 = 34$, so the mean number of children per family is one.

Q3: If one of these households is chosen at random, what is the probability that the family living there will have two children?

There are 4 households with 2 children out of the 34 families, so the probability that the family living there will have two children is $^4/_{34} = ^2/_{17}$.

Exercise 6.2

1 What is the probability that in these households a randomly chosen child is:
   (a) the only child;
   (b) one of three children in the family;
   (c) one out of four?

There are two main facts that need to be learnt about probability. The first is that a probability must always be between zero and one. The second involves remembering when to multiply the probabilities and when to add them. The situation is not always straightforward and it is best to practise this using a good textbook. Here is a very rough general rule in the examination:

> AND = MULTIPLY
>
> OR = ADD

Q4: A game of Ludo does not start until a six is thrown with a fair die. What is the probability that the die has to be thrown four times before the game can start?

This means that there are three occasions in which the result is not a six. There are five ways out of six that this can happen, so the probability is $^5/_6$. This is an AND situation, so we need to multiply:

$^5/_6 \times ^5/_6 \times ^5/_6 \times ^1/_6 = ^{125}/_{1296}$

Exercise 6.3

1 A fair coin is to be tossed repeatedly until a head appears. What is the probability that it has to be tossed five times?

2 Cards from a shuffled pack are selected until a spade appears. What is the probability that this happens with the second card?

3 A box contains 3 red balls and 7 white balls. They are selected randomly without being replaced until a white ball is chosen. What is the probability that this happens when the third ball is chosen?

Part One
Structures and Stresses

Some tensile strengths

Material	MN/m2
Brick	5.5
Dry wood (along grain)	103
Traditional cast iron	70–140
Traditional wrought iron	100–300
High-tensile engineering steel	1500

The ancients (and some moderns) built bridges without knowing, or much caring about the physics of stress and strain. They applied common sense, and, generally, it worked.

Stress is how hard a material is being forced apart, measured in:

$$\frac{\text{FORCE (IN NEWTONS)}}{\text{CROSS-SECTIONAL AREA OF MATERIAL}}$$

Strain is how far a material is being forced apart, measured in:

$$\frac{\text{INCREASE OF LENGTH}}{\text{ORIGINAL LENGTH}}$$

The **tensile strength** of a material is the stress required to break it, measured in MegaNewtons:

1 MEGANEWTON = 1,000,000 NEWTONS PER SQUARE METRE (MN/M²)

The SI unit of energy is used more now:

1 JOULE = ENERGY OF 1 NEWTON ACTING ON 1 METRE

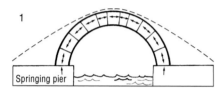

1

Springing pier

Horses and carts do not like hump-backed bridges; and railways do not like slopes of any kind. Hence, the segmented arch. Here the thrust of force is greater on the abutments. These have to be of rock, or other strong material, which may not always be available. An alternative, therefore, is the multi-arched bridge. Here the problem is the obstruction to navigation and the rush of water undermining the starlings.

We do not know when bridge-builders first constructed an arch to span a gap. The downward force (stress) is spread all round the arch. The rise is half the span. This is fine when spanning a ravine; otherwise sloping approaches are necessary.

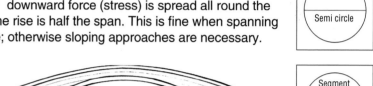

Semi circle

Segment

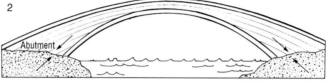

2

Abutment

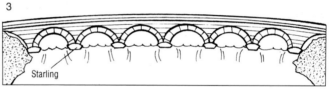

3

Starling

Rise (radius)

Span (diameter)

Cast iron became available in the 1770s. Though this is brittle, like stone, it can be cast in open, lattice form, rather than solidly. Being lighter, therefore, than stone, there is less downward force on the abutments. An alternative to the road/railway carried over the arch is to carry it underneath, suspended by cables of wrought iron.

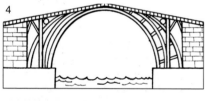

4

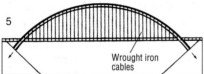

5

Wrought iron cables

This became available in the 1790s; but again, the downward stress was strong, so either a bowspring girder bridge was built, especially for railways, where the level had to be rigid, and each unit could be self-contained; or the cables could be slung from towers.

With the Bessemer process of 1856, steel replaced iron. Roadways (suspension bridges are ill-suited to rail) could be much lengthened. Steel is also used in reinforced and prestressed concrete, giving it great tensile strength.

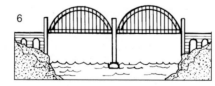

6

7

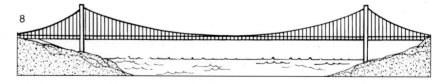

8

1 **Give a named example of each of the eight bridges pictured above.**
2 **Find out, explain, and illustrate how concrete is reinforced and prestressed.**

Part Two
Telecommunications

Electric current in copper wire gives way to fibre-optic cables, and fixed line-links to satellite communications. It was Arthur C. Clarke (scientist and science-fiction writer) who forecast, in 1945, that an artificial satellite at 35,803 kms above the equator, would orbit the Earth at rotation speed, and therefore be 'stationary'. The rest is history.

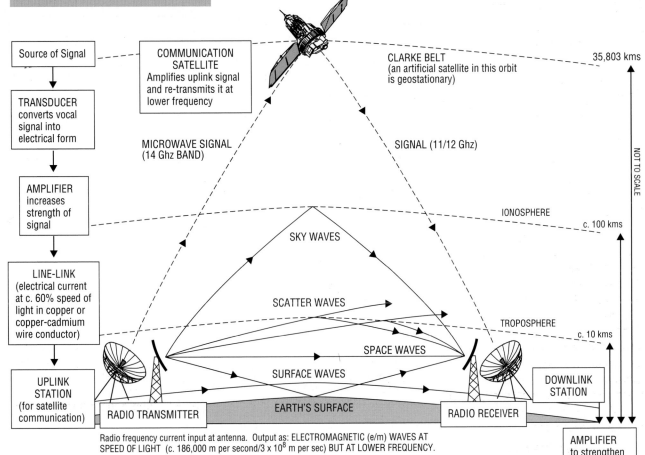

Radio frequency current input at antenna. Output as: ELECTROMAGNETIC (e/m) WAVES AT SPEED OF LIGHT (c. 186,000 m per second/3 x 10^8 m per sec) BUT AT LOWER FREQUENCY.

SURFACE WAVES – for world-wide communications in low-frequency* (LF) wave-bands (less than 300 kHz) and broadcasting in medium band (MF: 300 kHz – 3 MHz).

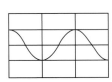

SKY WAVES – for high-frequency (HF: 3 MHz–30 MHz) radio communications including long-distance radio-telephone links, and sound broadcasting.

SPACE WAVES – for sound and television broadcasting, fixed and mobile telephone systems in very high (VHF: 30–300 MHz), ultra high (UHF: 300 MHz–3 GHz) and super high (SHF: 3–30 GHz) wave-bands.

COMMUNICATIONS SATELLITES – for multi-channel telephone systems, TV signals, and data, in UHF and SHF wave-bands

SCATTER SYSTEMS – for multi-channel telephone systems, in UHF and SHF bands

* frequency = number of cycles per second, measured in Hertz (Hz):
1 Hz = 1 cycle per second
Kilohertz = 10^3 Hz = 1,000 Hz (1 kHz)
Megahertz = 10^6 Hz = 1,000,000 Hz (1 MHz)
Gigahertz = 10^9 Hz = 1,000,000,000 Hz (1 GHz)

Which is which?

1 Aerial or dish transmitter or collector of electromagnetic signals.
2 A device that converts energy from one form into another.
3 Subdivision of the radio-frequency spectrum.
4 Complementary (one-way) channels providing bi-directional communication.
5 Wave-like electromagnetic radiation at very high frequency.
6 A circuit that increases the power or voltage of a signal.

A AMPLIFIER
B ANTENNA
C CIRCUIT
D MICROWAVE
E TRANSDUCER
F WAVE-BAND

Part Three
Water Supply

The supply of water is intimately connected with our health and well-being. The ownership and profits of the water companies have given rise to controversy in recent years; pollution, and neglect of the supply-system have also given cause for anxiety.

Official apathy only mirrors public apathy. So long as no public alarm was sounded, the government did little. Now, with alarm over water, health and environmental issues daily growing greater, the government at last stirs itself to wear a green mantle, though it hardly sits easily on those who claim that the profit motive and market forces alone can guarantee public health and clean water. So can we blame the government for its laissez-faire approach when our own communal attitude has been, until recently, barely less lethargic, despite the growing body of evidence that people are being harmed – in some cases, chronically – by substances such as lead, alum, fluoride, pesticides, fertilisers and sewage-borne bacteria, which are present in our water as a result of deliberate policy, apathy, greed, or negligence?

Nor can we simply blame the water authorities for our doubts as to the quality of what flows through our taps. On the whole, it is clear, they do their best. As for the high level of illegal sewage discharges, government cash restrictions during the last decade have made it hard for authorities to invest in repair, new plant, or alternative techniques of disposal. And despite the growing concern of many people, it is true that most of the water supplied in this country remains perfectly potable, and that treatment efficiently removes the most dangerous bacteria. When did you last meet someone dying of typhoid or cholera?

Totally safe water supply cannot be guaranteed. Removing nitrates in particular is expensive and difficult. Contamination due to faults in the supply-line between treatment-plant and domestic consumer is hard to deal with, save by adding chlorine or chloramines. Likewise it is difficult, given the huge increase in agricultural and industrial use of chemicals, to guard against or even to test for the subtle presence in water of some of these toxins. Even were the money made available, the tests required to isolate such substances would still remain time-consuming and complex. Even where such tests prove positive, it is difficult even for a well-funded agency to prevail over the powerful sectarian and vested interests that entrenched industries and agriculture represent.

(Stuart Gordon Macdonald, *Down the Drain*, 1989)

1 What does each of the following words mean, in the above context?
   (a) 'laissez-faire'; (line 7)
   (b) 'lethargic'; (line 8)
   (c) 'potable'; (line 21)
   (d) 'toxins'. (line 30)
2 To be 'green' is to be 'environmentally aware', but what does it mean for the government to 'wear a green mantle', do you suppose? (line 4)
3 Why might being 'green' conflict with support for the play of 'market forces'?
4 Which of the substances in the first paragraph might have been introduced into the water supply by 'deliberate policy' and which by 'negligence'?
5 Who incurs blame for the poor state of our water, in this article?
6 How would you yourself apportion such blame?

Part Four

Technology and Society

Technology covers a multitude of applied arts and sciences from bookbinding to cryogenics. All involve machinery of some sort and aim to improve our lives. Sometimes, technology solves one problem only to create another. **Have we become too confident, in your view, that for every problem we encounter there will be a 'technological fix'?**

1

Nuclear power poses some threat to public health, but no more so than many other technologies of which our industrial society is comprised and a lot less than most. It provides a potential target for terrorist attack, but there are many other non-nuclear targets where the threat is more credible and the possible consequences more terrifying. It can be misused to make weapons of war rather than used for the benefit of mankind, but then again that also applies to many other industries.

(Ian Blair, *Taming the Atom*, 1983)

2

A floppy disk can store only five real-life images, but a single CD can store 5000 such images. The floppy can store only three seconds of high-quality audio, but the CD can store an hour. It's this remarkable power of the CD ROM disc to digitally store video images, audio, data, and computer code in any combination that underscores its vast potential .... A single CD can hold an incredible amount of information.

(William H. Gates in Steve Lambert and Suzanne Ropiequet, eds, *CD ROM – The New Papyrus*, 1986)

3

During a discussion as to whether automatic machines rob human beings of employment, allusion was made to the fact that the spread of modern telephone installations in America is so enormous that even the entire female population between the ages of twenty and forty would not provide sufficient telephone operators if the old hand-operated switch-boards were still in use.

(Heinz Gartmann, *Science as History*, 1960)

4

We must come clean and admit that many VDU-related jobs are mostly dull, routine and repetitive. We have taken away from the human operator, even those previously engaged in low-grade and repetitive clerical work, many of the tasks which contribute to job satisfaction because the computer can do them better or faster, without thinking of the effect of what is left. The consequence is poor operator performance (i.e. a high input error rate ...).

(Graham Wright, *Mastering Computers*, 3rd edn, 1988)

5

Hydrogen and Solar energy do not pollute; when hydrogen is used to supply heat or energy, water is the by-product. Such systems produce none of the dreaded CO_2, no sulphur to cause acid rain, and no harmful pollutants to cause smog. Our solar energy will be around for a few billion more years ... and we would obtain hydrogen from water, and that won't run out either as water is the by-product of burning hydrogen.

(John O'M Bockris *et al*, *Solar Hydrogen Energy*, 1991)

6

Everywhere large water projects are both the consequence of and the justification for authoritarian government. From India to Turkey, to Paraguay, soldiers stand guard over dam construction sites and herd refugees to their new homes. It is no surprise that ... soldiers such as Nasser and Gadaffi and the military commanders of South America have been so prominent in the promotion of large dams.

(Fred Pearce, *The Dammed*, 1992)

7

The vision is now a reality. Though it has taken nearly 200 years, the Channel Tunnel has at last been built. ... Considerable effort has been made to minimize damage to the environment; and the final Tunnel incorporates within its structure and service every safety measure that can be perceived as being within the range of risk which people are prepared to accept as part of life.

(Donald Hunt, *The Tunnel*, 1994)

8

Genetics is often seen as a threat and to interfere with our inheritance as a curse on the future. In fact, the new biology has brought little but benefit. Ironically enough, Mary Shelley was pregnant when writing *Frankenstein* and produced a child which died when a few months old. She herself suffered from a severe depression, as did many of her relatives. Today's genetics might have helped to understand her child's illness and her own mental state.

(Steve Jones, *The Language of the Genes*, 1993)

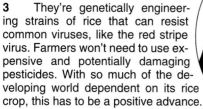

Part Five
Genetic Engineering

The Human Genome Project is a $2 billion programme to map the sequence of around 100,000 genes. Researchers claim to have identified genes responsible for aggression, schizophrenia, liver disease, dwarfism, and even grammar! **How far do we dare meddle with the genetic make-up of plants, animals and human beings?**

1 The problem with genetic screening for legitimate medical purposes is that the data may fall into the wrong hands. Insurance companies, for instance, could make use of the data to identify premium-payers with a genetic make-up that predisposes them to potentially fatal diseases.

2 Ask a sufferer from Alzheimer's Disease, Huntingdon's Disease, or Amyotrophic Lateral Sclerosis whether they approve of the identification of the rogue genes that may lead to the defeat of these debilitating conditions. I think you'd find that they do.

3 They're genetically engineering strains of rice that can resist common viruses, like the red stripe virus. Farmers won't need to use expensive and potentially damaging pesticides. With so much of the developing world dependent on its rice crop, this has to be a positive advance.

4 What's the point of spending so much research time on genetic tests to screen for this 'bad gene' and this or that rare disease when lifestyles are responsible for several of our diseases, and the biggest threat to life of all is simple starvation.

5 We've always used animals as means to our own ends. There is really no difference between 'creating' sheep whose milk contains a chemical for use in the treatment of emphysema, and breeding them for their fleece, or for their meat.

6 It's a short step from genetic screening for *information*, to the modification of 'defective' genes for the *improvement* of the organism, or the species. The human body isn't a biochemical computer program. There's more to life – there's more to *people* – than DNA.

7 It's not a question of whether or not you splice genes: as always in disputes of this kind, the question is where to draw the line. No-one is going to object to 'tweaking' genes for heart disease and kidney failure; but what about genes for male homosexuality, dyslexia, even shyness?

8 There can't be anything wrong, surely, with engineering drugs based on bacterial proteins that will puncture cancer cells. This sort of work is done in test-tubes, and on computer screens. We can do some very precise things with chemically-cultured smart drugs.

The Periodic Table

Democritus (c.460–370BC) had suggested that matter is made of tiny particles, each of them indivisible (Greek: *a* = not + *tomos* = cut). The idea lapsed, and the medieval belief was that everything was made of a mixture of four elements: earth, air, fire, and water.

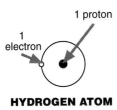

1 proton

1 electron

HYDROGEN ATOM

John Dalton (1776–1844) listed twenty substances that he believed to be indivisible elements; but during the 19th Century, lots more were discovered. Chemists began to tabulate them by atomic weight. It was found, for example, that an oxygen atom, with eight protons and eight neutrons is sixteen times heavier than a hydrogen atom which has only one proton. (Electrons contribute little to atomic weight.)

Proton:	elementary particle having positive charge
Neutron:	elementary particle having no charge
Electron:	elementary particle having negative charge

Dimitry Mendeleyev (1834–1907) arranged all the known elements in 'periods' (horizontally) according to their atomic weight. He had the good sense to leave gaps where known

elements did not fit the sequence, but where he suspected they did exist. Thus, he correctly predicted the existence of Germanium, fifteen years before it was discovered, in 1886.

John Newlands (in 1864) and Mendeleyev (in 1869) both noted that every eighth element in the sequence had similar chemical properties. Mendeleyev's table took account of this by arranging the elements in such groups, vertically, although this disturbed the neat order.

In 1913, **Henry Moseley** (1857–1915) discovered that when the elements were arranged according to the number of protons in their nuclei (i.e. by their atomic number), they fell naturally into periods and groups, without need for adjustment.

The atom can be thought of as a nucleus containing a number of protons (bonded tightly with a varying number of neutrons), orbited by an equal number of electrons. These electrons surround the nucleus with between one and seven shells. The Helium (He) atom, for example – like the Hydrogen (H) atom – has one shell; Lithium (Li) has two; and Argon (Ar) has three.

There is a limit to the number of electrons that can orbit on each shell: two is the limit on the inner shell, eight on the second,

eighteen on the third and so on, as shown here:

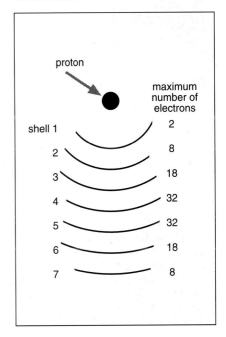

proton

maximum number of electrons

shell 1	2
2	8
3	18
4	32
5	32
6	18
7	8

We have not found – nor as yet created – an element with all 118 possible electrons on the seven shells. Uranium, with ninety-two electrons, is the element with the highest number of electrons that occurs in nature. Lawrencium, with 103 electrons, has briefly been created in a cyclotron (a type of particle accelerator).

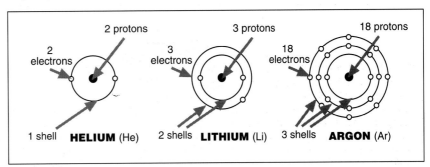

2 protons

2 electrons

1 shell **HELIUM** (He)

3 protons

3 electrons

2 shells **LITHIUM** (Li)

18 protons

18 electrons

3 shells **ARGON** (Ar)

ITEM

It is the number of electrons on the outer shells that determines the chemical characteristics of an element: whether it reacts with water, or forms a brightly coloured compound, or is found in nature, or has the properties of a metal. It is, therefore, the number of electrons on the outer shell of an element that determines its place in the horizontal sequence of periods in the table below; it is the number of its shells that determines its place in the vertical sequence of groups.

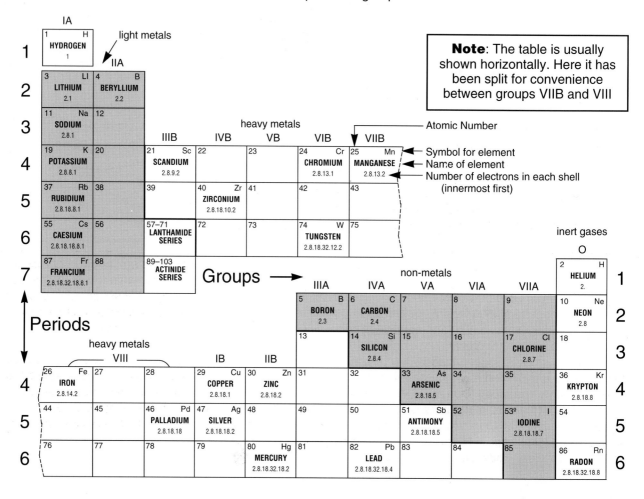

Note: The table is usually shown horizontally. Here it has been split for convenience between groups VIIB and VIII

Most of the boxes have been left unlabelled; but enough labels and other data are given to allow you to identify which elements correspond to the following atomic numbers:

1 – 7
2 – 18
3 – 22
4 – 50
5 – 79
6 – 88

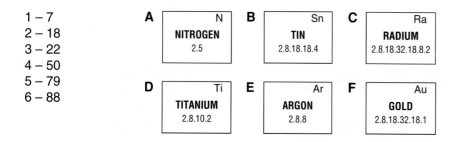

A		B		C	
	N		Sn		Ra
NITROGEN		**TIN**		**RADIUM**	
2.5		2.8.18.18.4		2.8.18.32.18.8.2	

D		E		F	
	Ti		Ar		Au
TITANIUM		**ARGON**		**GOLD**	
2.8.10.2		2.8.8		2.8.18.32.18.1	

Part One
The Solar System

To the Greeks it seemed that the sun and moon were relatively close to the Earth and revolved round it. The stars were thought to be fixed in position. The bright planets – Mercury, Venus, Mars, Jupiter and Saturn – were observed in motion against the background of the fixed stars, and these too were supposed to orbit the Earth.

Ptolemy (c. 90–168) proposed the most advanced version of the geocentric (Earth-centred) theory. The orbits of the planets were thought to be circular, but he observed that their motions were irregular; and tried to explain this by reference to 'epicycles'.

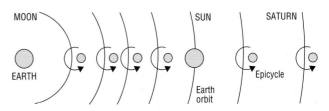

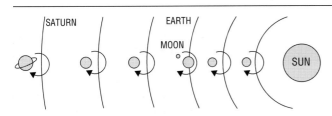

Copernicus (1473–1543) in his *Revolutions of the Heavenly Orbs*, 1543, put forward the heliocentric (sun-centred) theory. The 'Copernican Revolution' is well-named; but its author retained the Ptolemaic theory of circular orbits and epicycles.

Tycho Brahe (1546–1601) thought the sun and moon orbited the Earth, but the planets orbited the sun. His assistant **Johannes Kepler** (1571–1630) realized that planets moved in ellipses (1st Law), and that a planet accelerates as it nears the Sun (2nd Law). Kepler worked out a mathematical relationship between a planet's distance from the sun, and the duration of its orbit (3rd Law).

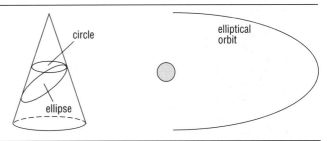

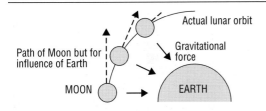

Isaac Newton (1642–1727) explained in his *Principia* why planets do not travel in straight lines. Using Kepler's 3rd Law he proportioned a body's distance from the sun to the sun's gravitational pull on it. He saw that this force was identical to the force of gravity on Earth.

Edmund Halley (1656–1742) deduced from ancient observations that 'fixed stars' were in fact in motion at a great distance from Earth. **William Herschel** (1738–1822) discovered Uranus in 1781. Observations of a planet from two widely-spaced points on Earth, against a background of remote bodies, made it possible (using trigonometry) to calculate planetary distances. **Friedrich Bessel** (1784–1846) thus estimated the distance from Earth of a star in the constellation Cygnus, in 1838.

Neptune was discovered in 1846, and the existence of Pluto was inferred in 1930.

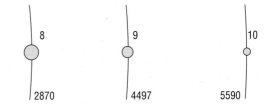

Mean distance from sun (in millions of kilometres)

A Which is which in the above diagram?

A Asteroids	**F** Neptune	**B** Earth	**G** Pluto	**C** Jupiter
H Saturn	**D** Mars	**I** Uranus	**E** Mercury	**J** Venus

B Who did what?
1 Devised inverse square law.
2 Recognized that the motion of the sun was not epicyclic.
3 Delayed publication of his theory until his death.
4 Calculated 'sidereal periods'.
5 Advanced a part geocentric, part heliocentric theory.

A BRAHE
B COPERNICUS
C KEPLER
D NEWTON
E PTOLEMY

Part Two
The Bang and Beyond

In 1932 Edwin Hubble discovered that the wavelength of the light from distant galaxies was shifting to the red end of the spectrum (the red shift). This suggested that the galaxies were receding – that we live in an expanding universe that issued from a big bang some 15 billion years ago. The basic fuel of the Universe is hydrogen: matter consisted entirely of hydrogen and helium, the lightest elements (see Item T, p.139–140). We owe all the heavier elements to supernova explosions.

THE MILKY WAY GALAXY

Contains about 400 billion stars. Ours (the sun) is c. 4.6 billion years old. It has protons enough to last another 5 billion years or so. It will have 'shone' for 10 billion years. As a red giant it will last a billion more years.

A GALAXY is a cloud of dust and gas rotating about a centre of clustered stars.

Galactic centre
Solar system

100,000 light years

ONE LIGHT YEAR is the distance travelled by light (at 186,000 miles per second), in one year – about 6 million, million miles. The nearest star to the sun is Proxima Centauri, 4.31 ly away.

A STAR begins life as such a cloud ('nebula') that collapses, under gravity, becoming denser and hotter.

Protostars

NUCLEAR FUSION begins. The temperature at the core is 15–60m°F. At this temperature, protons collide to form Hydrogen nuclei, and again to form Helium nuclei. The energy of mass is transformed into the energy of motion.

The protons in the core are exhausted in a contracting, yet ever hotter shell. Helium nuclei now fuse at super-high speed and are converted to carbon.

Star in the main sequence
At the outer edge the temperature cools to 2,000– 25,000°F in the (yellow) visible part of the spectrum

White Dwarf

Black Dwarf inert, invisible

Red Giant

A PROTOSTAR that achieves a mass more than 1.4 times the mass of the sun has a higher core temperature and a *much* higher rate of hydrogen burning. It is highly luminous, but relatively short-lived. It fails to balance the force of gravity and nuclear fusion as smaller stars do – and survive at constant size. Big stars collapse under gravity, then explode in a supernova that flares brilliantly for some months, leaving only a neutron star so dense it may collapse to infinity in a black hole.

Supernova

Neutron star

The envelope of the star absorbs the heat energy from the centre and expands, and cools. What had looked yellow is now red, as light is now emitted at a shorter wavelength. The outer layers of rarefied gas evaporate into space leaving only the fast-cooling inner core, crushed by gravity to a white dwarf – a dense mass of carbon nuclei and electrons. The latter prevent its shrinking further.

Which is which?
1 An interstellar cloud of dust and gas, dense or otherwise.
2 A cloud of gaseous matter that grows dense and hot as it implodes.
3 The fate of a main-sequence star that runs out of hydrogen at the core.
4 A singularity from which no electromagnetic radiation can escape.
5 The highly luminous end of a star about a critical mass.
6 The compressed core of a supernova, denser than a white dwarf.

A BLACK HOLE
B NEBULA
C NEUTRON STAR
D PROTOSTAR
E RED GIANT
F SUPERNOVA

Part Three
Black Holes

Put at its simplest, a black hole is a region of space from which the escape velocity is greater than the speed of light. Most people today know about escape velocity from hearing and reading about space rockets. The strength of the Earth's gravity, for example, is such that any rocket, bullet or cricket ball, say, thrown 5 upwards with a speed of less than 11 kms per second, must be pulled back to Earth. This can be expressed neatly in energy terms: if the kinetic energy that a particle has through its motion is less than the potential energy of the gravity field acting on the 10 particle, then it cannot escape. But once this escape velocity is reached, any particle thrown outwards from the Earth can keep on going. Or at least, it can escape from the Earth. A rocket at the same distance from the Sun as the Earth would need a velocity of 41 kms per second to escape from the greater gravitational 15 pull of the Sun and leave the Solar system. Because the Moon's gravity is weaker than that of the Earth, escape velocity is much less and that is why Apollo lunar modules could manage with such small rockets.

When you measure or calculate the escape velocity needed at 20 the surface of an astronomical body like the Earth or the Sun, both its mass and its density are important factors. The mass, obviously, because mass is what produces the gravitational field our rocket has to escape from; and the density because the more dense an object is, then the closer its surface is to its centre. ... 25

As the mass goes up, so does the escape velocity, and in a surprisingly short time we find that the speed of light is needed to escape from the gravitational field we have produced. This is true whatever theory of physics or mathematics we use. But Einstein's theory tells us, and experiments confirm, that noth- 30 ing can travel faster than light. So if we have an object so massive that light cannot escape from it, then nothing can escape, and the inside of the black hole is almost a self-contained universe. Almost, but not quite, since, of course, things can still get in from outside, even if nothing inside can ever get out.

(John Gribbin, *Our Changing Universe: The New Astronomy*, 1976)

1 From what does a rocket have to 'escape' after it is launched, in order to achieve 'escape velocity'?
2 From the references in the passage, what do you understand by:
   (a) 'kinetic energy'; (line 8)
   (b) 'potential energy'? (line 9)
3 Why is the escape velocity from the Sun so much greater than that from the Earth?
4 Why do you suppose Gribbin refers to the time before an escape velocity of the speed of light is reached as 'surprisingly short'? (line 26)
5 How does Gribbin (implicitly) define a 'self-contained universe'? (line 32-3)

Use any of the following extended quotations as a point of departure from which to answer any or all of these questions: **Is there life out there? Does it matter to us whether there is or not? If there were, what message would we want to transmit to it?**

1

We, with all our complexities, are the result of quite normal and common phenomena in the universe. This is a prime conclusion gleaned from decades of astronomical, chemical, and biological research. The nuclear reactions that make the stars shine create the elements of planets and life: carbon, nitrogen, oxygen, phosphorus, silicon, iron .... Our theories suggest strongly that in some of these planetary systems planets similar to Earth will exist often with liquid water on them, as well as a protective and nurturing atmosphere.

(Frank D. Drake, 'Extraterrestrial Life', in William J. Kaufmann, *Universe*, 1968)

2

Even if intelligence arises on as many as a million planets in our galaxy, there will still be very few intelligent species around *at the present moment* unless high intelligence, once it arises, persists for more than 10,000 years, for the following reason. The age of our galaxy, the time span throughout which intelligence can emerge is very long indeed – about 10,000 *million* years. Unless intelligence lasts once it arises, there will be very little overlap in time between its brief emergence on one planet and its emergence on another planet.

(Fred Hoyle, *Astronomy Today*, 1975)

3

Interstellar communication on a grand scale cannot be ruled out, though at present we are probably technologically too primitive to intercept any such signals. After all, a primitive man in a jungle would be quite unaware of two explorers communicating with each other on a walkie-talkie. The ages of stars and planets could run into thousands of millions of years, and this is a long enough time for the evolution of life elsewhere to much more sophisticated forms than those seen on the Earth.

(Jayant Narlikar, *The Structure of the Universe*, 1977)

4

Many astronomers like to argue that life must exist elsewhere because there exist so many sites where it could do so. The overriding opinion of biologists, on the other hand, is that the probability is essentially nil, because the number of evolutionary pathways leading to biological dead-ends is at least as large as the number of sites. Our argument destroys this potential paradise for extra-terrestrials. The universe would have to be just as large as it is to support even one lonely outpost of life. The global structure of the universe is unavoidably bound up with some of the smallest details of life on earth.

(John D. Barrow and Joseph Silk, *The Left Hand of Creation*, 1984)

5

Does extraterrestrial life appear in a form analogous to what we know on Earth? It seems unlikely that extraterrestrial organisms would resemble living species on Earth (particularly in view of the diversity of the latter). On the other hand, we can assume that extra-terrestrial life, like life on Earth, is based on carbon chemistry .... On Earth, slight variations in environmental conditions have caused substantial variations in the living world, to the point of altering the biochemical parameters of some organisms. However, it remains probable that some biochemical processes are universal.

(Philippe de la Cotardière, ed, *Larousse Astronomy*, 1987)

6

Mars has been well investigated by both American and Soviet probes. The American Mariner series provided us with our first close-ups of this planet, pictures that were to dispel any expectations that life could exist there. Mariner 4 was the first successful Mars fly-by, approaching to a distance of 9,600 kilometres in July 1965. The pictures it sent back ... showed heavily-cratered lunar-like regions, chaotic terrain and desert-like flat areas, all suggesting that Mars was a dead world.

(Carole Stott, *The Greenwich Guide to Astronomy in Action*, 1989)

Part Five
Space Travel

Answer the following question by reference to any of the opinions expressed below. **Ought we to invest in space research, and means of space travel, or would such investment be a crass waste of money?**

1 What justification can there possibly be for sending astronauts to Mars, or wherever, to colonize it, and – perhaps – to exploit it, when there's so much that we should be doing to reclaim *this* planet that we've done so much to spoil. It's a sort of irresponsible nomadism. Foul your nest, then move on somewhere else.

2 The Apollo programme was certainly the most exciting scientific project of the twentieth century. And it all happened within eight years of President Kennedy's announcing it. It was an adventure in which the whole 'global village' was involved. A successor project – with an international crew – would do more to unite nations in a common cause than any World Cup.

3 It almost doesn't matter what scientists do as long as they're given the chance to do science. Only in wartime has as much money been spent on science as governments have lavished on the space programme. The result has been a tremendous acceleration in the development of computers and satellite communications.

4 NASA has spent millions of dollars on planning a manned space station, without ever really considering what it's all *for*. There's nothing that manned space vehicles can do that robot craft can't achieve at a fraction of the cost. Sending people up just adds immense human complications to what should be a *scientific* enterprise.

5 The space race has been part and parcel of the arms race. The whole money-spinning enterprise has been political: the most visible feature of the rivalry between the so-called superpowers. 'My rocket is bigger that yours', one said to the other. 'Mine can stay up longer', the other said. It's time we left such bragging to little boys.

6 Man's urge to explore his universe could never be sublimated for long. There's no wilderness left in this world, no mountain that hasn't been climbed; so we're bound to look outward into space. If our own curiosity has been satisfied for the time being, our descendants will certainly want to renew the quest one day.

7 We've wasted fantastic sums of money on space research. The USA is the richest nation on earth, and it has squandered its resources – the world's resources – on prestige projects, when whole countries, whole continents go hungry. And the Soviet Union beggared itself in the process. It's obscene that we should get our priorities so horribly wrong.

8 We really only started to talk about 'one world', and 'spaceship earth', when the first astronauts brought those beautiful photographs back. It's ironical but true, that our concern for the state of this world has increased in synchrony with our exploration of space. There's no trade-off between the earth and space: we live in both.

ITEM

Pioneers

Below are the names of 52 'achievers' of one sort and another, and their birth and death dates. Alongside, is a list of achievements. Match each pioneer with his or her corresponding achievement from the alphabetic list.

1	André AMPÈRE (1775–1836)	A	Advanced the heliocentric theory.
2	Elizabeth ANDERSON (1836–1917)	B	Devised the gas-pressure law and the corpuscular theory of matter.
3	Nancy ASTOR (1879–1964)	C	Discovered new radioactive elements: polonium and radium.
4	Robert BADEN-POWELL (1857–1941)	D	Pioneer of the votes-for-women movement.
5	Antoine BECQUEREL (1852–1908)	E	Introduced assembly-line manufacture.
6	Robert BOYLE (1627–91)	F	Author of the theory of relativity.
7	Henry CAVENDISH (1731–1810)	G	Discovered bactericidal properties of penicillin.
8	Nicolaus COPERNICUS (1473–1543)	H	Agitated for humane conditions in prisons.
9	Marie CURIE (1876–1934)	I	The first female doctor in England.*
10	Charles DARWIN (1809–82)	J	Introduced vaccination against smallpox.
11	Paul EHRLICH (1854–1915)	K	Established the chemical composition of water.
12	Albert EINSTEIN (1879–1955)	L	Discovered the phenomenon of radioactivity.
13	Michael FARADAY (1791–1867)	M	Defined the laws of falling bodies.
14	Millicent FAWCETT (1847–1930)	N	Pioneered antiseptics in surgery.
15	Enrico FERMI (1901–54)	O	Demonstrated the relationship between electricity and magnetism.
16	Alexander FLEMING (1881–1955)	P	Devised an absolute scale of temperature.
17	Henry FORD (1866–1947)	Q	Established the relationship between heat and energy.
18	Benjamin FRANKLIN (1706–90)	R	Pioneer of synthetic drugs, including one against syphilis.
19	Elizabeth FRY (1780–1845)	S	Established the existence of radio-waves.
20	Galileo GALILEI (1564–1642)	T	Soldier and creator of the world order of scouts.
21	Heinrich HERTZ (1857–94)	U	Explained the principle of the lightning-conductor.
22	Edward JENNER (1749– 1823)	V	Established what happens in combustion.
23	James JOULE (1818–89)	W	Put forward the theory of evolution of species.
24	Lord KELVIN (1824–1907)	X	Defined laws of electromagnetic induction.
25	Antoine LAVOISIER (1743 –94)	Y	Built the first atomic pile.
26	Joseph LISTER (1827–1912)	Z	The first female Member of Parliament.
27	David LIVINGSTONE (1813–73)	AA	Early anthropologist in South Pacific.
28	Martin LUTHER (1483–1546)	BB	Pioneered hot-air ballooning.
29	Rosa LUXEMBURG (1870–1919)	CC	Identified microbes as agents of fermentation and disease.
30	Ernst MACH (1838–1916)	DD	Discovered X-rays.
31	Margaret MEAD (1901–78)	EE	Revolutionary German communist leader.
32	Gregor MENDEL (1822–84)	FF	Sailor and Antarctic explorer.
33	Maria MONTESSORI (1870–1952)	GG	Synthesised urea – an organic compound.
34	J.M. and J.E. MONTGOLFIER (1740–1810)	HH	Educationist who championed child-centred methods.
35	Isaac NEWTON (1642–1727)	II	Advanced the Quantum Theory.
36	Florence NIGHTINGALE (1820–1910)	JJ	Explorer of South-East and Central Africa.
37	Robert OWEN (1771–1858)	KK	Social reformer on behalf of children in factories and mines.
38	Emmeline PANKHURST (1858–1928)	LL	Built first practical powered aircraft.
39	PARACELSUS (1493–1541)	MM	Enlightened industrial employer.
40	Louis PASTEUR (1822–95)	NN	Champion of equality between the sexes.
41	Max PLANCK (1858–1947)	OO	Protested against abuses in the Roman Catholic Church.
42	Joseph PRIESTLEY (1733–1804)	PP	Pioneer of birth control and women's rights.
43	Wilhelm RÖNTGEN (1845–1923)	QQ	Made statistical analysis of the principles of heredity.
44	Ernest RUTHERFORD (1871–1937)	RR	Leader of militant suffragettes.
45	Robert Falcon SCOTT (1868 –1912)	SS	Pioneer of aerodynamics.
46	Lord SHAFTESBURY (1801–85)	TT	An early user of chemistry in the service of medicine.
47	Marie STOPES (1880–1958)	UU	Founded the profession of nursing.
48	William WILBERFORCE (1759–1833)	VV	Discovered carbon dioxide and oxygen.
49	Friedrich WÖHLER (1800–82)	WW	Establishd the essential structure of the atom.
50	Mary WOLLSTONECRAFT (1759–97)	XX	Defined laws of motion and gravitation.
51	Wilbur and Orville WRIGHT (1867–1948)	YY	Prominent engineer of the rigid airship.
52	Ferdinand Graf von ZEPPELIN (1838–1917)	ZZ	Leader of the campaign against slavery.

* if we except James Miranda Barry (1795–1865) who passed herself off as a man.

If you were to add, say, 10 more names to this list, whose would they be?

International Organizations

Part One

There are something like 4,500 international bodies – most of them formed since the Second World War. Many began life as groups pledged to defend their sovereignty against military aggression, and to promote peace. More recently, they have evolved as associations for the promotion of regional economic and social development. Military pacts have less significance now than development banks.

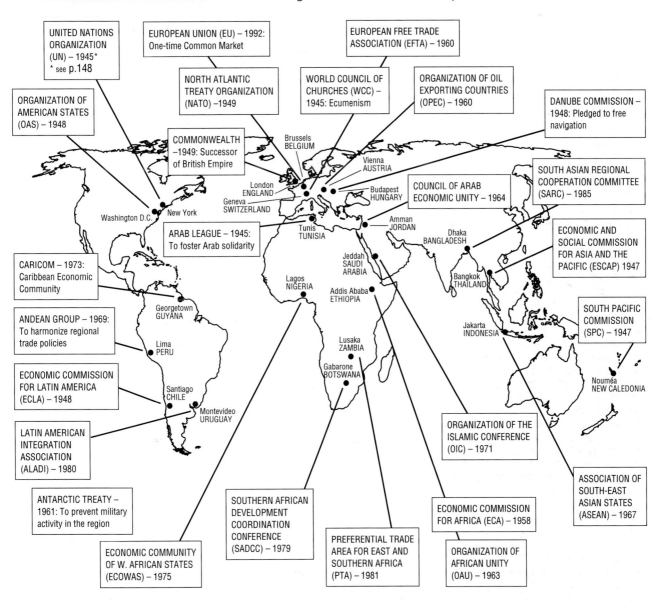

UNITED NATIONS ORGANIZATION (UN) – 1945*
* see p.148

EUROPEAN UNION (EU) – 1992: One-time Common Market

EUROPEAN FREE TRADE ASSOCIATION (EFTA) – 1960

ORGANIZATION OF AMERICAN STATES (OAS) – 1948

NORTH ATLANTIC TREATY ORGANIZATION (NATO) –1949

WORLD COUNCIL OF CHURCHES (WCC) – 1945: Ecumenism

ORGANIZATION OF OIL EXPORTING COUNTRIES (OPEC) – 1960

DANUBE COMMISSION – 1948: Pledged to free navigation

COMMONWEALTH –1949: Successor of British Empire

Brussels BELGIUM

Vienna AUSTRIA

SOUTH ASIAN REGIONAL COOPERATION COMMITTEE (SARC) – 1985

London ENGLAND

Geneva SWITZERLAND

Budapest HUNGARY

COUNCIL OF ARAB ECONOMIC UNITY – 1964

Washington D.C.

New York

Tunis TUNISIA

Amman JORDAN

Dhaka BANGLADESH

ECONOMIC AND SOCIAL COMMISSION FOR ASIA AND THE PACIFIC (ESCAP) 1947

ARAB LEAGUE – 1945: To foster Arab solidarity

CARICOM – 1973: Caribbean Economic Community

Jeddah SAUDI ARABIA

Lagos NIGERIA

Bangkok THAILAND

Addis Ababa ETHIOPIA

SOUTH PACIFIC COMMISSION (SPC) – 1947

ANDEAN GROUP – 1969: To harmonize regional trade policies

Georgetown GUYANA

Jakarta INDONESIA

Lima PERU

Lusaka ZAMBIA

ECONOMIC COMMISSION FOR LATIN AMERICA (ECLA) – 1948

Santiago CHILE

Gabarone BOTSWANA

Nouméa NEW CALEDONIA

Montevideo URUGUAY

LATIN AMERICAN INTEGRATION ASSOCIATION (ALADI) – 1980

ORGANIZATION OF THE ISLAMIC CONFERENCE (OIC) – 1971

ANTARCTIC TREATY – 1961: To prevent military activity in the region

SOUTHERN AFRICAN DEVELOPMENT COORDINATION CONFERENCE (SADCC) – 1979

ECONOMIC COMMISSION FOR AFRICA (ECA) – 1958

ASSOCIATION OF SOUTH-EAST ASIAN STATES (ASEAN) – 1967

ECONOMIC COMMUNITY OF W. AFRICAN STATES (ECOWAS) – 1975

PREFERENTIAL TRADE AREA FOR EAST AND SOUTHERN AFRICA (PTA) – 1981

ORGANIZATION OF AFRICAN UNITY (OAU) – 1963

International bodies have typically evolved thus:

1 MILITARY TREATY → 2 TRADE PACT → 3 COMMON MARKET → 4 ECONOMIC SOCIAL AND CULTURAL COOPERATION → 5 POLITICAL FEDERATION/ INTEGRATION

Of the twenty-five organizations referred to above:

1 Identify one that has military cooperation as its primary objective.

2 Name one that is a simple trade pact, at stage two.

3 Choose one that appears to have reached the 'common market' stage.

4 Which organization, or organizations, have a purely economic rationale?

5 Is there an organization whose reason for being might be described as 'cultural'?

6 What factors, in your view, could conceivably lead to political federation (stage 5)?

Part Two
The United Nations

1 January 1942	Twenty-six nations (dubbed the 'United Nations' by F.D. Roosevelt) sign the 'Atlantic Charter', a pledge to defeat the Axis powers.
21 August 1944	Representatives of thirty-nine nations discuss proposals for a United Nations Organization (UNO), at Dumbarton Oaks, Washington D.C.
26 June 1945	The UN charter is approved and signed by delegates of fifty nations meeting in San Francisco.
10 January 1946	The UN General Assembly meets for the first time in London. Trygve Lie of Norway is elected first Secretary General.
10 December 1948	The General Assembly adopts the Universal Declaration of Human Rights.

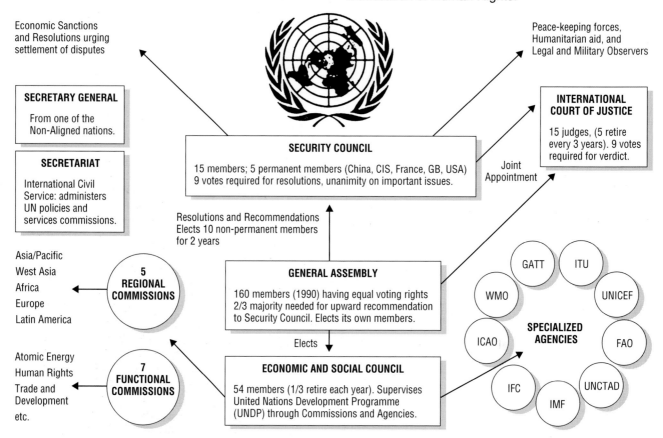

Economic Sanctions and Resolutions urging settlement of disputes

Peace-keeping forces, Humanitarian aid, and Legal and Military Observers

SECRETARY GENERAL
From one of the Non-Aligned nations.

SECRETARIAT
International Civil Service: administers UN policies and services commissions.

INTERNATIONAL COURT OF JUSTICE
15 judges, (5 retire every 3 years). 9 votes required for verdict.

SECURITY COUNCIL
15 members; 5 permanent members (China, CIS, France, GB, USA) 9 votes required for resolutions, unanimity on important issues.

Joint Appointment

Asia/Pacific
West Asia
Africa
Europe
Latin America

5 REGIONAL COMMISSIONS

Resolutions and Recommendations Elects 10 non-permanent members for 2 years

GENERAL ASSEMBLY
160 members (1990) having equal voting rights 2/3 majority needed for upward recommendation to Security Council. Elects its own members.

Elects

Atomic Energy
Human Rights
Trade and Development
etc.

7 FUNCTIONAL COMMISSIONS

ECONOMIC AND SOCIAL COUNCIL
54 members (1/3 retire each year). Supervises United Nations Development Programme (UNDP) through Commissions and Agencies.

GATT ITU
WMO UNICEF
ICAO **SPECIALIZED AGENCIES** FAO
IFC IMF UNCTAD

A What, in your view, has the United Nations Organization achieved over the past fifty years?

B What are the principal activities in which the UN is presently engaged?

C Which specialized agency does which?

1 Integrates bilateral trade agreements; works to liberalize trade.
2 Assists members in temporary balance-of-payments difficulties.
3 Improves production and distribution of food across the world.
4 Engages in programmes to prevent and eradicate diseases.
5 Gives support to insolvent nations by granting loans.
6 Organizes help for people dispossessed by war and natural disaster.
7 Harmonizes legislation on work practices and unemployment.
8 Promotes international cooperation to combat illiteracy.

A Food and Agriculture Organization (FAO, 1945, Rome)
B General Agreement on Tariffs and Trade (GATT, 1945)
C International Bank for Reconstruction and Development – or 'World Bank' (IBRD, 1946)
D International Labour Organization (ILO, 1919, Geneva)
E International Monetary Fund (IMF, 1947, Washington)
F United Nations Educational Scientific and Cultural Organization (UNESCO, 1946)
G United Nations High Commission for Refugees (UNHCR, 1952)
H World Health Organization (WHO, 1948)

Part Three
The Most Exploited Resource

The following passage is taken from a book written for the 1976 United Nations' Conference on Human Settlements, in Vancouver. If anything has changed since then, it is for the worse.

Consider the plight of the average small farmer in most developing nations. He probably does not own even ten percent of the land in Latin America. Forty percent of the land workers in India have no land at all . .... In most of the Indian subcontinent, the village is the limit for the cooperative – with perhaps no more than 150 members and not federated upwards in any way. This is too small a mass to afford modernization of methods or to provide any security for vital credit. In any case, the 'big man' of the village is in fact in charge even of the nominal cooperative, and in so far as it is used as a channel for government help, it is not difficult to guess in whose pockets the help ends up. Complete the picture with almost total isolation – dirt roads washed away in the monsoons, narrow mountain paths above dizzy Andean gulfs of emptiness, jungle tracks hacked and rehacked through the dense green curtains of clinging creepers, logs hollowed out for boats edging past rapids and alligators – and one has perhaps the faintest image of what life for the average five-acre man may be like, even if he is lucky enough to own his land, even if his health holds, even if his patient packhorse of a wife survives, even if his children live to help work the plot and secure his old age.

And having imagined it, one can ask whether it is a life that any human being will long persist in, once traditional fatalism begins to fade and rumours reach the distant places that cousin Jose has got his child into a primary school in Manila, that young Srinivas is earning $250 a year as an errand boy in Calcutta, that, after trouble with the landlord's agent, the Ramon family have simply given up and gone to Medellin where a cousin has started a small eating-house and hopes to be able to help them build a lean-to shack in return for help with marketing, serving, and washing up. So it goes – from one end of the universe of misery to the other. ... Yet these are men and women who can produce double the output per acre of sophisticated modernized farms. Collectively, they are probably the world's most neglected, most wasted, most exploited resource.

(Barbara Ward, *The Home of Man*, 1976)

1 Define the following words in the context of the passage:
   (a) 'federated'; (line 6)
   (d) 'nominal'; (line 9)
   (c) 'fatalism'; (line 22)
   (b) 'sophisticated'. (line 32)
2 What might Barbara Ward mean by her reference to 'modernization of methods'? (line 7)
3 The village is too small to provide 'security for vital credit'. What do you suppose Barbara Ward means by this? (line 8)
4 Who is the 'big man', do you think, referred to in line 8, and what appears to be his function?
5 What is the force of the description of the farmer's wife as a 'patient packhorse'? (line 19)
6 What would appear to be the solution, or solutions, to the picture of misery that Barbara Ward paints here, of the 'average small farmer in most developing nations'?

Part Four
Aid and Trade

We colonized overseas territories; we plundered them for their raw materials; we 'gave' them their independence; and we sent (and we still send) experts to 'develop' them. **Can the rich world live down its past and have dealings with the poor world on equal terms? Do grossly unequal wealth and opportunities between rich and poor make 'one world' an impossible dream?**

1

Aid is part of a hard-headed political bargain: donors possess certain surpluses of capital and trained people which they are willing to make available to recipients – at a price. The question then becomes one of what is the recipient prepared to pay for the development assistance which it seeks? But though aid may be part of such a bargain this does not rule out an element of humanitarianism as well, although it is advantage which *dictates* the action of governments.

(Guy Arnold, *Aid and the Third World: The North/South Divide*, 1985)

2

Until 1982 it was understood that there had to be, for a prolonged period, a one-way flow of resources from the advanced countries to the Third World to promote its development. The view went unchallenged in either official or private-sector circles, and was supported by every school of economic thought .... Since the debt crisis which broke in 1982, those flows have been reversed for each important group of countries in the Third World.

(Harold Lever and Christopher Huhne, *Debt and Danger: The World Financial Crisis*, 1985)

3

Private capital goes where private investors think they can make money. And that is seldom in underdeveloped countries. Certainly labour is cheap there – but it is generally the wrong type of labour – unskilled, undisciplined, unused to modern techniques. Moreover, other aspects of underdevelopment – soft administrations, interventionist economic policies, political instability – represent precisely that climate of uncertainty which is anathema to private investment.

(Peter Donaldson, *Worlds Apart*, 2nd edn, 1986)

4

There is a 'demonstration effect' which occurs when the presence of large numbers of tourists encourages consumption patterns which are inappropriate for the population as a whole. This can range from demands for expensive food imports to a newly found desire among the young to spend money on entertainment activities like gambling .... Finally, there is the pervasive influence of neo-colonialism.

(John Lea, *Tourism & Development in the Third World*, 1988)

5

Nation states have delivered to the 'markets' some of the power to set interest-rates and exchange rates and so, ultimately, levels and rates of employment and inflation. These powers can be reclaimed, but it is a distant prospect. The best that can be hoped for is the construction of a geopolitical and economic order which recognizes a dispersed-power principle. ... In its absence we remain prisoners of a new 'order' wedded to the anarchy and disorder of the markets.

(R.J. Johnston and P.J. Taylor, eds, *A World in Crisis?* 1989)

6

At one time there was the assumption that international tourism would inject much needed foreign exchange into the economies of developing countries and act as a stimulus to growth. The reality for many countries, however, has been marginal and may well have been outweighed by adverse social, cultural, and environmental impacts.

(Michael Barke, ed., *Case Studies of the Third World*, 1991)

7

Many examples around the world could be found besides Iraq to show how the deeds of their own and other people's leaders still plunge the most vulnerable of the world's people into misery and want; and how lacking, still, is the political will to recognize their rights and dignity as human beings by fixing – or enabling them to fix – a safety-net beneath them.

(Maggie Black, *A Cause for Our Times: Oxfam, the first fifty years*, 1992)

8

Peasant farmers in Ghana grow much of the cocoa used to make the chocolate eaten in Britain. ... This is a useful cash crop for farmers, as it can be grown alongside food crops. One in four Ghanaians are employed in growing and exporting cocoa, which provides 60 per cent of Ghana's export earnings. However, the World Bank has been encouraging several developing countries to grow and export more and more cocoa as a way of earning money to service their foreign debts. This has helped to create a glut of cocoa.

(John Madeley *et al*, *Who Runs the World?*, 1994)

Part Five
Population

In his essay *On the Principle of Population* (1798), Thomas Malthus warned that population growth would outstrip the food supplies necessary for subsistence. He urged sexual restraint and late marriage. Two hundred years later, we are still managing to feed most of the people most of the time. **Is there a population problem, and if there is what, in your opinion, should be done about it?**

1   It's not so much the absolute number of human beings on the planet that's so frightening, as the rate of growth. There were around 1000 million people in the world in Malthus' time. By about 1950, the figure was 2,500. Since then it's doubled. Of course the reason for this is that more people are surviving infancy, and then living longer. We'll have reached our limit within a century.

2   The problem is the imbalance between population growth rates in industrialized countries, and the less developed countries. There's been a marked downturn in fertility in the former, but high rates in the latter. Energetic family planning campaigns are needed to promote the desire for smaller families, and the use of effective contraceptive techniques in poor countries.

3   The world could actually support a much larger population than it does now, if only we distributed food and other goods more justly. Our family-planning programmes are a diversion of attention from our own gross over-exploitation of the world's resources in the greedy West.

4   You can preach birth control and distribute condoms until you're blue in the face, but you'll change nothing unless you raise people's standard of living. The poor need lots of children to ensure that enough survive to work for them and keep them in their old age. There's no other welfare system.

5   Bearing a child is probably the single most important thing that a woman does. The population problem apart, we should encourage people to think very seriously before bringing children into the world. The presumption should be against doing so, perhaps; and be in favour of male sterilization on demand.

6   The key variable in population growth, infant mortality and so on, is the education and welfare of women. Population policies have too often been run by men, accustomed to imposing their will on submissive women. If women were empowered, socially and economically, the population 'problem' would solve itself.

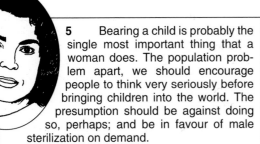

7   It is quite conceivable that many countries will have to go for the Chinese option, and the 'one child' policy. With one fifth of the world's population on 7 per cent of its land area, China had no choice but to curb family size. If this means limiting individual freedom of choice, in the public interest, so be it.

8   The real cost of runaway population growth is borne by the environment: by forests, and water resources, and soil and air quality. If *we* don't limit population pretty soon, crop-failure, disease, malnutrition, and man-made climate change will do it for us.

Answers

Answers are provided here to all multi-choice questions in Parts 1 and 2 and to comprehension questions of a 'closed' kind in Part 3. Answers are not provided to questions of an open-ended kind.

Unit 1 – Architecture

Part One – Classical

A 2   B 3   C 1   D 4   E 5

Part Two – Gothic

A 2   B 1   C 3   D 1   E 2
F 3   G 4   H 2   I 1   J 3

Part Three – Concerning Space

1   (a) attractiveness
    (b) parts which jut out
    (c) a variable whole
    (d) all the time and everywhere

2   ostentatious – pretentious, showy
    meretricious – vulgar

3   grand, dynamic lines

Item A – Inventors

1 R	2 D	3 T	4 J	5 U	6 C
7 G	8 P	9 Q	10 M	11 K	12 H
13 A	14 O	15 B	16 I	17 N	18 F
19 L	20 E	21 S	22 FF	23 JJ	24 DD
25 LL	26 CC	27 V	28 PP	29 NN	30 Z
31 KK	32 MM	33 II	34 AA	35 HH	36 BB
37 EE	38 X	39 GG	40 Y	41 W	42 OO

Unit 2 – Curriculum

Part One – The Division of Knowledge

1 B   2 D   3 E   4 C   5 F   6 A

Part Two – Subject Names

1   1 biology
    2 anthropology
    3 psychology
    4 astrology
    5 philology
    6 technology
    7 ecology
    8 zoology
    9 geology
    10 archaeology
    11 cosmology

2   A morphology — study of form of animals/words
    B biography — life story of a person
    C psychiatry — healing the mind
    D philosophy — systematic pursuit of understanding
    E pathology — study of disease
    F meteorology — study of weather patterns
    G economics — study of economy (money-movements)
    H geometry — study of measurement of shapes in space
    I cosmogony — theory of origin of universe
    J physiology — internal workings of organisms

3   (a) geomorphology — study of land-forms
    (b) geography — study of interaction of earth and life

(c) astronomy — study of the universe
(d) biotechnology — exploitation of the structure of organisms
(e) zoogeography — study of distribution of life forms

4   (a) E   (b) H   (c) A   (d) C
    (e) F   (f) B   (g) D   (h) G

Part Three – Arts and Sciences

1   (a) students of the arts
    (b) science
    (c) exploited by people
    (d) analysis of the world, and our part in it

2   The earth is not the most important part of the universe. It is not here for us to exploit. Nature takes/determines its own course. Facts not theories are the foundation of knowledge.

Item B – Affixes: Latin Forms

	1	2	3	4	5	6
1	1 A	2 F	3 D	4 E	5 B	6 C
2	1 B	2 E	3 F	4 A	5 D	6 C
3	1 A	2 C	3 D	4 E	5 F	6 B
4	1 D	2 C	3 E	4 A	5 F	6 B
5	1 B	2 A	3 E	4 D	5 F	6 C
6	1 A	2 F	3 D	4 B	5 E	6 C
7	1 E	2 A	3 C	4 F	5 D	6 B
8	1 B	2 A	3 C	4 F	5 E	6 D
9	1 B	2 C	3 A	4 E	5 F	6 D
10	1 A	2 D	3 C	4 E	5 B	6 F

Unit 3 – Economics

Part One – Economists

1 D   2 F   3 E   4 A   5 B   6 C

Part Two – The Money-Go-Round

1 J   2 H   3 B   4 A   5 C
6 G   7 E   8 F   9 I   10 D

Part Three – The Market

1   (a) codified (line 23)
    (b) sophisticated (line 4)
    (c) berated (line 31)
    (d) attributed (line 17)

2   Shaped the complex and sophisticated structure of economic activity.
    Turned individual to general advantage in the economic domain.

3   Both are 'natural'; neither can be forced.

Item C – Maths Introduction

Exercise 1.1

1   10m/s = 36km/h
2   360km/h = 100m/s
3   200m in 8 seconds is 25m/s. Multiply by 3.6 to get 90km/h.

31 MM	32 JJ	33 II	34 AA	35 E	36 NN
37 X	38 P	39 PP	40 G	41 M	42 CC
43 WW	44 OO	45 GG	46 SS	47 VV	48 RR
49 B	50 TT				

4   (a) 400,000km   (b) 40,000km   (c) 22.22km
5   340m/s = 20.4km/h.
    Mach 2 is 40.8km/h.

Exercise 1.2

1   A (2,0)
2   B ($\sqrt{3}/_2$, $^1/_2$)
3   C (0,2)
4   D ($-^1/_2$, $\sqrt{3}/_2$)
5   E (−2, 0)
6   F ($-\sqrt{3}/_2$, $-^1/_2$)
7   G (0, −2)
8   H ($^1/_2$, $-\sqrt{3}/_2$)

Unit 4 – Energy

Part One – Pioneers

1 H	2 C	3 E	4 B	5 J
6 A	7 I	8 F	9 G	10 D

Part Two – Alternatives

1	A 1	B 2	C 1	D 2	E 3	F 2
2	A 1	B 1	C 1	D 1	E 3	F 3
3	A 3	B 3	C 2	D 2	E 3	F 2
4	A 2	B 3	C 2	D 3	E 3	F 2
5	A 3	B 3	C 2	D 3	E 3	F 2
6	A 3	B 3	C 2	D 1	E 2	F 1

(You may find some or all of these 'answers' contentious.)

Part Three – The Power Concept

1   (a) you cite a parallel case
    (b) energy change from one form to another
    (c) limited
    (d) the most commonly-used example

2   That they produce an adequate quantity of light for the purpose.

3   In terms of kilowatt hours.

4   The resources are finite; time is infinite.

5   Because when power use was first measured, horses were the most available source of muscle power in large quantities.

Item D – Borrowings from French

1 N	2 G	3 Q	4 Y	5 GG	6 BB
7 FF	8 E	9 AA	10 V	11 D	12 A
13 M	14 K	15 Z	16 P	17 H	18 II
19 CC	20 EE	21 L	22 R	23 U	24 S
25 O	26 DD	27 F	28 C	29 T	30 X
31 J	32 I	33 B	34 W	35 HH	

Unit 5 – Environment

Part Three – Green Belts

1   Those surrounding London.

2   It has been developed.

3   It has a more official, health-based ring, viz. cordon sanitaire.

Item E – Similes

1 UU	2 C	3 H	4 J	5 D	6 XX
7 F	8 K	9 S	10 I	11 FF	12 O
13 LL	14 BB	15 N	16 R	17 HH	18 T
19 U	20 QQ	21 DD	22 Y	23 L	24 Z
25 Q	26 A	27 V	28 EE	29 W	30 KK

Unit Six – Europe

Part One – Past and Place

336 BC	Corinth
AD 410	Rome
AD 732	Tours
1066	London
1295	Venice
1453	Istanbul
1492	Granada
1517	Wittenberg
1523	Stockholm
1541	Geneva
1579	Utrecht
1588	Cadiz
1642	Oxford
1690	R. Boyne
1769	Ajaccio
1789	Paris
1801	Copenhagen
1812	Moscow
1812	Vienna
1855	Sevastopol
1860	Naples
1871	Berlin
1914	Sarajevo
1917	St Petersburg
1937	Guernica
1938	Munich
1955	Warsaw
1956	Budapest
1968	Prague
1975	Helsinki
1986	Kiev
1989	Bucharest

Part Two – EU Institutions

1 E	2 G	3 A	4 H
5 D	6 B	7 F	8 C

Part Three – War and Peace

1   (a) GB, USA, USSR
    (b) They are numerous, viz. Mark V, 9 – 'My name is Legion, for we are many', and a legion consists of 3,000-6,000 men.
    (c) friendship
    (d) heart-felt

2   Both literally and sincerely.

3   To guarantee Russian security and Polish independence.

4   *Optimism:*
    l. 18   'every hope ... settlements'
    l. 27   'I cannot conceive ... good solution.'

    Pessimism:
    l. 14   'vast array' (of problems)
    l. 37   'no pains ... patience grudged'

5   l. 7   answer to Polish question
    l. 9   'speediest possible destruction of Nazi power'
    l. 18   'harmonious settlements'
    l. 35   cordial association of Allies

Item F – Maths: Simple Percentages

Exercise 2.1

(a) 0.50   (b) 0.10   (c) 0.43   (d) 0.73

(e) 0.15   (f) 0.07   (g) 0.175   (h) 0.085
(i) 0.001   (j) 0.0001

Exercise 2.2

(a) $30   (b) £20   (c) $51.60   (d) £17.52
(e) £1.20   (f) 16.8cm (g) £1.40   (h) £55.25
(i) 5m   (j) 32 cents

Exercise 2.3

(a) 1.10   (b) 1.12   (c) 1.175   (d) 1.30
(e) 1.05   (f) 1.75   (g) 1.065   (h) 1.0825
(i) 1.0575   (j) 1.001

Exercise 2.4

(a) 0.88   (b) 0.85   (c) 0.10   (d) 0.825
(e) 0.70

Unit 7 – Government and Politics

Part One – Left and Right in British Politics

1 Con   2 Lab   3 Con   4 Lib   5 Lab
6 Lib   7 Con   8 Con   9 Lab   10 Lib

Part Two – The Houses of Parliament

1 E   2 C   3 F   4 A   5 J
6 D   7 H   8 B   9 I   10 G

Part Three – Cabinet Government

1 (a) executive is Prime Minister in Cabinet; legislative is parliament.
   (b) all-powerful
   (c) the part which calls for pomp and ceremony
   (d) the part which enacts and executes statute law

2 Indirectly – from a 'charmed circle' of MPs.

3 MPs are elected, and they choose the Prime Minister.

4 The Treasury is the pre-eminent department of state (the PM is its First Lord).

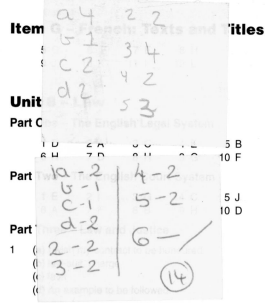

Item ... **itles**

Unit

Part C

1 D   2 A   ... 5 B
6 H   7 D   ... 10 F

Part

... 5 J
... 10 D

Part

1

2 To throw out the case.

3 A contract must be honoured under Venetian law.

4 literal, pedantic

5 She too is interpreting the law (even more) literally, pedantically.

Item H – Affixes: Greek Forms

1 symmetrical   2 parasitic   3 telepathic
4 euphemistic   5 monochromatic   6 epigrammatic
7 antithetical   8 peripatetic   9 amorphic
10 hypocritical 11 polyphonic   12 energetic
13 diagnostic   14 apologetic   15 ectopic

Unit 9 – Literature

Part One – English Literary Genres

1 D2   2 E2   3 G4   4 B2   5 C3   6 E1
7 G3   8 F2   9 E4   10 F4   11 G2   12 D3

Part Two – Literary Terms

Across
1 G   5 R   8 H   9 U   10 A   11 N
15 Z   16 K   20 D   21 X   22 I   24 W
Down
1 E   2 S   3 C   4 T   6 B   7 J
9 V   12 Y   13 L   14 O   17 O   18 Q
19 F   23 M

Part Three – The Case for the Novel

1 (a) praised extravagantly
   (b) fashionable nonsense
   (c) pretended, spurious
   (d) the most accurate

2 Combative to the point of sarcasm; using flattering, extravagant language.

3 To render life, no less.

4 Public (male) opinion would have scorned her.

5 With bored disdain.

6 These are the qualities generally associated with fiction.

Item I – Maths: More Percentages

Exercise 3.1

1 (a) $0.06 \times 0.80 = 0.048$; 4.8%
   (b) $0.10 \times 0.75 = 0.075$; 7.5%
   (c) $0.098 \times 0.88 = 0.08624$; 8.624%
   (d) $0.112 \times 0.60 = 0.0672$; 6.72%

2 (a) £2000 $\times$ 1.125 = £3524.68
   (b) £550 $\times$ 1.0610 = £984.97
   (c) £3000 $\times$ 1.05525 = £11440.18
   (d) £50 $\times$ 1.1156 = £96.08
   (e) £2500 $\times$ 1.06254 = £3186.07

Unit 10 – Media

Part One – A Map of the Media

1 F   2 H   3 E   4 G   5 A
6 B   7 C   8 I   9 D   10 J

Part Three – TV Ads

1 (a) time-tabling of programmes
   (b) publicly supported in the national interest
   (c) freedom of programmers to choose material
   (d) subtleties

Item J – French: Inferring Meaning

1 D   2 B   3 C   4 A   5 D
6 B   7 C   8 A   9 D   10 B
11 B   12 A   13 C   14 A   15 D

Unit 11 – Medicine
Part One – Medical Milestones
1 C	2 F	3 D	4 E	5 B	6 A

Part Two – Anatomy of Ailments
1 E	2 C	3 G	4 D
5 H	6 B	7 A	8 F

Part Three – The Hippocratic Oath
1 (a) counsel (l. 16)
   (b) covenant (l. 7)
   (c) precept (l. 7)
   (d) regimen (l. 12)

2 Medicine; he attributes to it an almost divine origin.

3 Its practitioners are members of a family, united by commitment.

4 abortion; involuntary euthanasia

6 confidentiality

Item K – Literary Terms and Examples
1 O	2 M	3 G	4 E	5 U	6 S
7 L	8 T	9 N	10 I	11 C	12 Z
13 R	14 Q	15 J	16 Y	17 K	18 X
19 V	20 P	21 F	22 W	23 A	24 D
25 B	26 H				

Unit 12 – Music
Part One – In Time
1 E	2 H	3 G	4 B
5 C	6 A	7 D	8 F

Part Two – The Orchestra
1
A 5	B 16	C 22	D 14	E 15	F 6
G 21	H 12	I 19	J 7	K 2	L 3
M 13	N 10	O 24	P 11	Q 4	R 18
S 17	T 20	U 8	V 23	W 1	X 9

2
A 4	B 6	C 2	D 1
E 7	F 8	G 3	H 5

Part Three – Popular Music
1 (a) Lambert is loosely quoting from the Psalms in lines.3–5; but the psalmist had never dreamt that it would be such music.
   (b) appalling gap/silence (ironic)
   (c) over-indulgence in sound
   (d) a pleasant sensation in the ear

2 'actually' (disbelieving)
   'spared' (as if suffering)
   'ghastly' (hyperbole)
   'atmospheric' (reductive)

Item L – Proverbs
1 C	2 K	3 V	4 P	5 H
6 U	7 Y	8 Q	9 L	10 F
11 M	12 A	13 B	14 I	15 X
16 T	17 D	18 O	19 G	20 R
21 N	22 W	23 S	24 J	25 E
26 II	27 WW	28 EE	29 Z	30 BB
31 HH	32 LL	33 VV	34 UU	35 QQ
36 XX	37 TT	38 SS	39 DD	40 AA
41 KK	42 CC	43 NN	44 JJ	45 FF
46 GG	47 MM	48 RR	49 PP	50 OO

Unit 13 – Painting
Part One – Painters, Periods and Places
1 J	2 A	3 E	4 I	5 D
6 F	7 B	8 C	9 G	10 H

Part Two – Impressionism and After
1 E	2 G	3 A	4 F	5 B
6 J	7 H	8 D	9 C	10 I

Part Three – We the Patrons
1 (a) offer a challenge
   (b) self-styled experts
   (c) some specific commission, commemorative or in tribute
   (d) the grit that issues in the pearl; the idea that gives rise to art.

2 We are the ones who ask them to do something in particular (l.5).
   We are indifferent or interested (l.35)

3 The artist must do more than reproduce old work.

4 A genuine attempt to do a 'concrete job' or 'task'.

5 They are a sop to critics, but they may be suggestive.

Unit 14 – Philosophy
Part One – Schools of Thought
1 C	2 F (or B)	3 A	4 G
5 D	6 H	7 E	8 B

Part Two – A History of -isms
1 H	2 G	3 I	4 J	5 C	6 A
7 B	8 F	9 D	10 E		

Part Three – No Man's Land
1 (a) One considers, guesses, wonders.
   (b) To infer from nature or some manifestation of supernature.
   (c) in-born, instinctive
   (d) unavoidably, inescapably, relentlessly

Item N – Greek and Roman Gods and Heroes
1
1 H	2 L	3 A	4 D	5 N
6 I	7 P	8 G	9 O	10 F
11 B	12 C	13 J	14 E	15 M
16 K				

2
1 S	2 U	3 Q	4 W	5 X
6 Y	7 R	8 Z	9 T	10 V

Unit 15 – Psychology (Cognitive)
Part One – Learning
1 E	2 C	3 B	4 F	5 A	6 D

Part Three – Infant Conditioning
1 (a) brisk, imperative
   (b) the light of the sun
   (c) jumped in surprise; were suddenly roused
   (d) fixed, moulded

2 It is a matter-of-fact narrative, 'scientific', unemotional.

Item O – French: Text and multiple-choice questions in English
6 D	7 C	8 A	9 B	10 C

Unit 16 – Religion

Part One – World Religions

1 Judaism
2 Christianity
3 Islam
4 Hinduism/Buddhism
5 Buddhism
6 Judaism
7 Islam
8 Christianity
9 Buddhism
10 Hinduism

Part Two – Protestantism

1 F	2 E	3 D	4 A	5 G
6 C	7 J	8 I	9 B	10 H

Part Three – Varieties of Religion

1 (a) particular, individual
  (b) concedes, admits the antagonist is right
  (c) God, fate, genetic inheritance
  (d) irritable

2 Ingredients of a personality and life-stance

3 That it is one answer (among many) to the questions that life poses.

4 No one religious answer is sufficient – the truth may be composite.

Item P – Maths: Star Problems

Exercise 5.2

1 (3,1) 2 (5,3) 3 (2,2) 4 (1,–4)
5 (2,2) 6 (–2,–2) 7 (–3,–4) 8 (3,4)

Unit 17 – Science

Part One – Scientific Method

1 Animals sleep/Fido sleeps/Fido is an animal.

2 The Copernican theory of the universe.

Part Two – Scientific Terms

Across		Down	
2	Compound	1	Sulphur
4	Quanta	3	Metal
6	Entropy	5	Neutron
9	Volt	7	Solid
10	Molecule	8	Gene
15	Isotope	11	Element
18	Cell	12	Hormone
19	Radon	13	Positron
20	Energy	14	Alkali
21	Kinetic	16	Sodium
22	Titrate	17	Electron
23	Amino	18	Crystal
24	Neon		
25	Valve		

Part Three – Humane Science

1 (a) ephemeral (changing) (line 28)
  (b) last, absolute, final (lines 23, 24, 28)
  (c) objective (line 1)
  (d) arrogant (line 31)

2 Stage of evolution, structural complexity and cognitive development.

Item Q – Classical Allusions

1	1 M	2 H	3 P	4 L	5 A	6 R
	7 B	8 N	9 D	10 Z	11 E	12 Q
	13 I	14 J	15 C	16 X	17 F	18 W
	19 Y	20 K	21 V	22 O	23 T	24 U
	25 S	26 G				
2	1 H	2 E	3 D	4 A	5 G	6 C
	7 J	8 I	9 F	10 B		

Unit 18 – Society

Part One – Stratification

1 (a) IIIN (b) 4

2 (a) E (b) 9

3 (a) II (b) 3

4 (a) I (b) 1

5 (a) VII (b) 8

6 (a) C1 (b) 5

Part Two – Schooling and Sifting

1 F	2 D	3 A	4 E	5 B	6 C

Part Three – Homelessness

1 (a) accommodated, adapted to, legitimated
  (b) neglected, run-down
  (c) transient, passing
  (d) demonization (making outcast)

2 They combine to form an earthquake metaphor indicating an unpredictable and deep-rooted problem.

3 A ginger group identifies the problem, publicizes it, and provokes to a solution; a pressure group campaigns and lobbies for action.

Item R – French: Text and multiple-choice questions in French

1 B	2 C	3 D	4 A	5 A
6 C	7 D	8 C	9 A	10 A

Unit 19 – Sport and Leisure

Part Three – Mass Entertainment

1 (a) working-class
  (b) lack, shortage
  (c) encouragement, stimulus
  (d) incapable of being satisfied

2 To distinguish it from rugby football.

3 That it was superficial, glossy, insubstantial.

Item S – Maths: Statistics and Probability

Exercise 6.1

1 Median £3.35

2 Mode 8 hours

3 Mode Size 14

4 Mean 5' 10"

Exercise 6.2

1 (a) $^{11}/_{34}$ (b) $^{2}/_{34}$ (c) $^{1}/_{34}$

Exercise 6.3

1 $(^1/_2)^5 = ^1/_{32}$

2 $^3/_4 \times ^1/_4 = ^3/_{16}$

3 The probability of red and red and white is
$^3/_{10} \times ^2/_9 \times ^7/_8 = ^{42}/_{720} = ^7/_{120}$

Unit 20 – Technology

Part One – Structures and Stresses

1 Pons Fabricius and other bridges in Rome

2 Ponte Vecchio, Florence

3 Blackfriars Bridge, London

4 Ironbridge, Coalbrookdale

5 Sydney Harbour Bridge

6 Royal Albert Bridge, Saltash

7 Clifton Bridge, Bristol

8 Humber Bridge

Part Two – Telecommunications

1 B   2 E   3 F   4 C   5 D   6 A

Part Three – Water Supply

1 (a) non-interventionist
   (b) inactive, lazy
   (c) drinkable
   (d) poisonous substances

2 It permits the appearance of greenness cloaking grey inactivity.

3 Being green implies limiting industry's freedom to pollute, funding, surveillance.

4 Deliberate policy: fluoride
   Negligence: pesticides, etc.

Item T – The Periodic Table

1 A   2 E   3 D   4 B   5 F   6 C

Unit 21 – Universe

Part One – The Solar System

A   1 E   2 J   3 B   4 D   5 A
     6 C   7 H   8 I   9 F   10 G

B   1 D   2 E   3 B   4 C   5 A

Part Two – The Bang and Beyond

1 B   2 D   3 E   4 A   5 F   6 C

Part Three – Black Holes

1 The gravitational pull, firstly of the earth, and subsequently of the sun.

2 (a) Power of doing work possessed by a body in virtue of its motion.
   (b) Power of doing work possessed by a body in virtue of its mass in relation to the mass of other bodies.

3 Sun's mass (and therefore its gravitational pull) is much greater.

4 He has referred to escape velocity of 11km per second and 41km per second; the speed of light is a massively greater 299,792km per second.

5 One that is separable in respect of its energy, its gravitational field and gives no luminous evidence of itself to the rest of the universe.

Item U – Pioneers

1 O	2 I	3 Z	4 T	5 L	6 B
7 V	8 A	9 C	10 W	11 R	12 F
13 X	14 D	15 G	16 Y	17 E	18 U
19 H	20 M	21 S	22 J	23 Q	24 P
25 K	26 N	27 JJ	28 OO	29 EE	30 SS
31 AA	32 QQ	33 HH	34 BB	35 XX	36 UU
37 MM	38 RR	39 TT	40 CC	41 II	42 VV
43 DD	44 WW	45 FF	46 KK	47 PP	48 ZZ
49 GG	50 NN	51 LL	52 YY		

Unit 22 – World

Part One – International Organisations

1 NATO

2 Andean Group, EFTA

3 CARICOM, ECOWAS

4 ECLA, ECA, OPEC

5 Arab League, WCC, OIC

6 Common language, common currency, political will, decision-making apparatus at ministerial level, economic parity, common traditions.

Part Two – The United Nations

1 B   2 E   3 A   4 H
5 C   6 G   7 D   8 F

Part Three – The Most Exploited Resource

1 (a) organised or linked structurally to other groups
   (b) so-called
   (c) acceptance of the apparently inevitable
   (d) using the latest technology

2 Use of fertilisers, machinery, irrigation systems.

3 Money-making potential as evidence that it is worth investing in.

4 The elder, the biggest landowner, the biggest employer of labour; his function is to act as a conduit between government and village.

Index